WOMEN:
THE MISUNDERSTOOD
MAJORITY

**CONTEMPORARY CHRISTIAN
COUNSELING**

WOMEN: THE MISUNDERSTOOD MAJORITY

M. GAY HUBBARD, Ph.D.

CONTEMPORARY CHRISTIAN COUNSELING

General Editor
GARY R. COLLINS, PH.D.

Library of Congress Cataloging-in-Publication Data:

Hubbard, M. Gay, 1931–
    Women : the misunderstood majority : contemporary concerns in counseling women / M. Gay Hubbard.
        p.   cm.—(Contemporary Christian counseling series)
    Includes bibliographical references and indexes.
    ISBN 0–8499–0834–5.
        0–8499–3380–3 (pbk.)
    1. Women—Pastoral counseling of.   2. Women—Psychology.
    3. Women—Religious life.   I. Title.   II. Series.
    BV4445.H833   1992
    253.5'082—dc20   92–22779
                                                                                CIP

3 4 5 6 7 8 9 LBM 7 6 5 4 3 2

Printed in the United States of America

In memory of my mother
Aurolyn Wiseman Fetrow
1906–1938

Contents

Acknowledgments

Many people helped me with this book, and it is my privilege to acknowledge their support and assistance.

The book began as an act of faith by David Pigg, Gary Collins, and my publishers. I am grateful for the opportunity that their willingness to risk has given me, and for the encouragement they have continued to offer throughout the project. Lois Stück has taught me why in every acknowledgment authors are quick to praise those editors who take an author's manuscript and make it into a reader-friendly book. I am grateful for her skill.

The energy to bring this task to completion has been generated by friends and family; I could not have done it alone. I am particularly grateful for those women who volunteered to make the book their project too, and prayed for me, specifically, consistently, and effectively: Laura Zach, Linda Chishlom, Linda Murray, Ruth Nichols, Marty Platt-Gowan, Dr. Miriam Dixon, and the staff at the First Presbyterian Church, Golden, Colorado.

There are others who have been interested in the book and have also prayed for me. One of the benefits of this work has been a renewed awareness of the network of friends with whom I have been blessed. Three of my colleagues, Laura Mae Gardner, Tim Dea, and Bonnie Messer, gave generous amounts of time in reading portions of the manuscript.

I appreciate also the continuing encouragement provided by the members of the Board of Christian Counseling Associates, who by their interest and prayers have supported my continuing counseling practice as well as the writing project. Willard Solfermoser offered not only friendship but also expert assistance when word processors were reluctant to perform.

My clients have been interested, patient, and supportive—men and women alike.

My family has been accepting and understanding of the long hours spent away from them and at the office.

My greatest debt of appreciation is to Joseph Hubbard, my husband and partner in professional practice. He has read the manuscript (some sections numberless times). He has given helpful suggestions, continuing encouragement, and faith in the value of the work. He has invested countless hours deciphering my revisions and corrections, and producing readable copy. His skill in word processing procedures made the continuation of my counseling practice possible while I was working on the book. In his contribution he has demonstrated by action what Christian marriage at its best is all about. I am enormously grateful.

Preface

In recent decades, women's lives have increasingly become the focus of social, political, and ecclesiastical forces seeking to control the speed and direction of social change. Despite wide differences in philosophy, power brokers in opposing camps too often hold one passionate belief in common: If only women can be persuaded (or coerced) to act in a certain way, then all will be well with the world.

Counselors (women and men) are themselves participants with their women clients in this conflicted, changing world. Counselors are subject, as are their women clients, to these competing forces and worldviews. And at the same time, women clients and their counselors are also active participants in the building and shaping of the social world to come. In this context of transition and conflict, counseling has become an even more difficult task; the problems that women clients bring to counseling have become even more complex.

There are many counselors, lay and professional, who are trying to help women develop more effective life management skills. However, it appears that a significant amount of this effort, while motivated by good intentions, is less helpful than it might be for two reasons: (1) The majority of counselors, lay and professional, enter the helping role with insufficient understanding of women as women and of the social reality of women's life experiences. (2) Counselors (women and men) participate in the helping role with insufficient understanding of their beliefs about women with a resulting lack of awareness of the ways in which these unexamined beliefs influence their relationships with women and shape the counseling process.

This book is designed to provide information at both of these troublesome points. I have explored some of the common misbeliefs about women that can confuse and entangle both women clients and their counselors. I have also attempted to summarize some of the findings and present debate in psychology of women that will help women and their counselors to think more clearly about women as women, the challenges they face, and the options that frame their choices.

The sheer number of gender-related studies and the complexity of the theoretical debates provides a formidable challenge for anyone setting out to compose a workable summary. In choosing which material to include and which to leave out, my goal has been to provide practical information for both women clients and their counselors to better understand women's gender-distinctive needs and characteristics and the social reality of women's life experiences, and then to be able to act on this information.

The reader will quickly become aware that I am critical of individuals who do not make their presuppositions and value systems explicit and open to the reader's examination. I want to avoid replication of this error. In this book, examination of misbeliefs about women and of the present sex and gender research reflects the following beliefs:

- Scientists have often used theoretical models and presuppositions that reflect primarily the male life experience and stereotypical, culturally determined views of women. As a consequence, the conclusions of their studies can (and often do) represent simultaneously both a statistically sound measurement of a variable and an *invalid* description of women's characteristics and life experiences.

- The spiritual dimension of the whole person can be incorporated in both research and counseling in a manner that respects the client's chosen belief system *without proselytizing and without violating the integrity of the counseling or research process.*

- Christian spirituality makes psychological sense. For my readers and colleagues who do not share my faith, I trust that my discussion of both the misbeliefs about women and the psychology of women will have value despite the fact that we may not share a common worldview. What we do share, however, is a common desire to understand better our women clients and to serve them competently and compassionately. It is my belief that as we become more knowledgeable, discerning participants in the help-giving, help-receiving process, the lives of all of us will be enriched.

Chapter One

Women as Consumers of Counseling Services

IF YOU ADVERTISE YOURSELF AS A COUNSELOR and open an office, whom is your first client likely to be?

A woman.

Why?

Because women are the major consumers of counseling services.[1] No one can explain why this is so with any degree of certainty. Emotional problems such as hysteria and depression, severe anxieties, phobias, and eating disorders are found more frequently among women. Conversely, substance abuse, antisocial personalities, and paranoid personality disorders are found more often among men. However, the individual who seeks assistance with a problem, whatever its specific nature, is most likely to be a woman,[2] although there is some troublesome evidence that women are not well understood, particularly within Christian counseling.

The psychology of women is still a young field of study within the science of psychology. Much remains unknown, and

1

since women's studies have been associated with feminist issues, much of what *is* known about the psychology of women
is not widely applied to counseling women within the evangelical community. Such information apparently is disregarded, without study, because it is presumed to reflect a
nonbiblical world view.

There is additional troublesome evidence that women in
therapy are often treated with less respect than are male clients. Therapists (male and female), for example, listen less
carefully to women clients and remember less of what women
say.[3] Women are more likely than men to have medication prescribed for similar symptoms.[4] When medication is prescribed
for a woman, it is more likely to be medication of the type that
can seriously alter personality and patterns of thinking.[5]

At least 5 percent of women clients have been victims of
sexual advances by their male therapists.[6] One unverified estimate suggested that such incidents are severely underreported
and may in fact run as high as 15 percent.[7] However, one study
in the early 1980s reported some reduction in the frequency of
acknowledged sexual contact between male therapists and
women clients.[8]

Such attitudes of destructive disrespect are often accompanied by seriously inadequate counselor information about
women in general.[9] Many counselors are unaware of research
dealing with the incidence and nature of psychological disorders in women. Many are poorly informed, if at all, in areas of
sexuality, pregnancy, and menopause.

Most therapists (male and female) graduate from professional training programs (including pastoral counseling
courses) never having had a single course dealing with
women, the population who will provide the majority of their
clients. In considering the implications of such lack of preparation, one writer has commented, "The problem of uninformed therapists may be more substantial than the problem
of biased therapists."[10] For women seeking counseling, neither
option appears particularly comforting.

Despite these serious problems, women are likely to continue to be the major consumers of psychotherapeutic services.
It is clear, however, that counselor ignorance of the psychol-

ogy of women, sometimes coupled with unprofessional and unethical practices, can lead to therapy that is hazardous to women's spiritual and mental health.

WOMEN AS PRIMARY CONSUMERS OF COUNSELING SERVICES

As one writer commented, our culture so much approves of women as the primary consumers of therapeutic services that psychotherapy and marriage are seen as the two socially approved institutions for American women.[11]

Traditionally most women see male counselors. Throughout the health care system, services for women are largely controlled and administered by men. In the area of psychotherapy, women have represented the majority of patients and the minority of therapists.[12] There is no indication that these trends are significantly different in Christian counseling.

One possible explanation for the increased incidence of psychological disorders among women is the existence of some as yet unidentified biological factor, although this appears to be an unlikely explanation.[13] Using data from public mental hospitals, outpatient psychiatric clinics, and general hospitals, W. R. Gove examined the ratio of women to men and analyzed the data in relation to four marriage categories: married, widowed, never married, and separated/divorced. He discovered a puzzling and intriguing fact. When females were *married*, they were more likely than males to receive psychiatric treatment. In all other categories, however, there were more men than women.[14]

Gove concluded that women are indeed more likely than men to be receiving treatment for "personal discomfort" or "mental disorganization" (Gove's categories), but this higher rate of disorder among women seemed to be due to the relatively high rate of mental illness among *married* women.

A supporter of the biological explanation for this increased incidence might argue that women who are likely to develop psychological disorders could be more likely to marry. However, this argument fails to explain Gove's further finding that widowed and divorced women are less likely than men to receive treatment.[15] Biology does not seem to provide an answer for the difference in sex ratios in psychological disorders.

It should be noted, however, that the physical health of married individuals, both men and women, tends to be better than that of their unmarried counterparts. Public health statistics indicate that although men do realize a somewhat greater health advantage from marriage than women, both married men and women appear to be physically healthier than do unmarried individuals.[16]

A second possible explanation for the number of women in treatment is that women are more willing to seek help. Perhaps men and women are equally likely to have psychological disorders, but women may be more aware of their problems[17] and therefore more likely to seek help.

Women might also show higher rates of treatment because it is more acceptable for women to be sick. Men are culturally expected to maintain the myth that they are strong and in control of their bodies and emotions, while women are given cultural permission to admit that they have problems.

Additionally, it is possible that women may appear more frequently for treatment because the therapeutic process itself is more compatible to women than to men. It is more culturally acceptable for a woman to be dependent upon someone else, to assume the role of the weak, submissive client with a strong, dominant therapist. Since the therapist is likely to be male, the role of the weak, submissive client is one that the male is culturally likely to reject, particularly in relation to another male.

Explaining women's increased incidence of psychological disorders by their increased willingness to seek help does have a certain appeal. However, Gove's work again indicates that there is little if any evidence to support this explanation.[18] When they have "disorders" (Gove's category), women appear to be no more likely than men to seek professional help. If anything, women may be slightly less apt to do so.

Women's alleged willingness to seek help does not then appear to provide an adequate explanation for women as the majority of consumers of mental health services. This leaves a third explanation that suggests the problem is the result of the way in which mental health is defined for women.

PSYCHOLOGICAL CONCEPTS OF WOMEN'S MENTAL HEALTH

A study by Broverman and her associates examined traits characteristically associated with masculinity and femininity.[19] Practicing therapists (both male and female) were each given a list of 122 character traits. Some therapists were asked to choose from the list the characteristics that best described a mature, healthy adult *man*. Others were asked to choose characteristics of a mature, healthy adult *woman*, and some to choose the characteristics that best described a mature, healthy *adult* (sex unspecified).

Analysis of the data indicated a high correlation between ratings of the healthy adult man and the healthy adult. The correlation was lower between the healthy adult woman and the healthy adult.

Does this indicate that a woman cannot win? If a woman earned a high rating as a healthy woman, she could not simultaneously earn a high rating as a healthy adult since the characteristics necessary to earn a healthy adult rating were masculine in quality. Conversely, if a woman earned a high rating as a healthy adult, she could not simultaneously earn a high rating as a woman. In short, she could be a healthy adult or a healthy woman, but she could not be both.

Broverman's study has been criticized for the way femininity was measured.[20] Even so, the study provides supporting data for Chesler's blunt summary, "Since clinicians and researchers, as well as their patients and subjects, adhere to a masculine standard of mental health, women by definition are viewed as psychiatrically impaired—simply because they are women."[21]

Some critics have suspected a male bias in the categories of the *Diagnostic and Statistical Manual of the American Psychiatric Association* (DSM-III-R).[22] After completing a careful review of relevant studies, however, others have concluded that diagnostic bias, if present, does not provide an adequate explanation of the increased incidence of psychological disorders for women.[23]

This debate has led to a troublesome realization: We do not yet know how to define a mentally healthy woman.

Broverman's study,[24] despite some technical limitations, showed how the mentally healthy woman had been identified up to that time. A woman had been declared mentally healthy if she demonstrated conformity to the culturally accepted picture of the stereotypical woman. This stereotyped picture was not the result of scientific research regarding mental illness. It was, instead, a composite derived from cultural norms, yet it was used as the accepted standard by which mental health professionals judged the mental health of a woman. A woman was judged to be well if she conformed to the stereotype and ill if she did not.

How did this stereotype come to be accepted and regarded as science? This occurred primarily through the writings of Sigmund Freud and the theory and practice of psychoanalysis. Because Freudian theory has so powerfully affected psychotherapy for women, it is important to understand Freud's concept of women.

Freud believed women to be inferior for several reasons. Matlin has summarized Freud's beliefs about women as follows:

1. Women experience more shame and envy than men because they lack penises.
2. Women show *narcissism*, which is an excessive concern with their bodies, as well as a tendency toward *masochism*, which is pleasure derived from pain.
3. In adolescence, women shift the focus of their sexuality from the clitoris to the vagina, a shift that is equated with a transition from activity to passivity. Furthermore, a woman who continues to enjoy clitoral stimulation in adulthood cannot obtain mature femininity. . . .
4. Because women never fully resolve the Oedipus complex, their final level of moral development is not as advanced as it is in men.
5. Penis envy can be partially resolved by having a baby; the desire to have children is therefore a sign of mental health.[25]

In Freud's studies the mentally healthy woman appeared as passive, dependent, childlike, and resigned to her biologically inferior status. Consistent with these concepts, classical psychoanalysis viewed the purpose of psychotherapy as the production of a passive, dependent woman who accepted her subordinate, inferior position without protest.

It is difficult to estimate the damage this concept has done. It has reinforced cultural stereotypes that are destructive to women and for decades has shaped the thinking of the professionals (primarily, although not exclusively, males), who by virtue of their positions in the mental health system are the arbiters who are authorized to declare a woman emotionally well-adjusted or mentally ill.

As the study of the psychology of women has grown and psychotherapy for women has received more attention, it is not difficult to see why the popularity of classical psychoanalysis for women has sharply declined.[26] Criticism of the Freudian model, however, did not in itself provide answers to some troublesome problems.

When researchers examine the increased ratio of women to men with psychological disorders, they continue to be faced with a cluster of complicated questions. Have women seeking treatment developed problems because they were seeking to fit the cultural stereotype? Have some of these women been diagnosed as having mental or emotional problems simply because they are different than the stereotyped concept of the feminine woman? Are these women healthy but diagnosed as having mental or emotional problems because they do not conform to the stereotyped concept of the healthy woman prescribed by Freudian theory? Or, in a yet to be defined way, is something really wrong with lots of women? If so, what is it? And why has it gone wrong for women in a way that is different from men? How does the variable of marriage fit into the puzzle?

These questions continue to trouble researchers and counselors alike. Nevertheless, after completing his research, Gove concluded, "The evidence strongly suggests that the higher rates of mental illness among women in our society reflect real differences and are not artifactual."[27]

In a response to Gove's paper, however, Marilyn Johnson points out the possible distortion of incidence rates that may have resulted from the definitions of mental health that Gove used in his research.[28] She argues further, as do two other major researchers,[29] that the questions themselves have been incorrectly formed and suggests that we must make new questions before we can reach definitive answers.

WOMEN AS CONSUMERS

The summary of what we know about women as consumers of mental health services raises serious unsolved problems.

1. More women than men come for counseling. We do not know why.
2. The ratio of women to men includes a puzzlingly high proportion of married women. We do not know why.
3. Mental health for women has been defined in a double-bind fashion that has pitted being feminine against being healthy. This has made serious problems for women and their therapists, most of which are not yet recognized nor solved.
4. The mental health system has been, and continues to be, controlled primarily (although not exclusively) by males. The majority of professionals (male and female) have no training in psychology of women. For the most part they are graduates of traditional training programs which incorporate many aspects of Freudian theory with its implicit antagonism toward women.
5. There is some evidence that the therapeutic process as it is traditionally practiced is destructive to women.

Given this discouraging scenario, a counselor may well wonder where to begin. But one can start by focusing on what women themselves say are the reasons for which they seek help.

According to one therapist who works almost entirely with women:

Over the past ten years of working with women in therapy I have heard the same stories repeated over

and over again: stories of women who are chronically depressed; of women who lack self-esteem—or
a sense of self at all; of women who are sexually un-
responsive; of women who feel lost without men; of
women who live with men who abuse them but
whom they love too much to leave; of women who
live with men they no longer love but are terrified to
leave; of women who want to be in a stable relationship with a man but cannot sustain one; of women
who feel empty and lost and don't know what they
want—except to feel better.[30]

I would add stories of women who are single mothers,
struggling to support children on a poverty level income;
middle-aged, newly divorced women, struggling to reenter
the work world or enter it for the first time; women who are
dealing with the bitter scars of incest and sexual assault—
sometimes within the marriage relationship itself; women
whose inner world is composed of unbearable, unmanage-
able anxiety; women whose daily temptation is to embrace
death by choice, and leave the world in which they no longer
wish to live; angry women who feel forbidden to own their
rage; despairing women; women whose bodies will not conceive; women whose bodies have conceived a child for whom
there are neither physical nor emotional resources; women
for whom the burden of family has become too heavy to
carry; women alone, for whom loneliness appears the pun-
ishment for some nameless inadequacy that they feel helpless
to change.

I have listened to the stories of women who are embezzlers,
who are shoplifters, who are substance abusers, who are frantic with the care of aging parents; women who were severely
neglected, and who now, in turn, cannot adequately mother
the children they have borne; women who are struggling with
their sexual identity and with the desire to act out their sexuality inappropriately; women who with pain and shame have
acknowledged injuring their children; women who have be-
haved abusively to their mates; women who are struggling
with inequities, injustice, and discrimination in the workplace;

grandmothers who are facing a second cycle of mothering with grandchildren who have been abandoned by their parents; grandmothers who are separated from grandchildren through the decision of a court or of an alienated adult child; women whose work world is filled with bias and harassment; women whose retirements have stripped them of the meaning of their work; women who work with no hope, no future in the drudgery of dead-end jobs.

Hurting women who come to the Christian counselor for help are not substantially different from those coming to other therapists. Women, Christian and non-Christian alike, suffer as women in some tragically parallel ways. Christian women, however, often bring two additional problems that may be unique to them. First, many of these women carry an additional burden of self-imposed guilt. For many women both the nature of their problems and their inability to solve these problems without professional help is to them proof that they are spiritual failures.

Additionally, many women come with a religiously encouraged distrust of the therapist and of the therapeutic process. For example, a recent Bible study that was widely distributed by a major radio pastor indited all psychotherapy as a humanistic effort to replace the ministry of the Holy Spirit. The study guide states,

> Our counselor must be God. . . . Techniques, theories, and therapies will never restrain the flesh because they appeal to the flesh. Solutions to personal, family, and church problems are found in God's counsel ministered through the Spirit of God. We must turn to the Spirit of God, learn to walk in the Spirit, and understand the power of the Spirit. We must reject man-centered, humanistic, psychological solutions to problems.[31]

It is sad that many Christian women have been taught that seeking a therapist's help is not only proof that they have failed spiritually, but that all therapists and therapeutic processes are, by definition, dangerous to their spiritual health and well-being. It takes time, skill, patience, prayer, and the intervention of the Holy Spirit to establish a trusting, healing relationship with a woman who fears that the therapist is the enemy of her soul.

FINDING A PLACE TO START

When the counselor begins work by focusing on the story of the woman who has come for help, two factors quickly emerge. Although these factors are fairly evident, they are often overlooked by the counselor who has not been trained to be sensitive to the unique characteristics of problems that women bring to the therapy process.

The first problem lies with the woman's attitude toward her own story. Despite her pain, a woman who comes for therapy often regards herself as having little real importance. She regards her life experiences as having little or no significance that merits the attention of others or, for that matter, of herself. She often begins her story with the assumption that her first task in the therapeutic hour is to discover what the counselor thinks is important and then tell the counselor what the counselor indicates is important to hear. Most women begin counseling with the belief that they are themselves unable to know with certainty what is significant about their own life experiences.

The counselor is then faced with two challenges: (1) to encourage a woman to tell her own life story and, in telling, hear *herself* tell her story and give it meaning; and (2) to learn as a counselor to hear the woman's story with an open mind and to begin the therapeutic work from the point in the woman's life story where *she* invites participation.

If a counselor listens in this way, it will quickly become clear that every woman brings to her therapeutic work a belief about what it means to be a woman and what she believes living life as a woman is all about. If women are to work out their sense of health and wholeness as women, each must be helped to face her own belief system so that it can be consciously examined to see if it is indeed true.

I have come to think of the belief systems that women bring to therapy as having a strong element of mythology or misbelief mixed in with major elements of truth. A woman may believe, for example, that she is physically unattractive, and indeed, by the standards of her culture, that may be true. In most instances, however, such a woman will have an accompanying belief of which she is unaware, and which is *not* true. She believes, "I am physically unattractive, and that makes me of less value as a woman." It is this second part of her thinking, this belief that her value as a women depends upon her physical beauty, which is untrue. This is a *misbelief*. I have come to think of misbeliefs such as this as women's *mythology*.

This mythology is so covertly interwoven in women's stories that it is not always readily heard or identified. The indirect expression of the mythology is not the only reason for this difficulty, however. The mythology is often difficult to identify because the therapist (male or female) also believes the old mythology in whole or in part. These misbeliefs about women are so commonly circulated in our culture that they become an unconscious part of our thinking long before we reach graduate school or seminary.

Because the professional training of therapists, including pastoral counselors, does not include study of the psychology of women or deal directly with issues specifically relevant to therapy with women, the therapist's belief system about women survives the professional training system without examination. Therapists then often begin therapy with women in a condition much like their women clients. Therapists (male and female alike) are influenced by a belief system of which they are unaware and which is therefore unexamined and difficult to identify.

Examination of some components of this belief system is a necessary beginning point for any therapist who desires to become more competent in helping women.

NOTES

1. N. F. Russo, ed., *A National Agenda to Address Women's Mental Health Needs* (Washington, D.C.: American Psychological Association, 1985).

2. William R. Gove, "Mental Illness and Psychiatric Treatment Among

Women," *Psychology of Women Quarterly* 4 (1980): 345–62. Juanita Williams, *Psychology of Women*, 3rd ed. (New York: Norton, 1987), 448–50.

3. T. C. Buczek, "Sex Biases in Counseling: Counselor Retention of the Concerns of a Female and Male Client," *Journal of Counseling Psychology* 28 (1981): 13–21.

4. L. S. Fidell, "Sex Differences in Psychotropic Drug Use," *Professional Psychology* 12 (1981): 156–62.

5. L. S. Fidell, "Put Her Down on Drugs: Prescribed Drug Usage in Women" (Paper presented at the Western Psychological Association Meeting, Anaheim, Calif., April 1973).

6. J. C. Holroyd and A. M. Brodskey, "Psychologists' Attitudes and Practices Regarding Erotic and Nonerotic Physical Contact with Patients," *American Psychologist* 32 (1977): 843–49.

7. A. M. Brodsky, "A Decade of Feminist Influence on Psychotherapy," *Psychology of Women Quarterly* 4 (1980): 331–44.

8. K. S. Page, B. G. Tabachnick, and P. Keith-Spiegel, "Ethics of Practice: The Beliefs and Behaviors of Psychologists as Therapists," *American Psychologist* 42 (1987): 993–1006.

9. J. A. Sherman, C. Koufacos, and J. A. Kenworthy, "Therapists: Their Attitudes and Information About Women," *Psychology of Women Quarterly* 2 (1987): 299–313.

10. Margaret W. Matlin, *The Psychology of Women* (Fort Worth, Tex.: Holt, Rinehart and Winston, 1987), 395.

11. Williams, 465.

12. A. M. Brodsky and R. T. Hare-Mustin, "Psychotherapy and Women: Priorities for Research," *Women and Psychotherapy* (New York: Guilford, 1980), 385.

13. Matlin, 391.

14. W. R. Gove, "Sex, Marital Status, Psychiatric Treatment: A Research Note," *Social Forces* (1979), 89–93.

15. W. R. Gove and J. F. Todor, "Adult Sex Roles and Mental Illness," *American Journal of Sociology* 78 (1973): 812–35.

16. Catherine K. Riessman and Naomi Gerstel, *Social Science and Medicine*, quoted by Bryce J. Cristensen, "The Costly Retreat from Marriage," *The Saturday Evening Post* (January/February 1990), 32.

17. See Matlin, 387–89, for a discussion of the implications of Gove's work.

18. Gove, "Mental Illness and Psychiatric Treatment Among Women," 345–62.

19. I. Broverman et al., "Sex-role Stereotypes and Clinical Judgments of Mental Health," *Journal of Consulting and Clinical Psychology* 28 (1972): 1–7.

20. M. L. Smith, "Sex Bias in Counseling and Psychotherapy," *Psychological Bulletin* 87 (1980): 392–407.

21. Phyllis Chesler, *Women and Madness* (New York: Doubleday, 1972).

22. M. Kaplan, "A Woman's View of DSM-III," *American Psychologist* 38 (1983): 786–92.

23. R. D. Phillips and F. D. Gilroy, "Sex Bias in Counseling and Clinical Judgments of Mental Health: The Broverman's Findings Reexamined," *Sex Roles* 12 (1985): 179–93.

24. Broverman, 1–7.

25. Matlin, 397.

26. Hannah Lerman, *A Mote in Freud's Eye: From Psychoanalysis to the Psychology of Woman* (New York: Springer, 1986). See also Hannah Lerman, "From Freud to Feminist Personality Theory: Getting Here from There," *Psychology of Women Quarterly* 10 (1986): 1–18.

27. W. R. Gove, "Mental Illness and Psychiatric Treatment Among Women," in *Psychology of Women: Ongoing Debates,* ed. Mary Roth Walsh (New Haven, Conn.: Yale University Press, 1987), 110.

28. Marilyn Johnson, "Mental Illness and Psychiatric Treatment Among Women: A Response," in *Psychology of Women: Ongoing Debates,* ed. Mary Roth Walsh (New Haven, Conn.: Yale University Press, 1987), 119–26.

29. B. P. Dohrenwend and B. S. Dohrenwend, "Sex Differences and Psychiatric Disorders," *American Journal of Sociology* 81 (1976): 1447–54.

30. Miriam Greenspan, *A New Approach to Women and Therapy* (New York: McGraw- Hill, 1983), 161.

31. John MacArthur, Jr., *Whatever Happened to the Holy Spirit?* in John MacArthur's Bible Studies (Panorama City, Calif.: Grace to You, 1989), 17.

Chapter Two

Mental Health and the Mythology of Women

APPROACHING THERAPY WITH WOMEN BY LISTENING without prejudice to the woman's story is, admittedly, a radical idea. It is so radical in fact that for the most part it is not done.

Probably most therapists (male and female) would vigorously resist this charge. They would insist, to the contrary, that they do listen carefully to what the woman client says. As we noted earlier, however, some studies indicate that even at the simplest level of listening, therapists (male and female) do not pay attention to women's stories in the way in which they attend to men's stories. Therapists then remember less of what they do hear if it is a woman's story.

Additionally, therapists filter what they hear through diagnostic grids that reflect a professional presupposition about what women are really like. In listening, therapists also filter what they hear through their belief system about women, which for the most part is unconscious and unexamined. One nationally known therapist of women recently noted, "Every

15

therapist, whether feminist or 'Freudian,' will express, in the course of treatment, her or his own values and visions for women. There is no 'value-free' therapy."[1]

Therapy is not and cannot be value-free for the woman (or man) client any more than it can be for the therapist. For both the woman client and her therapist, culturally defined notions of masculinity and femininity consciously or unconsciously influence what will be considered to be healthy or natural for men and women. Both the woman and her therapist must deal with this mythology at a conscious and deliberate level or these belief systems will seriously interfere with the healing process.

In seeking to become aware of women's mythology, both in myself as a therapist and in my women clients, I have sought to listen from the woman's point of view to literally hundreds of women's stories over the years.

In the process, I have identified a number of misbeliefs that women clients frequently hold about themselves as women and about the life tasks and experiences of women. The following list is far from exhaustive. It does, however, identify some of the most common and powerful of these misbeliefs. It includes some that have long historical roots and some that have particular relevance for Christian women.

MISBELIEFS WHICH SOME WOMEN AND THEIR THERAPISTS HOLD:

1. Women are of less value than men.
2. Women's work is of less value than men's work.
3. Women are more emotional than men, less logical, more intuitive, and, consequently, less capable decision-makers. They talk more than males and think less.
4. Women's sense of self and sense of achievement are relationally based and therefore inferior. Because women's sense of self and of achievement are relationally based, women are dependent upon a significant other person, preferably a male, to affirm and confirm them.
5. Women are passive, weaker, more fragile, and more vulnerable than males, and therefore less able to achieve significantly or to function independently. Women cannot, by definition, have enough of the "right stuff" to

achieve nor to function independently. If a woman becomes a high achiever, by male norms, or exhibits high levels of independence, she is viewed by definition as having become less womanly.

6. Women are irrational, unstable, and changeable.

7. Women are deceitful, untrustworthy, and manipulative.

8. A good woman can by love alone change a man's or family's dysfunctional behavior.

9. A good woman cares only for others, disregarding her own needs.

10. A good woman's needs will be met by others spontaneously without her request because she has selflessly cared for others.

11. Relationships and emotional intimacy are the *only* sources of life satisfaction for the good woman.

12. A woman's body is her primary source of identity and worth. Her worth derives from her beauty, fertility, her sexuality, which is designed principally to provide sexual satisfaction for the male.

13. Power and true femininity and/or spirituality cannot co-exist. The good woman, if she is spiritually mature and psychologically well-adjusted, cannot, by definition, be a powerful woman.

14. The good woman can be readily identified by her piety, purity, domestic skills, and highly submissive attitude toward males—the cult of True Womanhood.

15. The good woman is most satisfied when occupying a woman's proper place and finds her true fulfillment as a woman in being a submissive wife and self-sacrificing mother.

16. Marriage and family relationships are primarily the woman's responsibility. If marriage and/or family relationships deteriorate, it is the woman's fault. It then becomes her responsibility to fix what is wrong.

17. A good Christian woman is responsible for the man's sexuality, faithfulness, and self-control.

18. Christian women are uniquely responsible for our national welfare and survival. It is God's will that they preserve our nation from moral destruction by confor-

mity to traditional roles. Nontraditional roles for women threaten national survival.

19. Christian women draw their value only from their roles as wives, mothers, and helpers of males. This is God's design and His will for their lives.

Evidences of Mythology in the Counseling Process

When Kate came for her first appointment, I asked what she wanted to happen in her life as a result of counseling. She thought about my question for a moment, then said seriously, "I want counseling to help me become a good woman, able to live life in the right way."

Most women who come for counseling will identify a less philosophical goal, but whatever their stated purpose, like Kate, most will have a mental image of what a "good woman" is like. Most will also have some idea about how to act in "the right way" as a woman.

Some women like the good woman image that they bring to the therapeutic process. Even if this concept is positive, however, such a concept can be troublesome if the woman thinks of it as an unreachable ideal.

Other women do not like the good woman image they have developed, but they feel vaguely guilty about this dislike. They will say, "I just don't like women very well. I don't know what's the matter with me. I guess I have a poor self-concept." Nevertheless, they exhibit uneasiness about any attempt to examine or change this concept. It is as though they think, "My concept of the good woman is right, even if I don't want to be a woman in that way. It is something about *me* that's wrong."

Even when women come to counseling with little conscious awareness of their concept of the good woman, this image is powerful in shaping the content and process of therapy. Every woman brings the myth of the good woman along with her own individual myths to therapy. These myths, like ghosts, are present in every therapy hour.

An examination of the general mythology of women reveals that women are rarely viewed simply as ordinary human beings. Freud contributed powerfully to this aspect of the myth.

He once asked a female colleague, "The great question that has never been answered and which I have not yet been able to answer, despite my thirty years of research into the feminine soul, is 'what does a woman want?'"[2] In 1933 in his last paper on female psychology, Freud spoke of femininity as a riddle.

It is difficult to estimate the degree to which this attitude discouraged the scientific study of women and perpetuated the myth of woman as the mysterious, unknowable other, the polar opposite of the strong, active, logical male. However stereotyped, Freud's attitude became part of the view of women that was advanced as psychological science. This attitude was incorporated into the Terman scales, which formed one of the foundational measures of femininity on which subsequent measures throughout nearly four decades of research were based.

This concept of woman as the mysterious other is a curious paradox. Women are viewed as symbolizing the sacred, yet as embodying the profane. They are pictured as the source of temptation and sexual sin, yet presented as the defenders of virtue, morality, and sexual purity. Women are portrayed as weak and vulnerable, yet so powerful that their failure to conform to proper roles can prove the downfall of a great nation.

Not long ago, a young woman came to me for assistance with the trauma following a date rape. After tearfully recounting the circumstances surrounding the event, she said, "My pastor told me that whenever anything like this happens, it's the woman's fault, that I must have tempted him in some way!" In this incident the myth of the woman as the irresistible sexual temptress came directly into the therapy hour by way of the pastor's opinion. Thankfully, not all pastors perpetuate this myth. The example serves, however, as clear evidence that the mythology of women shapes the way in which we view women in the church as well as in the culture at large.

THE MYTH OF WOMEN'S VALUE

Many women come to therapy identifying problems in self-esteem as the presenting problem. But often underlying the woman's personal sense of limited self-worth is her belief that by being born female she has been assigned permanently to the world of second-class citizenship. The difficulty is not that women are of less value. The problem is that they have been taught to think that they are of less value and often have been treated so.

For many Christian women, there is an additional, painfully conflicted aspect to this devalued role. A Christian woman is likely to be exposed to a theology that affirms her worth as an equal recipient with men of the image and the grace of God. In contrast, however, she is treated as constitutionally deficient as a woman and therefore of less value than the males in her environment, both within and outside the church. Which of these messages is she then to believe? Because actions have greater impact than words when the messages are incongruent, devaluing behaviors (in the church and out) decrease the woman's belief in her God-given worth, no matter how respectful the theological message of her church may be.

Therapeutic issues are complex and sensitive for the woman who has emotionally resigned herself to a devalued position in relation to men. Such a client cannot be instructed that God loves her and that she therefore need no longer be depressed. Neither can she be advised that her identity is improperly formulated, and that she should alter her theology to permit a more positive self-concept. Development of a biblically congruent sense of positive self-esteem is a long and complicated counseling task.

If the depression and depleted sense of self-esteem are treated medically with antidepressants or therapeutically without reference to the underlying belief system or social system (including the marriage), then progress will be slow or nonexistent. When the mythology is part of the pathology, it cannot be therapeutically ignored.

For the woman who is more directly confronting the myth of her devalued worth, therapeutic work is not easier, but it is more straightforward. Examination of the myth remains, however, equally essential to the woman's progress. Issues of self-esteem inevitably entail grappling with this myth.

MYTHS ABOUT WOMEN'S WORK

The idea that women's work is less valuable than men's is again a difficult myth with which to deal. It is true that in the culture at large, women's work *is* less valued in comparison to work traditionally done by males. This is not a phenomenon limited to any one culture; it is a universal fact.

Mary Stewart Van Leeuwen has suggested several explanations of the lower social status of women's work as compared to that of men.[3] Whatever the reason may prove to be, women's work is treated as though it is of less value than that of men. Such treatment is a demonstrable fact of life for women. That is no myth. The myth lies in the assumption that this treatment reflects an underlying truth that women's work is in reality less valuable than men's.

A very bright, capable young client once came for assistance with a persistent low level of depression. In one session I described some research in which the identical piece of writing had been highly valued if the alleged writer was thought to be male and less highly valued if the alleged writer was assumed to be female.

"How does this help you think about your struggle with your work?" I asked.

"I think it makes me sadder, and more angry," she replied slowly. "If I understand what you said, it means that I am not just a jealous, emotional woman. If I write a brief, and George writes a brief, they will likely think George's brief is better just because he's a man."

This young attorney went on to work out some creative and effective ways for herself as a Christian to deal with the injustice she was experiencing in her work world. Her problem began with her recognition that the devaluing of her work was indeed a fact. The solution to the problem began when she realized that for her to act as though her work *was* of less value was to participate in a destructive piece of women's mythology.

The majority of women work in low-paying jobs, many of them at minimum wage. Many women spend major portions of their waking hours working as homemakers where they receive no pay at all. Much of women's work is direct service to others (waitress, beautician, clerk) or care of children. It is difficult for a woman to affirm the worth of her work in the face of poor working conditions, low pay, or no pay at all. It is a rare counseling case in which the issue of work, its significance and value, is not a part of a woman's therapeutic struggle.

EMOTIONAL WOMEN, THE CHALLENGE OF DECISION-MAKING

Women often come to the therapeutic process with the deeply embedded myth that they are unable to make good decisions. Many women also have been taught that God knows that as women they are constitutionally unable to make capable decisions and that they must go to a male (father, husband, pastor, therapist, physician) who will help them. The myth suggests that these wise males will explain women's emotional inner storms to them, then tell them what to do with their "female" feelings and lives.

Therapeutic issues for such women are sensitive and complex. The presenting issue is usually depression, sometimes accompanied by an overwhelming sense of fatigue, an inability to get anything done. For such women therapy must deal carefully with the myth, since it is tangled with the woman's sense of how the good woman expresses her faith. If the woman believes that she demonstrates faith in God by denying her own ability to make capable choices, then helping the woman establish options for choice intensifies her sense of helplessness. Choosing is the thing that both her faith and her self-image forbids her to do.

For women able to deal more directly with doubts about their decision-making capacity, the myth of the emotional woman who cannot choose competently needs to be faced straight on. Simply helping a woman identify options for choice can produce high anxiety if the woman believes she has a seriously impaired capacity to choose which she cannot change. By first confronting the myth, options for choice can then be identified and exposed in the context of the woman's fear of choosing.

The Myth of the Incomplete Woman
and the Necessary Male

One old and powerful myth is that a woman is incomplete in herself because she is female and that she needs a male to make her life and herself complete. The myth teaches women that regardless of the quality of her friendships or the depth and strength of relationships she may have, she is incomplete without a male (father, husband, lover, employer, therapist) to provide meaning for her life. This myth makes its appearance in many forms when we counsel with women.

It is ironic for Christians that this myth stands the biblical account in Genesis on its head. In the Creation story, it was Adam who was incomplete without Eve. The myth, however, insists that a woman cannot experience an authentic sense of self or achievement without a significant other person, preferably male, to affirm and confirm her.

Current research indicates that women do appear to experience a need for affiliation and connection that is different than the male experience.[4] Van Leeuwen[5] has provided some challenging insights regarding the possible differential effects of the Fall, which take into account this gender-related difference between males and females.

One circumstance in which this myth often emerges openly is in counseling a woman entangled in an extramarital affair.

A very attractive, professionally successful woman came for counseling complaining of depression. Further exploration revealed that the depression was related to her disappointment and frustration with her lover, her married employer with whom she had maintained an intimate relationship over an extended period of time. She gave an angry, tearful, detailed account of her frustration and hurt in the relationship and the ongoing injury to her conscience it entailed.

"Why do you stay?" I asked gently.

"Well—," she paused. After a thoughtful moment, she said, "I suppose it's partly because I think a woman's better off with a man than she is alone, even under conditions like this."

For Christian women, sometimes there is an additional tangle with the idea that God's will for every woman is a husband. For

these women, to be without a husband is to have missed God's
plan for their lives.

THE MYTH OF THE UNRELIABLE, UNTRUSTWORTHY WOMAN

It would be difficult for most of us to count how many times
we have heard the phrase, "You can't trust a woman." It would
be equally difficult to count the jokes we have heard based on
some woman changing her mind, her hairdo, the furniture, or,
in these days of plastic surgery, her face. Women, the myth
says, are unstable, changeable, and unpredictable. Additionally, they are deceitful, manipulative, and untrustworthy.
There is a joke that also explains why males continue in relationships with these unreliable creatures. It is because "the
ladies, God bless them, you can't live with them, but you can't
live without them."

Women come to therapy with a lifetime of smiling politely
at such jokes, having learned that if they object they will be
publicly rated a very poor sport or, even worse, be suspected
of dangerous feminist leanings. The therapeutic issue is, however, neither amusing nor philosophical. It strikes at the core
of identity issues for women and raises for many women painful questions of their inherent capacity to make and keep
commitments and to sustain responsible behaviors under difficult circumstances.

The myth of the manipulative woman who seeks out of self-
ishness to secretly, deceptively get her way is a major
troublemaker for women, particularly when faced with mastering negotiation skills as a part of conflict resolution.

A woman, second-generation missionary, returned from the
mission field because she was seriously depressed. Exploration revealed that for a long period of time she had been
required to work closely with a coworker who was domineer-
ing and opinionated and who had mercilessly exploited her
passive compliance. My client had made no effort to negotiate
any of her needs with this coworker nor to defend the boundaries of her personal space.

Asked why she had chosen passively to endure as long as
she had, she gave an enlightening response. "I thought it was

better not to do anything," she explained carefully, "because I knew it would make trouble."

"Would that have been a bad thing to do—make trouble?" I asked.

"Well, yes," she said, then added hesitantly. "My father used to say that whenever there was trouble on the compound, at the bottom of it every time you would find some sneaky woman trying to get her way."

A form of the myth that Christian women sometimes are taught suggests that God will provide stability for her instability through her submission to the authoritative male in her life.

THE MYTH OF A WOMAN'S POWERFUL LOVE

Many women are troubled by the myth that a good woman can change a man's (or family's) dysfunctional behavior by love alone. This myth continues to be a chronic troublemaker for women in therapy.

Women who are co-dependents and who function as enablers are often truly astonished to discover in therapy that love cannot alter another's dysfunctional behavior. For such women the concept of permitting individuals to experience the consequences of their behaviors feels like a betrayal of their chosen good woman role.

One woman came for therapy because she was depressed. Her depression was related to seventeen years of marriage to an alcoholic husband. We discussed the possibility that she would no longer call his employer and report him sick on those days he was unable to go to work because of his drinking. Initially, she refused to consider acting in such an unloving way. She explained that she thought that God's Word promised her that if she just loved her husband, God would change him. Her responsibility was only to love unconditionally, and her husband's recovery was assured.

Pastors have numberless stories of ill-advised marriages that, despite their wise counsel to the contrary, have occurred under the spell of this myth. The woman believed that evidences of incipient violence, an ungovernable temper, substance abuse, gambling, or financial irresponsibility were not really significant. Certainly, the woman believed, the man would change in response to the powerful love of a good woman, and she was determined to be that woman.

Belief in this myth makes a woman seek help for a troubled marriage because in her thinking it is *she*, not her troubled spouse, who has failed. The myth has taught her to believe that he would not have become or remained such a troubled individual if only she had loved enough.

THE MYTH OF THE UNSELFISH SAINT

The good woman, so this myth goes, cares only for others, disregarding her own needs. For the woman who believes this myth, disregarding her own needs is her functional definition of unselfishness. To attend to her own needs is selfish, so since good women are not selfish, she must never attend to her own needs.

Again, therapeutic issues are complex and sensitive for such women. To attempt to help them identify their needs without dealing with the myth only intensifies their inner tension. To have needs and to respond to them, even by so simple an act as identifying them, is the very thing the myth of the good woman forbids them to do.

Often for Christian women, this myth is tangled with the idea that taking up one's cross and following Jesus requires the believer to embrace a death to self that entails absolute denial of personal needs and individual preferences.

"I don't *have* any needs or wants," a woman told me one day at the close of a women's retreat. "I've been crucified with Christ, and after you've experienced the Cross, then ideas about women's needs such as you have presented here today simply aren't relevant any more."

A further refinement of the myth of the unselfish saint holds that while the unselfish saint may on occasion have some needs, it is not necessary for her to pay attention to them personally nor ask another to do so. If she is a good woman, unselfishly caring for others' needs, others will in turn spontaneously meet her unspoken needs without her request.

Often in therapy if a woman shows resistance to asking others to meet her needs, the problem is this form of the myth. She may feel that she has been unselfishly caring for others, therefore she has a right to expect that others will know and meet her needs even without her spoken request.

THE MYTH THAT RELATIONSHIPS ARE ALWAYS ENOUGH

This myth is again difficult to deal with since it distorts the truth about the importance of relationships to women. Women do appear to have a need for connection and affiliation which is different from that experienced by males. But the myth teaches women that relationships, if they are truly good women, are *all* that they need.

This myth appears in many complex forms. One circumstance in which it frequently surfaces is in therapeutic work with many professional women, including women who are artists, musicians, and writers. The myth forbids them, in effect, as good women to invest in their art, music, writing, or work the time, energy, and significance that emotionally they desire to give it. Conflict about their gifts and work revolves around their struggle with this myth.

A former client who is a gifted young artist tells of a conversation with her mother centered around this myth. My client had been asked to show her work at an important local gallery, but when she stopped by her mother's house to share her excitement, the conversation went something like this:

Susan: "Mom, I'm really pleased with how my life is going. I'm beginning to feel as though I'm getting somewhere with my art. I've been asked to do a show at Christmas at the Metropolitan Gallery."

Mother: "That's nice, Susan." Long pause. Then, "How are you and that nice young man doing, honey? Be careful not to talk too much about your show."

Mother was carefully reinforcing the myth that only relationships count—especially relationships with the opposite sex. According to the old mythology (and mother), only relationships bring a lasting sense of joy and of accomplishment. Being

a gifted artist is irrelevant to the important business of being a
woman.

Almost without exception clinical issues of enmeshment
entail some form of this myth. The intrusive mother, the cling-
ing wife, the depressed empty-nester, these often are women
who are struggling with the myth that forbids them to include
some significant nonrelational achievement in their lives.

Women sometimes recognize this struggle in another
woman and comment, "She would feel better [i.e., be less de-
pressed] if she just had something interesting to do." That is
indeed correct, but the problem is that the myth forbids her to
develop something significant and exciting to do. The myth
holds that for the good woman, relationships are all that one
needs; they alone are enough.

THE MYTH OF THE BODY AS A WOMAN'S SOURCE OF IDENTITY

This myth has been a source of trouble for women for centuries, and both Freud and Hollywood have furthered the trouble.
Women are taught to believe that identity and achievement for
a woman is biologically based. Women come to therapy having
been taught to evaluate themselves and their lives from a biological point of view. "Am I beautiful? Am I sexually attractive?
Am I thin? Can I conceive a child? Am I successfully resisting
the aging process?" And, recently, "Do I have a hard, athletic
body line with no apparent feminine curves?"

Theoretically, Christian women should experience less pressure in this area, but sadly the myth is equally powerful and
equally destructive within the church. For example, in the
church there are increasing numbers of women who are single,
or married and childless (by choice or circumstance). For others, parenting is a painful and difficult experience. These
women often find Mother's Day to be a nearly unbearable or-
deal. There the church perpetuates the myth that the good
woman is married, fertile, and deeply fulfilled by the parenting
process.

The good woman is also thin. In one widely known organization that sponsors community Bible studies, a woman is
prevented from moving into leadership unless her weight falls

within established norms, no matter what her knowledge of Scripture may be nor what evidences of spiritual maturity she may display. Those norms forbid too much weight, but no woman can be too thin to serve. In my community a woman I knew to be anorexic did in fact hold office; her assistant was a recovering bulimic. The tragedy of such behavior is, of course, twofold. Obesity becomes the focus of unfair discrimination while the desperate need for help evidenced by the anorexic woman and her bulimic assistant are ignored.

A local marriage enrichment series sponsored by a nationally known parachurch organization held a session for wives only that focused on diet and grooming tips presumably to enable a woman to secure and hold her husband's interest and approval through her appearance. While the women were receiving this instruction, the men, in a husbands-only session, were instructed in financial planning and money management.

This emphasis on biologically based significance in women's lives can also be seen in a common response to women living in violent and abusive marital relationships. Many churches are becoming more knowledgeable about the nature of domestic violence and more concerned about the welfare of women who find themselves caught in such relationships. Women are still frequently told, however, that their husbands' violence and abuse can be cured if only the women will provide more sexual satisfaction.[6] The woman's body and her physical availability to the man become the focus of attention, rather than the woman's pain or the violence which holds both husband and wife in its terrible cycle.

The myth that a woman's worth and identity is biologically based lives on in the church as well as in the culture at large.

THE MYTH OF POWERLESSNESS

This myth presents a double bind for women. It teaches that power and true femininity and/or spirituality cannot coexist. The good woman, if she is spiritually mature and psychologically well-adjusted cannot, by definition, be a powerful woman.

As Broverman's research indicated, women come to therapy facing the cultural double bind. They can be immature and dependent, and a culturally approved female, or they can be powerful and independent, but at the cost of losing a significant aspect of their womanliness.

For Christian women, again, there can be an additional painful tangle with the idea that the biblical norm for all women is avoidance of power and/or assignment of all power to men. The myth teaches that the good, godly woman demonstrates dependency, submissiveness, and powerlessness, at least in her relationships with men, and she does this because this is God's assigned role for her life.

Therapeutic issues surrounding this myth are enormously difficult for most women to work through. As therapists we must work to insure that psychological health and spiritual maturity *are not* defined in solely masculine terms. Women must be free to develop characteristics of maturity and uses of power that are distinctively feminine. But at the same time, women must be free to develop standards of feminine maturity that are not controlled by cultural requirements for dependency and powerlessness. A therapist who sees women must be sensitive to the destructiveness of this myth and the difficulty of the double bind that it poses for women, which can be particularly painful for women in more conservative churches.

THE CULT OF TRUE WOMANHOOD

By the mid-nineteenth century, American society had developed a firmly held definition of the good woman. She was pious, pure, utterly submissive, and dedicated solely to her domestic duties. This definition of the good woman was advocated with such fervor that historians commonly refer to this concept as the cult of True Womanhood.

According to historian Barbara Welter,

> The attributes of True Womanhood, by which a woman judged herself and was judged by her husband, her neighbors and society, could be divided

into four cardinal virtues—piety, purity, submissiveness and domesticity. Put them all together and they
spelled mother, daughter, sister, wife—woman.
Without them, no matter whether there was fame,
achievement or wealth, all was ashes. With them she
was promised happiness and power.[7]

Welter also described the fervor with which this idea was
promoted. "If anyone, male or female, dared to tamper with
the complex of virtues which made up True Womanhood, he
was damned immediately as an enemy of God, of civilization
and of the Republic."[8]

Another historian, Barbara MacHaffie, has discussed how
the troublesome nature of the cult of True Womanhood seriously impaired the full participation of women in the Christian
community.[9] Some aspects of this troublesome tradition affect
counseling with women particularly within the evangelical
community.

Many Christian counselors as well as many women clients
believe remnants of the cult of True Womanhood. Most therapists, and most of their clients, have little knowledge of church
history or of the history of women,[10] so they fail to realize that
the cult of True Womanhood does not rest upon a biblical foundation. It was developed to serve a socioeconomic, ecclesiastical
agenda. Selected biblical truths were interpreted, organized, and
promoted to serve social and political goals consistent with a
male-dominant culture. Because these ideas may appear scrip-
tural, they can influence the goals of therapy without the
therapist or client being aware of the actual nonbiblical basis
upon which the cult of True Womanhood rests.

An additional problem with the cult of True Womanhood is
its mix of truth and falsehood. The cardinal virtues of True
Womanhood (piety, purity, submission, and domesticity) contain a particularly complicated combination of wheat and
chaff. It is easier to see the chaff in this concept of the good
woman if we begin first with the kernels of truth that the idea
contains.

For evangelical women, piety is often conceptualized in
terms of personal devoutness and theological orthodoxy. As

such, piety has a high value. When she comes for counseling, the evangelical woman will often include an increase in her personal devotion to God as a part of her goals for growth. She will express a desire for counseling in a form consistent with an orthodox expression of her faith. The evangelical woman would likely agree, at least in the context of Christian counseling, that the good woman is a pious one.

Similarly, sexual purity is important to the majority of these women. Some of them, of course, report difficulty or failure in living out their sexual value system. Such difficulty and failure is often a part of the presenting symptoms which they bring to counseling. Yet, despite these personal struggles, and the social changes which have accompanied the sexual revolution, sexual purity retains a high value for evangelical women. The evangelical woman would likely agree with advocates of the cult of True Womanhood, that a good woman is characterized by sexual purity, which is generally defined as celibacy outside the marriage relationship and fidelity within it.

Care of family and nurture of children are also deeply held values within the evangelical community. Tension in family life is often a precipitating circumstance which leads a woman to seek help from a counselor. As participants in families, evangelical women continue to value domestic skills. They view homemaking as an important contribution to the community at large as well as to their immediate families.

Evangelical groups today, as MacHaffie notes, are widely associated with a position advocating the subordination and silence of women.[11] Within the evangelical community, however, there are significant exceptions to a rigid application of this concept. Both in groups and in the lives of individual women, there is growing emphasis upon mutual submission and greater participation of women within the life and government of the church.[12] Nevertheless, many evangelical women agree, at least in principle, that the good woman is submissive, although *submission* would likely be defined in a way quite foreign to nineteenth century thought.

In view of these points of agreement, it may appear strange that the cult of True Womanhood is cited here. Given the general consensus regarding the value of piety, purity, submission, and domesticity, why would the cult of True Womanhood be listed as a myth with potential danger to the therapeutic process? There are reasons for this objection based both in theology and in science.

The problem is twofold. It entails (1) the emphasis of the cult of True Womanhood upon women as females rather than women, and (2) the way in which it defines women's nature.

The cult of True Womanhood presented women's nature (whatever that was) as utterly different from that of men. These differences were for the most part conceptualized as negative characteristics or as deficiencies. She was weak, illogical, dependent, childlike, and without sexual needs. Astonishingly, however, despite this allegedly deficient nature, the woman was characterized as a noble being who was far more responsive to God than was the man. Piety, purity, submission, and domesticity were viewed as special requirements for women because of this allegedly unique female nature. Scripture was then summoned to support this point of view in whatever prooftexting fashion was necessary to support the argument.

This view of women's nature certainly does not fit with our present understanding of women as they are pictured through developmental and gender research. It is not difficult to see why the cult of True Womanhood and its definition of *the feminine* is discarded out of hand by scientists.

Theologically, the concept is equally wide of the mark. In the broad context of the Christian faith, personal devotion to God, sexual purity, and care of family are values and responsibilities equally applicable to men as to women. Mutual submission to one another within the family of God is required of both men and women. Both men and women are required, additionally, to be subject to those civil authorities appointed to rule over them. Piety, purity, family care, and a spirit of submissiveness are behaviors required of all believers in obedience to the Scripture, rather than as responses to social roles. Behaviors that demonstrate these values are therefore equally desirable in both men and women.

In the conventional understanding of Scripture, men and women are equally sinful. They must depend equally upon the ministry of the Holy Spirit to draw them to God. They are equally dependent upon the Holy Spirit to work out that transformation of character and behavior which is the mark of the mature believer.

The cult of True Womanhood conceptualizes the nature of women as being different in their potential for response to God. As a result of this different nature, women are expected to have different rules for obedience than do men. Many evangelicals would regard this point of view as a dangerous step toward what the apostle Paul called "another gospel."

At this point I trust that it is clear that whatever remnants of the cult of True Womanhood that survive are dangerous. Such concepts seriously distort the biblical call to discipleship which is incumbent upon *all* believers, male and female alike. Additionally, it presents a definition of femininity that has no basis in fact as established by scientific study of women.

Ways in which these remnants may occur in the therapy hour include the idea that women find fulfillment (and, by implication, true mental health) *only* in their proper sphere as wives and mothers. It also appears in the idea, still circulating, that women are uniquely responsible for the man's sexuality ("It was my responsibility to say 'no.'"), marital fidelity ("He's seeing another woman. What did *I* do wrong? I should have loved him more!"), and self-control ("He blew up and spanked Susan too hard. But it was really my fault. I should have kept her quiet."). It also occurs in the form of a persistent low-level depression associated with the woman's sense that she is keeping the rules but is experiencing a continuing sense of disappointment with life.

A woman recently came for therapy reporting that she was depressed. While describing the circumstances of her life, Laura said, "I'm keeping a model home. My kids are great, and doing well in school. My husband gets good meals, clean clothes, adequate sex, the lawn mowed, and reasonably good conversation when he can stay home long enough and awake long enough to join in. I'm a submissive wife, an at-home mother, a model housekeeper, and an active participant in my church. I'm doing what I'm supposed to do. Why am I so unhappy? Why do I feel so frightened that this may be all there is?"

Laura will come up for further discussion in a later chapter. Here I want only to point out that piety, purity, submission, and domesticity were insufficient to serve as the bottom line for this woman's life, despite the inherent value of these characteristics. Fidelity to the cult of True Womanhood cannot provide women an adequate answer to the question, "Is this all that there is?"

Remnants of the cult of True Womanhood are often incorporated in an overemphasis on the importance of the woman's participation in relationships. The belief that a woman's unique nature makes her the responsible one in relationships may be a source of serious spiritual problems as well as adjustment difficulties.

Mary Stewart Van Leeuwen suggests that the Fall affected men and women in different ways. This has resulted in the tendency in men to abuse power. In women it has resulted in a willingness to have peace at any price in order to preserve relationships. Women, Van Leeuwen suggests, are tempted "to reduce all of womanhood to nurturing relationships at the expense of hearing the word of God and keeping it." In so doing, women abandon the exercise of what Van Leeuwen views as "responsible dominion."[13] Van Leeuwen is not alone in her concern about the ways in which emphasis on relationships may affect women's sense of spirituality and social responsibility.

In *Gender, the Myth of Equality*, James Neely discusses what he views as the female tendency to neglect knowledge of society and its institutions, and to reject personal involvement in social issues. He describes this tendency as "disallowing the Logos."[14]

It is not clear if in fact these are sins to which women are uniquely vulnerable. But if so, ideas growing out of the cult of True Womanhood that restrict women from responsible participation in all areas of life (including the church) make a major contribution not only to women's psychological distress but also to their spiritual failure to thrive.

Since we cannot yet define mental health for women in an objective, global way relevant to all women, it appears most beneficial to begin therapy with women with the goal of structuring the counseling process so that the woman can hear her own story and work out her own definition of wholeness and health for herself. For the Christian woman, this would entail working out her sense of self and focus of life within the context of her faith and her understanding of obedience to the Word of God and to the church.

When the counselor and woman client attempt to follow such an approach, both are faced with the task of identifying and dealing with (1) the old mythology or belief systems about women that thread through the woman's story and (2) her understanding of herself and her life. Because professional training programs do not address the psychology of women, therapists (male and female) may find that their own entanglement with the old mythology may seriously interfere with the therapeutic process. Examining aspects of the old mythology is a helpful step toward becoming a more competent therapist with women clients. It is disconcerting to discover, however, that while the old mythology continues to thrive and cause trouble, a new mythology has begun to flourish and to provide additional problems for both the woman and her therapist.

NOTES

1. Harriet Golhor Lerner, *Women in Therapy* (New York: Harper and Row, 1988), 110.

2. Sigmund Freud as quoted in Juanita Williams, *Psychology of Women*, 3rd ed. (New York: Norton, 1987), 8.

3. Mary Stewart Van Leeuwen, "Making Baskets or Building Houses," *Daughters of Sarah* 15 (September/October 1989): 3–7.

4. Jean Baker Miller, *Toward a New Psychology of Women*, 2nd ed. (Boston: Beacon Press, 1986).

5. Mary Stewart Van Leeuwen, "The Christian Mind and the Challenge of Gender Relations," *The Reformed Journal* (September 1987).

6. Jim Alsdurf and Phyllis Alsdurf, *Battered Into Submission* (Downers Grove,Ill.: InterVarsity, 1989).

7. Barbara Welter, "The Cult of True Womanhood," in *Dimity Convictions: The American Woman in the Nineteenth Century*, ed. Barbara Welter (Athens, Ohio: Ohio University Press, 1976), 21.

8. Ibid.

9. Barbara J. MacHaffie, *Her Story: Women in Christian Tradition* (Philadelphia: Fortress Press, 1986), 2. MacHaffie's discussion of the cult of True

Womanhood occurs in Chapter 6, "Women Organizing for Mission and Reform," 93–106. MacHaffie also discusses the Cult of True Womanhood in Chapter 8, "American Women in Catholicism and Sectarianism," 117–28.

10. MacHaffie's book is a brief, easy-reading history of women in Christian tradition with a valuable bibliography of suggested further reading. It is a helpful resource for a therapist seeking to understand more clearly the historical context of the mythology of women as it has been articulated through the centuries by the church.

11. MacHaffie, 107.

12. Christians for Biblical Equality, currently led by the classical scholar Dr. Catherine Kroeger, is one such group. Information and publications can be secured by writing: Christians for Biblical Equality, 380 Lafayette Freeway, Suite 122, St. Paul, MN 55107–1216.

13. Mary Stewart Van Leeuwen, *Gender and Grace: Love, Work, and Parenting in a Changing World* (Downers Grove, Ill.: InterVarsity, 1990).

14. James C. Neely, *Gender, The Myth of Equality* (New York: Simon and Schuster, 1981). See also Joan Winfrey, "Gender Studies: A Review of the Literature and Some Implications for the Church," *Journal of Biblical Equality* 1 (1989): 50–60.

Chapter Three

The New Mythology

LIKE THE OLD MYTHOLOGY, THE NEW MYTHOLOGY is equally difficult and troublesome to identify and manage. While listening to women's stories, I have identified new misbeliefs which have arisen in the current wave of social change. The list below is far from exhaustive, but it does include some of the most common and powerful of these new misbeliefs which, like the old mythology, can influence and interfere with the counseling process.

MISBELIEFS HELD BY SOME WOMEN AND THEIR THERAPISTS

1. Women are *no* different than men. Genuine differences are limited to genital structure and functioning; all other differences are the result of gender-role socialization.
2. Life patterns and life priorities for women are best when they replicate those of white male middle-class norms.

3. Achievement is the *only* source of self-esteem and life satisfaction for the fully mature woman.
4. Women are healthiest and happiest when they develop and use power in ways similar to those demonstrated by males.
5. Mental health for women requires the assimilation of masculine traits and characteristics.
6. Relationships are of no more value to women than to men except to the degree the woman is socialized to believe that they are.
7. Marriage and family are of incidental value to the fully mature woman and so are to be incorporated into her life solely on the basis of personal and career convenience.
8. Conservative religious beliefs are inevitably destructive to women's growth and achievement.

As with the old mythology, not all counselors nor all women clients believe these aspects of the new mythology. However, individual threads of these concepts are often interwoven with women's stories in such a way that they are difficult to see unless this mythology, too, has been subjected to careful thought.

THE MYTH OF SAMENESS

One of the particularly troublesome ideas of the new mythology is the concept that differences between men and women are limited to biological differences in genital structure and functioning. This myth argues that all other differences are the result of culture expressed through gender-role socialization and should therefore be disregarded or eliminated.

The question of sex and gender differences is complex and presently the source of sharp disagreement between scientists. Biology, psychology, anthropology, medicine, sociobiology, and theology, among other disciplines, currently struggle with the question. Researchers and scientists viewing similar types of data can (and do) come to widely differing conclusions.[1]

Because of its importance and complexity, material on gender differences will be reviewed in a separate chapter. In considering gender differences in the context of the new mythology, the point is not the content of the research but rather the human tendency to substitute an opposite but equally erroneous idea for an old mistake. When this happens the new position is often held with equal prejudice and error.

The old mythology argues that men and women are so different that women are the "absolute other." Since women are absolutely *different,* the old mythology requires that women live by different rules and roles and function differently in relationships.

The new mythology argues that men and women are absolutely the *same.* Since women are absolutely the same, this new mythology then insists that they need the same rules and roles and function in the same manner in relationships.

The truth appears to be that each of these pieces of mythology is seriously incorrect, at least in this all-or-nothing form. To believe either without qualification is to put oneself at odds both with science and with Scripture. That is certainly a poor place from which to begin the counseling process.

There appear to be elements both of error and of truth in each myth. Men and women in some ways are more *alike* than different; in other ways they are more *different* than alike.

The old mythology points to differences between men and women as *the truth* through which all other truth must be understood; it has resulted in dangerous distortions and rigid stereotypes which have been destructive to women. The new mythology points to likenesses between men and women as *the truth* through which all other truth must be understood; it is proving to be equally dangerous. It is already resulting in distortions and new equally rigid stereotypes which are also destructive to women.

A number of years ago a woman came to me for counseling. She was a brilliant young attorney and a new believer who was struggling with translating her faith into her workplace. She was also beginning to struggle with her identity as a woman within the context of her new faith. Integration into the life of her new church was proving difficult. We soon discovered that among her difficulties was the fact that she had run head-on into the old mythology.

She was being taught that the good Christian woman was, in every relationship and circumstance of life, emotional, soft, receptive, and dependent. Her role as a woman was always to be the responder rather than the initiator. The difficulty was that Anne was a prosecuting attorney in a district attorney's office. Her responsibilities included the preparation and prosecution of those cases in which sexual crimes against children were alleged to have occurred. In that setting, for Anne to have always acted as the emotional, soft, receptive, gentle responder would have been worse than inappropriate. It would have effectively prevented her from carrying out her job.

Additionally, while Anne had secured a good position immediately out of law school, she sensed that her advancement was now being slowed by systematic discrimination against her within the office. This discrimination appeared to be rooted at least in part in the perception of the other attorneys that she was a woman, and worse, a woman who had "gone religious." They were convinced she was too soft and sentimental to do her job with the toughness required for competency as a prosecuting attorney. Her church, in addition, was suggesting that Christians ought never to be involved with the civil court system. It had been suggested to Anne that for her as a woman to serve as a prosecuting attorney was a serious mistake, the result of her failure to accurately discern God's will for her life.

Anne said, "I feel I am being told to be like the child victims I seek to serve: vulnerable, defenseless, and helpless to seek justice for myself or for those kids who have been hurt."

The old mythology was clearly injurious to her. It could have hindered her faith had she not sought help for the issues that it raised.

This case is interesting because this client also met the *new* mythology with equally difficult issues and equal destructiveness.

After a period of time, Anne worked out a good sense of her identity as a woman along with a powerful sense of her calling as an attorney, both within the context of her faith. She went on her way with my prayers and expectation that she would indeed do well.

Several years later I received a call from a woman whose voice I recognized although her name was unfamiliar. It was Anne with a new name taken at the time of her recent marriage. She asked for an appointment.

When she came in, she said, with a smile, "Well, you're not going to believe what the problem is this time."

She had done well in her career. She had eventually left the district attorney's office and had accepted a partnership in a law firm specializing in domestic cases. She had married a pediatrician whom she had met in the course of her volunteer legal work for an organization serving inner-city children. She was the mother of a new baby, a daughter whom she and her husband had christened Sarah.

The problem, as you may have guessed, was the new mythology. In her firm her work was becoming suspect because she was "taking this mothering business too seriously." From the viewpoint of the senior partner, she was showing a suspicious lack of professional commitment to her career because she wanted to work fewer hours and maintain a more consistent schedule in order to have time with her child.

In an uncomfortable conference with the senior partner, Anne had been told that she would be expected to work the same number of hours as men in the firm and under exactly the same conditions. She would be expected to place no more importance upon family than was considered appropriate and desirable for male attorneys. The senior partner's parting comment had been that in his office no differences were made between men and women. Everybody was treated the same.

There are, of course, many complex issues involved in the second situation that Anne brought to me, not the least of which is the awkward fact that *same* is not always *equal*. But the significance of the case includes the clarity with which it demonstrates that the myth that men and women are the same created as much difficulty and distortion as did the myth that men and women are absolute opposites. Neither the old mythology nor the new is an adequate basis for therapeutic work with women.

THE MYTH OF THE MALE PRIORITY SYSTEM

The myth that women are no different than men has been closely allied with the myth that the right way for a woman to live life is by assuming the priority system traditionally characteristic of the white male middle class. This myth threads its way through women's stories in a variety of disguises. Sometimes it comes through the advice (or pressure) of the significant men in a woman's life.

Claire came to me for assistance because she was depressed and chronically fatigued. She noted with wry humor that she *should* be having a midlife crisis, since that was her age-appropriate complaint, but she was just too tired to have one no matter how hard she tried. Further inquiry indicated that Claire, at least on the surface, was a fortunate participant in the good life, American style.

A physical examination indicated that Claire was in good health. She was a mature believer, active in her church. She and her husband had been married twenty-four years. Her adult children were struggling somewhat to get settled in careers and relationships but were, for the most part, doing well. While Claire and her husband were not wealthy, financial need was not a major source of stress.

"Claire, tell me. What do *you* think the problem is?" I asked her one day.

"Well," Claire said hesitantly, "Jerry is really mad at me because I don't want to work. He says I'm just lazy, and being home all these years has spoiled me."

"But you do work," I pointed out. "You work in your home, and also outside your home three days a week."

"Yes," Claire said, "but Jerry doesn't mean like that. He means have a real job, and really do something with my life. He thinks I'm depressed because I've never really done anything with myself and that I won't be happy until I do. Besides, he thinks the extra money would be nice."

Clearly, Claire was experiencing internal conflict about the goals she needed to set for the middle years of her life. In seeking to work out this life task, however, she had become entangled in the new mythology, packaged in the message she was receiving from her husband.

Claire's husband was genuinely concerned about her. His assumption was that Claire's happiness and well-being would be enhanced if only she would establish a career outside her home along with a commitment to her career that paralleled the life path he had taken. The issue was not in fact *work*. The issue was whether Claire's work would follow the male pattern and priority system.

In the counseling process, other painful issues in the marriage relationship began to emerge. The beginning point of progress for Claire, however, was uncovering this basic question: in order for Claire to be a good woman, doing life in the right way, did she have to develop a characteristically male attitude toward career? Did her priority system need to parallel that of her husband? The new mythology answers these questions, "Yes."

This new mythology is sometimes reflected in messages to women about money. If a woman is doing it right, money is important, and making more money is more important than most things. It is also reflected in attitudes toward time. The new mythology suggests that time a woman invests in work is well spent, but time spent in relationships is nonproductive. It implies a double message about power. The more people and assets the woman controls, the more powerful she is. The more powerful she is the better life she has, but the less feminine she is.

In the new mythology sex is defined for women, as for men, apart from relationships. Sex is a physiological tranquilizer, or, conversely, an emotional high, a pleasant means of brief intimacy without the cost of commitment. Sex is further viewed as an approved means for women to acquire power. Security is defined materially. Money, power, and position make women safe, but unfeminine. Relationships (particularly with husbands and children) make women vulnerable, hostages to fate.

The present emphasis in the pop psychology press focuses on women as loving too much, as being afraid of money, as afraid of success, and being as a class constitutionally co-dependent. This material reflects a strange mixture of the old mythology, the new, and some truth.[2]

Certainly in response to the old mythology many women do love in ways that are inappropriately self-neglectful. Some women do indeed assume the caretaker role in ways that enable others to avoid the consequences of their behaviors and to side-step the challenges of mature adulthood. It is true that many women do not understand money and so use money in ways that do not represent good stewardship either of their time, energy, or resources. Because of fear, many women do avoid development of their gifts and talents.

However, underlying much of this current focus on women's problems appears to be the new mythology. Since men (presumably) do not love too much, fear success, act co-dependent, nor fear money, the solution to the problem appears simple. If women would only do loving, money, success, and relationships right (i.e., like white, middle-class men) all these messy women's problems can be avoided.

It is true that male-type patterns and priorities have produced a world in which many men (particularly white, middle-class men) do control and enjoy a disproportional share of resources along with the alleged good life and mental health which these resources can provide.

However, it is not at all certain that by adopting the same behaviors and priorities women would automatically arrive at the same alleged utopia. Furthermore, there is substantial reason to question this alleged utopian nature of the male world. Men, if listened to, often report that their world of presumed privilege has its pain and deprivations, its limitations and loss. Reoccupation of Eden requires more than the right chromosomes, privileged social class, and a substantial bank account.

The Myth of Male Achievement

"Why can't a woman be just like a man?" fumed Professor Higgins. The answer appears to be because she is not one.

This awkward fact does not, however, appear to prevent the new mythology from telling women that they should nonetheless seek to achieve in male-defined ways, because these male achievement behaviors and performance values are the source of the good life and high levels of self-esteem that men enjoy.

According to the new mythology, achievement is *the* major source of well-being, satisfaction, and self-esteem which men allegedly enjoy in ways that women do not. Such achievement, defined according to male norms, is assumed to be the solution for the poor sense of self-esteem from which many women suffer. This exasperating pattern of truth and error is frustrating to unweave.

Achievement *is* a critical component of self-esteem for men and women alike, just as relationships are critical for both men and women. The idea that achievement is unimportant to women, or, conversely, that it is important to women in the same way it is for most middle-class men again polarizes the issue and puts it into a form that obscures and confuses the therapeutic issues for many women clients.

A young client became entangled in this myth through her father's well-intentioned efforts to assist in her career decisions. Her father was a highly placed government official who by his early fifties had reached most of his career goals, including substantial power, position, influence, and money. Mary came to see me because she was increasingly aware that she was sabotaging her efforts to become established as a journalist. This was occurring despite her father's use of his considerable influence to help her.

In listening together to Mary's story, we discovered that journalism—with the ultimate goal of an anchor position on a major network—was, at least in part, her father's dream for her, not her own.

Mary did indeed need to establish career goals. However, she needed first of all to separate her process of goal development as a woman from her father's masculine life pattern and his dream for her. When Mary explained to her father that she had decided to withdraw from journalism and develop a different career path, he was angry and bewildered.

He pointed out that he had been trying to help her do something of which she could be proud, which would enable her to feel really positive about herself and to utilize her considerable talents.

Unwittingly but in a very powerful way, Mary's father was passing on the new mythology. He was recommending achievement for his daughter, as defined by the male priority system which had shaped his life. Interestingly enough, he appeared largely unaware of the price this pattern had extracted. Shortly thereafter, his third divorce was finalized.

One of the most helpful resources to women struggling with the achievement aspect of the new mythology are men who are able and willing to acknowledge that the male-type career pattern is often as destructive to men as it can be to women. Unfortunately, the number of men able and willing to share such insight with women is still quite limited.[3] There is evidence, however, that some positive change is occurring,[4] and the numbers of such men are increasing.

Women often become anxious when dealing with the achievement myth in their therapeutic process. Questioning this achievement myth frequently places them in a position of rejecting a value system held and practiced by significant men in their lives. It can also at times place them at odds with other women who are strongly committed to business and professional goals.

The tension is further exacerbated if the woman is active in a church that conceptualizes the issue in a polarized form with only two options available to women: replication of the male life career pattern, or no achievement at all outside the traditional home. In this polarized form this concept incorporates the worst of both the old and new mythologies.

Women can achieve significantly in many areas, including fields such as law, medicine, and engineering, which were formerly closed to women. But contrary to the new mythology, they need not adopt the male system to do so. Counselors often have little awareness of the degree to which such issues are allied with the chronic fatigue and depression which women bring symptomatically to the therapeutic process.

THE MYTH OF THE VALUE OF THE MALE PATTERN OF POWER

Historically the issue of power has evoked ambivalent feelings in women. The new mythology suggests to women that they should acquire and use power in ways characteristic of men. When women are challenged with this alternative, the mix of the old fear and the new anxiety makes power an even more highly conflicted issue for almost all women, and often for their therapists as well. One therapist who specializes in work with women believes that power is the most significant therapeutic issue for contemporary women.[5]

The new mythology encourages women to adopt the male model of power in much the same way it encourages women to adopt the male model of achievement and life priority system. There is, however, substantial evidence to suggest that this idea is counterproductive for women (and for men).

In order to understand the complexity of the problem, it is helpful to review briefly the nature of the male pattern of power and then note two ways in which the recommendation of the new mythology can make trouble for women.

In the culturally approved male model, power is operationally defined as dominance *over* others, including the ability to control, limit, or destroy the power of others. Power in this model is a zero-sum game, that is, gain for one person entails a necessary, inevitable loss for other(s). Power is demonstrated in aggressive, competitive behavior in which ruthlessness is acceptable when necessary for winning.

The male pattern of power is achieved independent of relationships. It is won through tangible resources such as money, knowledge, physical strength, and control of social institutions. It is expressed through behaviors such as aggression, confrontation, competition, conflict, and hard-ball bargaining. The powerful person is expected to appear competent and without needs under all circumstances, to appear to be, in effect, totally self-sufficient.[6]

There are at least two serious problems for Christian women who encounter the new mythology regarding power. The first is psychological. The second is spiritual.

Women are socialized to a very different pattern of power. In the culturally approved feminine pattern, power is personal, and women are expected to win power through liking, loving, approval, and sexual influence. Women's culturally approved use of power is indirect, expressed through manipulation, sneakiness, avoidance of confrontation, and any method of influence that does not appear to involve direct use of power as practiced in the male pattern. This female style of helplessness calls on women to win power through appearing to be incompetent.[7]

The new mythology appears to suggest that women solve the issue of power by adopting the male power style to which, in the first place, they are not socialized, and which, in the second place, frequently entails significant negative consequences for women when they attempt without preparation to replicate the male power pattern.[8] To suggest that a woman adopt a role that is the opposite of that to which she has been socialized increases her inner sense of tension and identity conflict.[9] To suggest that she do so without understanding the consequences of such action is both unrealistic and irresponsible.[10] The penalty for the woman can be especially harsh within the church.

A therapist who works primarily with women has summarized the woman's dilemma as follows. "Feeling good means feeling powerful. But feeling powerful, for women, is closely associated with not feeling womanly, which is a fundamental threat to identity. Feeling good then becomes feeling bad. . . . society . . . makes it practically impossible for women to feel authentically powerful and feminine at the same time."[11]

Most powerful women reject out of hand the idea that power and femininity are practically impossible to combine. However, many of these women would concur that this combination is often difficult to demonstrate in a socially acceptable form, particularly within the evangelical church.

To suggest that women be limited only to stereotypic, culturally approved feminine forms of power is, of course, not the solution to women's problems. To require women to be passive, powerless, or devious is simply to reaffirm one of the most destructive components of the old mythology. To then cite the old mythology as a biblical norm provides further pain and confusion. However, recommending an unexamined adaptation of the culturally approved male model of power is neither psychologically feasible nor biblically sound.

For Christian women the most serious objection to the new mythology does not revolve around gender issues. Rather, the problem is the degree to which the culturally approved male model of power violates (for men and women alike) the letter and the spirit of the New Testament.[12]

Believers (men and women alike) are commanded to express power through servanthood and demonstration of a spirit of humility rather than through domination. We are to care for one another's needs rather than to compete for control of resources. We are to regard one another as equals in Christ rather than superiors and subordinates on the basis of the control we are able to exert over others.

Power is not regarded in the New Testament as a gender-relevant issue. The use of power is presented as one dimension by which the followers of Jesus (men and women alike) could be distinguished from the world. Jesus said that power used in service to others, as contrasted by power used in domination over others, marked those who followed him.

The issue for the woman of faith then becomes much larger than gender relevance. The overriding issue is fidelity to her faith in the way power is used in her life.

THE MYTH OF MASCULINE CHARACTERISTICS

The new mythology has also suggested to women that the solution to their problems as women is to adopt masculine characteristics. Here again the difficulty for both the woman and her therapist is that this idea is a mixture of truth and error.

We can easily dispose of the more obvious part of this error. Most women and their therapists alike would view the abolishment of the feminine self as a rather drastic solution to whatever difficulties a woman may be experiencing in her life. With rare clinical exceptions, women come to therapy because they want to experience life as women, not as men, but to experience life as women in less painful and more satisfying ways. Becoming more masculine is, for most women, much like a proposal to cut off one's head in order to cure a toothache.

The more powerful and difficult part of this error is not so apparent, nor so obviously incorrect. This error grew out of some of the most interesting research about women and women's mental health to come out of the early development of psychology of women.

As noted earlier[13] Broverman and her associates discovered that the culture at large, and mental health professionals specifically, had placed women in a no-win situation regarding mental health. Characteristics approved as evidences of masculinity were synonymous for the most part with characteristics of adult mental health while those for femininity were not. Women then appeared to be faced with the dilemma of choosing between being healthy adults or healthy women since, by definition, they could not be both.

One important effort to solve the problem came out of the work of Sandra Bem.[14] Bem attempted to discover if an individual could incorporate both masculine and feminine characteristics, and by doing so avoid the forced choice of masculine *or* feminine. This concept of combined traits, called androgyny, suggested that people (men and women alike) were most healthy mentally when they could demonstrate, as needed, those characteristics associated with both the feminine and the masculine roles. The concept of androgyny called for men to incorporate some characteristically feminine traits, and for women, in turn, to incorporate some characteristically masculine traits.

Initially, androgyny seemed like a good idea as it focused on combining the best of two worlds. As the 1980s drew to a close, however, the concept of androgyny has turned out to have serious problems, and to have considerably less promise than initially anticipated. Sandra Bem herself has abandoned her work on androgyny and moved on to a new paradigm she calls "gender schema theory."[15]

What went wrong with this idea? Several things.

For one thing, androgyny, at least as it was measured on the psychological tests designed to identify it, did not translate into clearly observable differences in behavior. In effect, people who were clearly androgynous on the test (i.e., achieved combinations of high masculine and high feminine scores) often failed to show in real life those behaviors hypothesized to demonstrate the trait of androgyny.[16]

Additionally, people who achieved high masculinity scores continued to show higher self-esteem and more positive self-images than did other people. People with high masculine scores were likely to be better adjusted and less depressed than other people. Androgynous people proved to have no special advantage over masculine people.[17] In short, it was the high masculinity scores, rather than the combination of masculine/feminine (androgyny) which appeared to give the advantage.[18] In our culture, which continues to value masculine qualities over feminine qualities, people with high levels of masculine qualities are better adjusted. One writer[19] noted that if we lived in a culture in which feminine qualities were equally valued with masculine traits, the androgynous individual might indeed prove to be better adjusted, but such is not the case in our present society.

The androgyny studies did not lead women further forward in solving their dilemma. The choice appeared to remain: assimilate high levels of masculine traits if you wish to achieve high levels of self-esteem. Pay the price of low self-esteem and the risk of depression if as a woman you retain high levels of stereotypically feminine traits unbalanced by masculine characteristics.

When the new mythology suggests to women that the route toward high self-esteem and personal competence requires that a woman incorporate masculine characteristics, the recommendation reflects an element of truth. However, it presents this truth in a potentially misleading way, and this again polarizes the masculine/feminine dichotomy.

The most helpful step beyond this Catch-22 appears to lie in a concept sometimes referred to as gender-role transcendence.[20] Gender-role transcendence proposes that individuals develop the capacity to choose life strategies on the basis of a personal value system rather than on the basis of gender-role.

In instances of gender-role transcendence, the individual

retains strong gender-role identity as male or female. Life strategies and personal behaviors, however, are based on inner values and judgments and are not limited to internalized social roles.

One description of an emotionally healthy woman suggested that she "takes risks and extends herself without placing too much emphasis on either success or failure."[21] If for the moment we accept this behavior as a characteristic of an emotionally healthy woman, it is clear that in order to demonstrate this behavior a woman would need to display at least two traits stereotypically considered to be masculine: she would need to be active and independent. In an individual with high levels of gender-role transcendence, however, the individual would choose to act in such a way not because she was choosing to be masculine, but rather because such behavior enabled her to reach a higher goal, such as obedience to her faith.

As an example from everyday life, suppose that a woman finds herself seated in a plane next to a male stranger with whom by necessity she will spend the next four hours. She is faced with a decision. Shall she initiate a conversation with this stranger, seeking a socially comfortable opportunity to share her faith? Or shall she make the decision on the basis of gender and choose the "proper" restricted response for a woman in public contact with a male who is a stranger? Gender-role transcendence would suggest that the decision would best be made on the basis of the higher goal (sharing her faith) rather than on the basis of conformity to a gender-based social role.

Gender-role transcendence has, of course, enormous appeal for Christians who take seriously the Apostle Paul's principle of equality in Christ. "There is neither Jew nor Greek, slave nor free, male nor female, for you are all one in Christ Jesus," Paul wrote to the Galatian believers.[22]

Paul was not suggesting, of course, that by virtue of becoming a Christian an individual stopped belonging to an ethnic group (Jew or Greek), a social class (slave or free), or a gender (male or female). Instead, he said that these distinctions, important as they are, should no longer control behavioral choices. While such distinctions continued to have great significance, they were no longer to serve as the primary basis for defining relationships. Philemon, for example, was no longer to relate to Onesimus on the basis of his slave status. Women were to be honored and included as equals in the church—five out of six passages in the New Testament mentioning house churches connect them to women.[23] Nor were such social distinctions to legislate moral choices. The right or wrong of eating together, Paul told Peter publicly (and angrily), could no longer be based on the old distinction of Jew and Greek.

Women who are Christians have the exciting challenge of working out an identity that does not deny nor demean the feminine but that does not permit cultural role restrictions to define a woman's pattern of thinking nor limit her behavioral choices. "It is for freedom that Christ has set us free," Paul wrote to the Galatian church.[24]

For Christian women who are seeking to make choices in the context of gender-role transcendency, such choices do not deny gender but make gender subservient to higher goals. While a mentally healthy woman will continue to affirm clearly her identity and worth as a woman, her priority system will reflect faith first and gender-role second.

This priority system appears to be precisely the point of Jesus' famous conversation with Mary and Martha the night he came to dinner at their home in Bethany. Remembering Luke's account of Mary's behavior and Jesus' response that night,[25] women may smile at the "new" idea of gender-role transcendence. This idea of gender-role transcendence actually was first new, and radically so, when Jesus lived it out and the Apostle Paul wrote it down. It is ironic that now, two thousand years later, studies in the psychology of women call us to consider again the exciting, definitive way this New Testament concept speaks to contemporary issues of women's identities and needs.

THE MYTH OF MINIMAL RELATIONSHIPS

As we have discussed above, many messages of the new mythology extend the idea that women's problems are often solved by adopting masculine characteristics, priority systems, and goals. This idea is also reflected in the new mythology message about relationships. The old mythology argues that relationships are *all* a woman needs. The new mythology argues that relationships are of no more importance to women than to men, except to the degree to which women are socialized to believe that they are. Here again the new mythology and the facts seem to be seriously at odds.

Women do appear to establish basic identity through relationships of intimacy and nurture that are different from those of men.[26] They appear to work out their moral dilemmas in terms of relational issues in a way quite different from the abstract principles utilized by men.[27] One important writer has studied developmental processes and concluded that masculinity is primarily defined through processes of separation, while femininity is defined through attachment.[28]

Another researcher has recently advocated development of a new approach to the psychology of women based in part on the degree to which relationships shape women's identities and the ways in which they live their lives. Jean Baker Miller suggests that this change of focus is necessary because traditional structures and categories through which psychologists study human development primarily reflect the male patterns of life. In Miller's judgment, these categories have been insufficient and misleading and have seriously distorted our understanding of women's life experiences.[29]

Theory and present research appear to indicate that women not only relate differently than do men; women also use relationships in formulating feminine identity in ways different than those utilized by males. In addition, women appear to differ from males in their continuing adult need for affiliation and intimacy.

The new mythology appears to regard these differences as evidence of socialized female deficiency in character or personality and to suggest that the problems of life for women can be solved simply by adopting the male way of relating. Again, the mix of truth and error can result at many points in utter frustration for therapist and client alike.

There are life circumstances where the ways in which women practice relationships can indeed cause serious problems. For example, as Van Leeuwen has pointed out, one serious problem for Christian women may be their willingness to disregard issues of justice in order to achieve relationships without conflict.[30] But the new mythology's implication that masculine patterns are inherently less problematic lacks substantive support. If, as Van Leeuwen suggests, the characteristic problem with the male pattern of relationships is abuse of power, then common sense would conclude that replacing the feminine pattern—which tempts one to disregard justice—with a masculine alternative—which tempts one to the abuse of power—is hardly a constructive solution to this human problem.

THE MYTH OF MINIMAL FAMILY

When women accept the new mythology proposal that women's choices regarding family should replicate the traditional patterns of males, everyone loses—men, women, and children.

Family issues for women will be dealt with in more detail in the discussion of women in transition (chapter 8). Here in discussing the new mythology, the point is, again, that replication of male patterns is no solution to the problems that women face.

In a carefully reasoned critique of the early stages of the women's movement, one of its founders noted, "I think we must at least admit and begin openly to discuss feminist denial of the importance of family, of women's own needs to give and get love and nurture."[31]

It is encouraging to see recognition of the importance of family from such a source. However, it is equally important to recognize within the evangelical community that while families are an important source of love and nurture for women, families often are also the source of stress and tension in women's lives and sometimes the source of violence, injury, and very real danger. Additionally, family responsibilities can pose a serious conflict of interest for working women who are living out new patterns of family life in a changing world.[32]

The new mythology recommends that women handle this conflict by adopting the culturally approved male pattern: restrict family to whatever small islands of time and attention the world of work permits. This is not, however, a constructive solution for women, for their children, or for the men whom these women love.

It is helpful to recognize from the outset that this pattern has not been a constructive solution for men either; this is a dysfunctional pattern for men as well as for women. As every counselor knows, what is good for GM, Eastman Kodak, or Wall Street (or for the institutional church, as many pastor's families will attest) is not by definition good for employees (men or women) nor for the family. It makes no sense to recommend to women that they adopt a pattern that already has demonstrated its destructive character for men as well as for their families.

The new mythology with its emphasis on incorporation of the stereotypically masculine is a poor solution for problems. It also has potential for making even more serious problems than may initially be anticipated.

Therapists who have undertaken serious study of the psychology of women have major theoretical differences, but there is a general concern regarding the danger of women seeking to replicate male models in the ostensible service of progress. Jean Baker Miller summarized her concerns in the forward of her book, *Toward a New Psychology of Women*, noting:

> The goal that women should become men or even become *like* men seemed disastrous to me for many reasons. Therefore, it seemed important to begin to create new images and visions and to explain the reasons why we needed new visions rather than imitations of old models. And the place to start was to describe the actual life activities and values of the vast majority of women.[33]

THE MYTH OF RELIGION AS A DEFICIT FACTOR

One of the important life activities and values of many women is the practice of their faith. It is interesting to discover that while the new mythology recommends to women

that religion is likely to be dangerous to their mental health
and therefore to be avoided, this is an area where psychology of women appears to demonstrate a strange combination
of puzzling silence and implicit bias.

In this piece of mythology, the mix of truth and myth is
again difficult to separate. Because this myth is often interwoven with scientific material, it is helpful to review some
examples in order to identify forms in which the myth appears.

One writer in a respected text on sex and gender issues includes a thoughtful discussion of gender and religion. In this
discussion James Doyle demonstrates a good working knowledge of church history and describes carefully the ways in
which Jesus broke clearly with the Jewish traditions regarding
women's place in society. Doyle goes on to describe sympa-
thetically women's participation and leadership in the early
church; he includes a remarkably fair and lucid discussion of
St. Paul's directions regarding women.[34] When Doyle reviews
the general history of women in the church, he states:

> In summary, we can conclude that religion, which is
> one of the more powerful social institutions, has
> looked generally upon women as the "other" or as a
> second-class participant in religious ritual. . . . over-
> all, even though women make up the majority of
> most churches' memberships, women continue to
> find themselves sitting in the churches' back pews
> listening to men, who for centuries have enjoyed the
> privilege of being up-front, nearer the sanctuary.[35]

Williams in another respected text, *Psychology of Women:
Behavior in a Biosocial Context*, limits consideration of religion
to a casual paragraph.[36] In this paragraph she notes religion
as a source of moral values encouraging the production of
children.

In *The Psychology of Women*, a widely used text, Matlin de-
votes two pages to "images of women in religion and
mythology."[37] The following quotation is included despite its
length in order to convey fairly the tone of Matlin's discussion.

Most religions include a description of how the world and its human occupants were created. For example, Jews, Christians, and Muslims share the story of Adam and Eve. In this story, God creates man "in his own image." In other words, God is a man and men came first. Later, God made Eve as a companion to Adam, and she was constructed from his rib. In other words, women are made from men, and women are therefore secondary in the great scheme of things. Males are "normal" and females are "the second sex."

Furthermore, Eve gives in to temptation and leads Adam into sin. Women, then, are morally weak and this weakness can contaminate men. When Adam and Eve are expelled from paradise, their curse shows an interesting asymmetry. Adam's curse is that he must work for a living, whereas Eve's curse is that she must bear children in pain. Eve's curse has two prescriptions for women: she must not seek employment, and childbirth must be an unpleasant experience. . . .

From the religions of the world and from mythology, we can derive several views of women that are not necessarily compatible with one another. . . . However, each image emphasizes how women are *different* from men. Once again, men are normal and women are "the second sex."[38]

It appears likely that Jew, Moslem, and Christian might have objections to the story of Creation and the Fall in the form and tone in which Matlin reports it. The point, however, is not how far from the orthodox mark Matlin's account may be, but the strength of her implied message that religion is inherently hostile to women in whatever form it occurs. A large portion of the power of Matlin's message lies in its context. This conclusion appears in a very fine book in which research regarding women is presented with scrupulous attention to balance and truth.

Doyle, Matlin, and Williams each are discussed here because they represent sound scholarship and careful writing.

However, despite their clear commitment to balance and truth, a peculiar omission has appeared.

Doyle is clearly correct; the church *has* been a source of discrimination against women. Williams, however casually, accurately notes the influence of the church on women's management of their fertility. And as Matlin notes, the church *has* used the creation story to justify disrespect for women. Yet despite the accuracy of this negative information, the myth of religion as hostile to women causes even careful writers such as these textbook authors to omit another important truth.

It is also a fact that women by the thousands attend church faithfully and report their faith to be a positive part of their lives.[39] While the negative impact of religion historically is increasingly reported, the positive impact of faith is increasingly overlooked.

The impact of women's faith is rarely studied scientifically. Researchers have paid little if any attention to this important facet of women's experience. Examples of such omissions are easy to find. An important study in 1980 reviewed the research related to psychotherapy and women that was available at that time.[40] The papers in the study covered five major areas and concluded with a report that incorporated priorities for future research for the National Institute of Mental Health.

This important study was carried out by experts whose interest and concern was a proper scientific understanding of psychotherapy with women. In this context it is highly significant that the issue of women's religious practice was omitted entirely. The powerful although unspoken conclusion appears to be that women's faith is irrelevant to the psychotherapeutic process.

Another equally important study but with a different theme was reported in 1985.[41] In this study, all of the presumably significant research regarding gender and personality theory was reviewed by invited researchers and theorists. The results of these studies and proposed directions for future research were outlined. Included was an important paper titled "Individual Differences in Moral Development: The Relation of Sex, Gender, and Personality to Morality."[42] Another paper was titled "Responsibility and the Power Motive in Women and Men."[43]

Again it is interesting to note what was omitted. There was no suggestion that women's religious practice was a significant factor for study. The unspoken but powerful conclusions of these studies appears to be that women's faith is irrelevant to the study of gender and personality even though factors such as moral development, responsibility, and use of power clearly are.

The new mythology appears to imply that religious faith, particularly in traditional form, is either hostile to women's welfare or irrelevant. This is, however, a presupposition, not a scientifically established fact. This presupposition is interwoven in scientific materials by writers and researchers who are unaware of their bias or who do not choose to acknowledge it. In an important policy paper, "Women, Spirituality and Mental Health," Maureen Hendricks has discussed critically this omission and unacknowledged bias.[44] Unfortunately, at the present time there appears to be little interest in research designed to establish the facts about the influence of women's faith and even fewer resources available to support such inquiry.

We must admit, sadly, that the church far too often *has* been the source of pain and discrimination against women. But it is also true that many women find their faith to be a source of strength and comfort and a practical help in dealing with life's most difficult situations. Many women report their faith to be a major part of their lives; further, they report their faith to be a powerful influence in their inner world. It is difficult to understand how for such women their faith can be considered irrelevant to formation of personality and to the process of psychotherapy.

In many ways the old mythology was detrimental to the spiritual and psychological health of women. But the new mythology, which argues for women to disregard or discard their faith in their pursuit of mental health, is equally harmful, certainly to clients whose faith is central to their lives.

It is one thing to say that the church has often been guilty of ignorance and prejudicial behavior against women. That, sadly, is so. It is also true that the church has often required women to demonstrate their faith in patterns of behavior which have been destructive to them. But it is quite another thing to imply as fact, as does the new mythology, that it is women's faith that has injured them. That simply is not true.

Both the old mythology and the new mythology are destructive to women and a major source of trouble for both the client and the therapist. Consequently, counselors and their women clients must grapple with both the old and new mythologies, recognizing each as having equal potential to interfere seriously with the counseling process.

Counselors often have a further set of beliefs that can interfere with therapy. These beliefs are frequently acquired in the process of professional training. They are further reinforced by conventional wisdom regarding counseling with women contained in journal articles and spread through informal exchange of information at professional meetings. Most of these beliefs, which are taken as fact, have little if any basis in sound research.

However, as therapists we often hold this belief system about the counseling process and about ourselves as therapists with the same firm, unconscious grip with which we and our women clients hold the cultural mythology about women. Just as it is important to examine the mythology about women, it is important to examine the therapist's mythology, although these beliefs overlap at various points.

NOTES

1. Beryl Lieff Benderly, *The Myth of Two Minds: What Gender Means and Doesn't Mean* (New York: Doubleday, 1987).

2. In a syndicated column, Carol Tavris commented on aspects of the old mythology present in the recent spate of co-dependent materials. See Carol Tavris, "Co-dependency: A Guilt Trip for Women," *The Denver Post*, 18 March 1990.

3. The number may, however, be growing. See chapter four, "The Quiet Movement of American Men," in Betty Friedan, *The Second Stage* (New York: Summit Books, 1986), 125–61. See also James Doyle, *The Male Experience* (Dubuque, Iowa: Brown, 1983).

4. J. H. Pleck, *Working Wives, Working Husbands* (Beverly Hills, Calif.: Sage, 1985).

5. Helen Collier, *Counseling Women: A Guide for Therapists* (New York: The Free Press, 1982), 261.

6. Discussion of the culturally approved male pattern of power and its implications for women is included in the work of both Helen Collier, ibid., 58–60, 169–70, 261, 265, and in James Doyle, *Sex and Gender: The Human Experience* (Dubuque, Iowa: Brown, 1985), 150–75.

7. Ibid.

8. N. Costrick et al., "When Stereotypes Hurt: Three Studies of Penalties for Sex-role Reversals," *Journal of Experimental Social Psychology* 11 (1975): 520–30.

9. L. S. Radloff, "Sex Differences in Depression: The Effects of Occupation and Marital Status," *Journal of Sex Roles* 1 (1975): 249–65, and Jean Baker Miller, "Women and Power," *Work in Progress*, no. 82–01 (Wellesley, Mass.: Stone Center, 1982).

10. A. Kahn, "The Power War: Male Response to Power Loss Under Equality," *Psychology of Women Quarterly* 8 (1984): 234–47.

11. Miriam Greenspan, *A New Approach to Women and Therapy* (New York: McGraw- Hill, 1983), 195.

12. A challenging consideration of the spiritual problems entailed in the culturally approved concept of power is incorporated in Cheryl Forbes, *The Religion of Power* (Grand Rapids, Mich.: Zondervan, 1983). Also helpful is Richard Foster's study, *The Challenge of the Disciplined Life: Money, Sex and Power* (New York: Harper and Row, 1988).

13. See chapter one, pages 5–6.

14. Sandra Bem, "The Measurement of Psychological Androgyny," *Journal of Consulting and Clinical Psychology* 42 (1974): 155–62.

15. Sandra Bem, "Gender Schema Theory: A Cognitive Account of Sextyping," *Psychological Review* 88 (1981): 354–64.

16. E. Lenney, "Androgyny: Some Audacious Assertions Toward Its Coming of Age," *Sex Roles* 5 (1979): 703–19.

17. Margaret W. Matlin, *The Psychology of Women* (Fort Worth, Tex.: Holt, Rinehart and Winston, 1987), 279–81.

18. N. M. Henley, "Psychology and Gender," *Signs* 11 (1985): 101–19.

19. L. A. Gilbert, "Toward Mental Health: The Benefits of Psychological Androgyny," *Professional Psychology* 12 (1981): 29–38.

20. M. Rebecca, R. Hefner, and B. Oleshansky, "A Model of Sex-Role Transcendence," in *Beyond Sex-role Stereotypes: Readings Toward a Psychology of Androgyny*, ed. A. G. Kaplan and J. P. Bean (Boston: Little, Brown and Co., 1976), 90–97. See also L. Garnet and J. Pleck, "Sex Role Identity, Androgyny, and Sex Role Transcendence: A Sex Role Strain Analysis," *Psychology of Women Quarterly* 3 (1979): 270–83.

21. Collier, 273.

22. Galatians 3:28 (NIV).

23. Acts 12:12; 16:40; Romans 16:3–5; 1 Corinthians 16:19; Philemon 1:2; 3; Philippians 4:2–3 (Euodia and Syntyche are cited as "fellow workers" with the Apostle Paul along with Clement).

24. Galatians 5:1 (NIV).

25. Luke 10:38–42.

26. Jean Baker Miller, "The Development of Women's Sense of Self," *Work in Progress,* no. 12 (Wellesley, Mass.: Stone Center, 1984).

27. Carol Gilligan, *In a Different Voice* (Cambridge, Mass.: Harvard University Press, 1982).

28. Nancy Chodorow, *The Reproduction of Mothering: Psychoanalysis and the Sociology of Gender* (Berkeley: University of California Press, 1978).

29. Jean Baker Miller, *Toward a New Psychology of Women,* 2nd ed. (Boston: Beacon Press, 1986), ix–xxv.

30. Mary Stewart Van Leeuwen, *Gender and Grace: Love, Work and Parenting in a Changing World* (Downers Grove, Ill.: InterVarsity, 1990).

31. Betty Frieden, *The Second Stage,* rev. ed. (New York: Summit Books, 1986), 22.

32. Jesse Bernard, "Women's Mental Health in Times of Transition," in *Women and Mental Health Policy,* ed. Lenore E. Walker, Sage Yearbooks in Women's Policy Studies, vol. 9 (Beverly Hills, Calif.: Sage, 1984), 181–95.

33. Miller, xi.

34. Doyle, 237–50.

35. Ibid., 251.

36. Juanita Williams, *Psychology of Women,* 3rd ed. (New York: Norton, 1987), 307.

37. Matlin, 247–48.

38. Ibid.

39. See *Women's Realities, Women's Choices,* Hunter College Women's Studies Collective (New York: Oxford University Press, 1983), 358, 372, 391.

40. Annette M. Brodsky and Rachel T. Hare-Mustin, eds., *Women and Psychotherapy: An Assessment of Research and Practice* (New York: Guilford, 1980).

41. Abigail J. Stewart and M. Brinton Lykes, eds., *Gender and Personality: Current Perspectives on Theory and Research* (Durham, N.C.: Duke University Press, 1985).

42. Ibid., 218–46.

43. Ibid., 247–67.

44. Maureen Hendricks,"Women, Spirituality, and Mental Health," in *Women and Mental Health Policy,* ed. Lenore E. Walker, Sage Yearbooks in Women's Policy Studies, vol. 9 (Beverly Hills, Calif.: Sage, 1984), 95–115.

Chapter Four

The Mythology of the Therapist

MOST COUNSELORS CURRENTLY IN PRACTICE have had limited opportunity to gain professional training focused on psychotherapy with women. As a result, most of us who regularly see women clients are faced with the need to find individual means to correct this deficiency. Examining our belief system about counseling women can be one helpful way to bring about such professional growth.

The following misbeliefs are not held by all counselors, but they are sufficiently common to merit careful evaluation.

MYTHS ABOUT THE COUNSELING PROCESS
WHICH CAN INFLUENCE THERAPISTS

1. Counselors' beliefs and attitudes about women have little influence on the content and outcome of the counseling process.
2. All approaches to counseling are equally helpful to women.

3. The risk of sexual intimacy between the male counselor
   and woman client is nonexistent in Christian counseling. Such unethical relationships happen only with
   non-Christians and result primarily from the inability
   of an inexperienced, male counselor to deal with a seductive female client.
4. The primary source of women's problems is women
   themselves. Socioeconomic factors and cultural attitudes
   toward women are relatively unimportant to the outcome of counseling.

In this chapter, each of these myths will be discussed in detail.

THE MYTH OF VALUE-FREE THERAPY

Traditionally the counselor has been seen as an emotionally distant, neutral authority who expertly interprets the
client's rage or despair while remaining personally
uninvolved and untouched by the client's pain. It has been
commonly assumed that this scientific stance of distance and
objectivity is necessary for the client's healing and personal
growth.

This assumption represents a professional belief rather than
a scientifically established fact. As one prominent therapist of
women has pointed out, "There is nothing more inherently
neutral or scientific or professional about emotional distance
than there is about emotional connection."[1]

Insistence upon emotional distance and unconnectedness
may reflect the culturally approved pattern of social interactions for males, adopted as the norm for the profession. While
this pattern of interaction may characterize many men, there
is no evidence that this is emotionally healthful for men (or for
women, if they adopt it), despite its powerful cultural man-
date. Further, there is no experimentally established evidence
to indicate that such a stance does in fact significantly aid the
healing process.

Nevertheless, the belief that emotional distance and neutrality are vital to the healing process has had a long tradition. It

has led to a further belief that since this stance is presumed to be desirable, it is therefore possible to achieve.

Consequently, counselors in training have often been taught to establish a hierarchical, distant, objective relationship with the client. As a part of their professional training, counselors were often taught to believe that the emotional withholding of the counselor from the client was essential to the neutrality and effectiveness of the healing process.

Counselors have then traditionally come to believe that what they were taught they *should* do, they *could* do, and, in fact, *did* do in relationship with their clients.

THE DIFFICULTY OF VALUE-FREE THERAPY

The truth is that such an uninvolved neutral role for the counselor is impossible, even if it were demonstrated to be helpful to the client (which it has not). When counselors (male or female) insist that therapy with their clients is indeed value-free and that they themselves are able to remain emotionally detached, rational observers, the situation reminds one of the story of the emperor who had no clothes. No matter how much we would like to think this to be so, the facts indicate otherwise.

One family therapist noted that we cannot *not* react out of our gender, class, sibling position, ethnic background, personal history, theoretical orientation, experience, and wisdom, or lack of it. Our choice is whether we do so consciously or unconsciously.[2]

Harriet Goldhor Lerner is a psychoanalyst on the staff at the Menninger Clinic whose work with women is internationally known. She notes, "The ways in which we formulate research questions, generate theory, and conduct psychotherapy are never separable from our own gender and family experiences, which include unconscious fears, wishes and assumptions about women. . . ." She concludes, "Every therapist, whether feminist or 'Freudian,' will express, in the course of treatment, her or his own values and visions for women. There is no 'value-free' psychotherapy."[3]

Such a conclusion is particularly notable coming as it does from an individual whose training in the psychoanalytic tradition might well have inclined her to a continuing belief in the traditional view of the therapist's role. However, as Lerner herself notes, her present views have developed as a result of working with women. Participation in therapy with women has led her to major revisions of previously held psychoanalytic assumptions. It has also led Lerner to increased consideration of women's problems within the context of the social and family systems of which her women clients are a part.[4]

Another therapist, also specializing in work with women, points out the importance of the therapist's belief system about women. Susan Sturdivant notes:

> It is values and beliefs that form the foundation of psychotherapy, not empirical facts, and we must come to grips with this. . . . In this light, one's beliefs may be seen to affect virtually all aspects of treatment, including the definition of mental illness, determination of the need for therapeutic intervention, interpretation of symptoms, [and] selection of goals. . . .[5]

It is not difficult to find evidence that this is true. Ten years after the Broverman studies, another investigator reviewed studies of sex-role stereotyping in mental health standards and concluded: "Data provide evidence that therapists' sex-role values are operative during therapy and counseling. Data indicate there is sex-role stereotyping in mental health standards and that sex-role-discrepant behaviors are judged more maladjusted."[6] In short, if a woman acts in a way that is inconsistent with stereotypic feminine behaviors, that nonstereotypic behavior is likely to be judged to be maladjusted even though, in fact, it may only be unconventional.

Therapists in the studies reviewed by Sherman believed that their clinical judgments of women clients' problems were not influenced by their personal beliefs and attitudes about women. Indeed, confidence in their ability to provide value-free therapy appeared to lead to a "bias about bias" on the part of both male and female therapists.[7]

Therapists with less stereotypical concepts of women have been found to view women as stronger and healthier than those therapists with more stereotypic views. Therapists with less stereotypical views have also been found to be more likely to focus on the therapeutic goal of supporting efforts to achieve change in the woman's life rather than emphasizing the woman's adjustment to her life circumstances as she finds them.[8]

We do know that the attitudes and beliefs that the therapist (male or female) holds about women *do* influence the therapeutic process. The issue is clearly not *if* but *how* and in what direction. Within Christian counseling, this question has received insufficient attention.

In this time of change and controversy over women's issues, women have good reason to feel distrustful of the counseling process. Many people are committed to continuing traditional roles for women as the only permissible expression of biblical truth. Other people are committed to altering traditional roles of women because this is seen as the only avenue through which full development of opportunities for women can be achieved.

Therapists who are unwilling to acknowledge that their own belief system influences therapy may seek unconsciously to produce the kind of woman that the therapist believes the woman *should* be.

The ethical issue of using the therapeutic process to serve the agenda of the therapist rather than to facilitate the goals of the client is a serious one. This is especially significant to Christian counselors both because of the ethics involved and because of the risk to the religiously committed woman client who may be particularly vulnerable to the authority of the counselor.

The less a counselor (male or female) knows about the psychology of women, and the less one has studied the sociology of women's life experience, the greater the risk to the therapist and to the woman client. When acting from little or no factual information, the counselor will inevitably make the content and process of therapy congruent with the mythology and belief system that the counselor holds.

This is one of the key areas of Christian counseling in which the value system of the counselor has a potential to influence dramatically the course of therapy without the therapist's conscious intent to do so, or without the therapist's conscious awareness that such influence has indeed occurred.

THE DANGERS OF THEOLOGICAL BIAS

Christian therapists (male or female) may be convinced that their view of the good woman is correct because it is (presumably) biblically based. Under such conditions, covert use of the therapeutic process to shape the woman client into the therapist's idea of a proper biblical woman may be viewed as permissible or even desirable. Presumption of such theological license can encourage the therapist's improper use of the therapeutic role and then permit such unethical behaviors to remain a dangerous and unexamined issue.

As a Christian with a lifelong commitment to a conservative evangelical expression of my faith, I believe that direct, open work regarding spiritual issues is an appropriate part of the therapeutic process. However, I do *not* believe that the use of the therapeutic process as a covert tool for gender-role socialization is either professionally ethical or spiritually honest. Whether the thrust of that socialization is toward traditional roles or toward nontraditional roles, it remains inappropriate and unethical. Proper goals of therapy for women must incorporate the *woman's* goals for her life *as she develops and establishes them herself* in the process of therapy. They must not reflect the agenda of the therapist established, consciously or unconsciously, to support his or her own value system.

It is increasingly common for a prospective client to ask the counselor to explain the theoretical orientation from which treatment will be developed. Given what we know about the impact of the therapist's belief system, it would be wise for prospective women clients to inquire, specifically and in detail, about the therapist's attitude and values regarding women. This is a critical factor, certainly as vital to the therapeutic outcome as the therapist's commitment to a given personality theory or method of treatment.

The issue of the counselor's value system is not, however, a simple one for Christians, nor is it limited to the issue of beliefs about women. There are counselors who are Christian but whose therapeutic work is based primarily upon models developed by psychologists with little or no interest in spiritual matters. There are other therapists who are Christian and who seek to practice out of a Christian model of counseling and psychotherapy that ignores, and sometimes rejects, secular research and methodologies. Still others, perhaps the majority, seek to practice out of a model that integrates both faith and science. However, for all of these groups the issue of value-free therapy is a moot point.

For us as Christians, our relationships and work as therapists not only cannot be value-free—*it must not be*. We are called in the context of the New Testament to a mutual respect of persons beyond gender and social role, and to relationships of caring and compassion that facilitate spiritual growth. None of us can be the value-free, rational, uninvolved observer recommended in the traditional role. As Christians, we are fellow sinners, fellow sufferers, and fellow pilgrims, although the spiritual journey of the client often differs widely from our own. Whatever our operational definition of a professionally proper role of the therapist may be, it must reflect these truths in some way in our work and relationships with men and women alike.[9]

THE MYTH THAT EVERYTHING WORKS

The effectiveness of psychotherapy has long been a hotly debated issue among mental health professionals. Some individuals argue that therapy has never been demonstrated to make a lasting difference in the lives of individuals. An early study critical of traditional psychotherapy became famous when its author pointed out how many people became well without having received any treatment at all.[10]

The standard response of psychotherapists to such criticism has been that therapy certainly does make a difference—at least to some degree, most of the time—and there is research to support their claim. Most therapists acknowledge, however, that measuring such change has been a frustrating, complicated process.

If we accept those studies that indicate that psychotherapy does make a difference,[11] we are then faced with the difficult question of *how* this change occurs. We are also faced with the equally difficult question of *what* makes this change occur when it does.

These questions have provoked sharp debate. In a recent statistical analysis of 114 separate outcome studies, two researchers have concluded that therapy has been in fact demonstrated to have a moderate, relatively uniform positive effect.[12] The same study also noted, however, that there are minimal differences in outcomes related to various treatment methods—dynamic, humanistic, behavioral, and cognitive. Therapy does make a difference, but it does not appear to be the specific theory or methodology employed that causes this change.

One problem with such studies is that they put large amounts of data together in statistically sophisticated ways which support such conclusions but which may inadvertently blur significant factors in establishing the big picture.

For example, is psychotherapy wonderfully effective for the rich and a dismal failure for the poor so that when the two groups are averaged together we get moderate positive effect? Is the dynamic approach wonderful for the well-educated intellectual and dreadful for the individual who is a high school dropout with a low-average intelligence? If men are (presumably) rational and women (presumably) expressive, do males do better with cognitive strategies and females with dynamic approaches? But what if the woman is a black teenage high school dropout, and the man is a middle-aged, white upper-class executive? What differences do these factors make? What is the significance of gender in the context of such age, ethnic, socioeconomic differences?

To complicate things further, what is the significance of the motivation of the client? Is it possible that therapy is successful, regardless of method, when clients are highly motivated and unsuccessful when they are not? Or is it possible that therapy is successful when the client and therapist achieve a good match—whatever it takes to make that happen—and that motivation is a result, not a cause, of a good client-therapist match? If client-therapist match is a crucial variable, what is the significance of gender? Does this mean that males should see only male therapists and females only female therapists? If that is so, what are the economic implications of such an arrangement for men, who are presently the majority of the therapists and supervisors, and women, who are presently the majority of the clients and less often a supervisor?

Given the complexity of the issues involved, it is difficult to find a point from which to consider the myth that all approaches to psychotherapy are equally helpful to women. Therapists who work with women commonly report a fairly strong consensus that some things appear to work better for women than do others; the myth that all approaches work equally well does in fact incorporate some serious error.[13] However, it is considerably more difficult to sort out what works for what women under what circumstances and why. In all the welter of confusion regarding the general effectiveness of psychotherapy, finding some facts about effective therapy with women is itself no small task.[14]

Common sense suggests that if a woman is Hispanic, a migrant worker, and depressed, effective assistance for her will be different in some ways than effective assistance for a white, upper-class woman who is a member of her local Junior League but who also is depressed. (Similar distinctions would, of course, have relevance in designing effective counseling for men.)

Effective therapy for women requires that we recognize that gender separates women into a distinctive subgroup of clients (as it does men). Dealing with women as a distinctive subgroup, then, requires the therapist to develop specialized skills, attitudes, and knowledge related to these distinctives.[15] However, while dealing with women as women it is also essential to recognize the enormous differences between individual women within the gender group.

Failure to deal adequately with these large intragroup differences appears to underlie much of the confusion and lack of conclusive results in gender-based research. Failure to consider these differences in combination (e.g., gender, age, ethnic group, *and* client-therapist match) has further trivialized research regarding psychotherapy, including therapy with women.[16]

Despite the somewhat uncertain conclusions of research regarding psychotherapy with women, after years of work with women, it is my sense that the following factors, if present, make counselors more effective with women:

1. Counseling for women is likely to be more effective if the therapist's attitude toward women is relatively free of stereotypes and reflects high levels of respect for the woman's ability to set her own goals for growth and achievement and to govern her life.
2. Counseling for women is likely to be more effective if the therapist develops a nonhierarchical relationship with the woman client that is characterized by equality and appropriate self-disclosure and governed by the structure of a *mutually defined* therapeutic contract.
3. Counseling for women is likely to be more effective if the goals of therapy include work with the issues of (a) caregiving and guilt, (b) powerlessness and victimization, (c) fear and dependency, (d) sex-role stereotyping, and (e) view of God.[17]
4. Counseling for women is likely to be more effective if the goals of therapy include work with the issues of anger *linked* with issues of justice, and skills of confrontation, negotiation, reconciliation, and peacemaking. Women must learn about anger, how to control and to express anger. Women profit from therapeutic efforts that link anger with issues such as justice, in addition to the conventional focus on conflicted relationships.
5. Counseling for women is likely to be more effective if the goals of therapy reflect concern for the woman as an individual, but within the context of the family and relational systems in which women work out their lives. Emphasis upon intrapsychic factors alone do not appear to be effective with the majority of women clients because, as Gilligan, Miller, and others have pointed out, women make decisions about themselves and their options for change within the context of their relational network. Such emphasis requires a clinically careful balance, however, to avoid fostering the woman's tendency to continue inappropriate patterns of dependency

and caretaking, and avoidance of responsibility for her own needs and decisions.

6. Counseling for women is likely to be more effective if the therapeutic goals include increased understanding of the ways in which culture (including the institutional church) impacts the lives of women generally and the client specifically.

THERAPY THAT DOES NOT WORK FOR WOMEN

Not all things work equally well for women. Those theories and therapeutic relationships that reinforce and reward women for passive, dependent responses are not good for them. (Cultural differences must, however, be carefully taken into account at this point.) Treatment goals that permit and sometimes encourage women to place responsibility for their lives on others, including the therapist, are destructive to women. Attitudes on the part of the therapist that reinforce the woman's concept that she is weak, inadequate, and incompetent to manage her life, perpetrate the old mythology rather than mental health for the woman. Beliefs and behaviors of the therapist that encourage the woman to place the control of her life in an external human authority rather than in her own God-given, Spirit-directed power to control her life diminishes the woman, and in diminishing, destroys.

Attitudes on the part of the therapist that reinforce the concept that the feminine self is inferior and must simply be endured as a genetic, sin-mutated deficiency, damage women. Conversely, the idea that the feminine self must be rejected in order to develop power and competence distorts women's therapeutic issues of identity in a destructive way and reflects the dangerous cultural notion that the masculine pattern is the preferred norm to be adopted as a way of life. Such attitudes embody aspects of both the old and the new mythology and are without question destructive to women's growth and development.

Goals of therapy that require the woman client to serve the value system of the therapist or the institutional church *without the woman's conscious knowledge and emotionally competent consent* are clearly detrimental to the welfare of the woman client. Further, in the generally understood canon of the therapist's professional responsibilities, such goals are unethical and irresponsible.

Therapy that through omission of spiritual goals discourages the woman's integration and development of her spirituality is destructive to women.

Therapy that refuses to acknowledge cultural discrimination against women is destructive to women. Failure to deal factually in the therapeutic context with the experience of discrimination encourages the woman client either to deny the reality of this aspect of her life experience or, conversely, to suppress awareness of such experience in service to the therapist's comfort or bias; this fosters the client's continued unconscious acceptance of the victim role. In contrast, to deal with the reality of discrimination in such a way as to exacerbate the woman's anger and to encourage the age-old battle of the sexes—making men, without exception, villains—is destructive to women. This approach encourages the maintenance of stereotypic concepts of men and calls women away from the New Testament goals of confrontation, forgiveness, and reconciliation.

What does *not* work for women is therapy that incorporates the old or new mythology.

THERAPY THAT DOES WORK FOR WOMEN

What *does* work for women is therapy that incorporates the radical concepts of the New Testament: that women are of equal value to men, and their femininity equally vital and necessary in the human task of imaging God; that women are equally capable and equally responsible to manage their lives in obedience to the will of God as revealed to us in His Word; that to be equal does not require that one be the same; that women (and men) are called to gender-role transcendence in living out the high calling of God in Christ Jesus; that such transcendence does not deny nor seek to alter the rich significance of gender difference but expresses these differences in obedience to our calling to see ourselves as one in Christ.

Good therapy for women recognizes and respects differences, including ethnic differences. Asian, Hispanic, Afro-American, and Anglo women are in some important ways different. Good therapy for women also respects socioeconomic differences. The worlds of the rich and the poor are not the same. Effective counseling recognizes age differences. To be old in a society that venerates youth is challenging, sometimes painful, and always complex. Effective counseling reflects individual goal and lifestyle differences. Some women teach school, run word processors, or wait tables. Some women make bread, do counted cross stitch, and exercise the option of being home when the kids return from school. Increasing numbers of women are trying to find ways to do parts of both in a whole new way in a world of sweeping social change. Good therapy deals with the tension of change without glorifying either the old or the new.

And good therapy for women recognizes and respects similarities. We are women with women's ways of seeing the world, of relating, of communicating, with women's goals and griefs, with women's needs and resources, with women's ways of connectedness, and with our paradoxical struggle to be separate and creatively alone. We have women's bodies and experience the cycle of menses and menopause, the struggle of managing fertility, and the challenge of valuing the female experience while rejecting the idea that our female bodies are our only source of worth or identity.

The question of good therapy for women cannot be answered simply by providing a same-sexed therapist,[18] nor by choosing a given approach to treatment, feminist, Freudian, cognitive, behavioral, or Christian. Good therapy for women comes from a therapeutic relationship in which the woman client is empowered to value her femininity without being bound by a culturally defined expression of it, enabled to direct and control her life consistent with her freely chosen value system, and challenged to integrate her womanhood and personhood in such a way that she can become all she by God's divine intent and gifting is meant to be.

THE MYTH OF THE SEXUALLY SAFE RELATIONSHIP

One of the most dangerous myths regarding therapy is the myth of the sexually safe therapy hour. This myth is particularly dangerous within the community of Christian counselors. We want to believe that within the context of the therapeutic relationship with a Christian that the woman client is automatically made sexually safe by the therapist's stated commitment to a Christian value system.

This simply is not so.

Within counseling relationships with many Christian therapists, women clients *are* sexually safe, some of them, thankfully, in a healing relationship in which for the first time in their lives they are enabled to experience emotional safety with a man. Unfortunately, this is not automatically the case. And within the Christian community, including professional affiliations of Christian counselors, there is often a deep reluctance to acknowledge the problem or to take action when unprofessional behavior occurs.

There is clear agreement between professionals that sexual contact between the professional and client is unethical, and specifically forbidden. Physicians, pastors and priests, psychiatrists, psychologists, social workers, and marriage and family therapists officially subscribe to a code of ethics that prohibits sexual contact. Similarly, the proposed code of ethics for CAPS (Christian Association for Psychological Studies, an association to which many Christian counselors belong) strongly prohibits sexual intimacy between therapist and client.[19]

How frequently does such forbidden behavior occur? Therapist/client sexual intimacy occurs in secret and in a relationship in which interpersonal power is unequally distributed. Consequently, the perpetrator is unlikely to feel willing (or compelled) to report the unethical behavior, and the victim is emotionally unlikely to be able to do so. This behavior, like rape and incest, is believed to be a highly underreported crime.[20] While such sexually inappropriate behaviors can occur between a woman therapist and male client, in the overwhelming majority of the cases the victim of such professional malpractice is a woman client.

Conservative estimates indicate that approximately 6–7 percent of therapists will acknowledge sexually inappropriate behavior with clients.[21] Peter Rutter based his study, *Sex in the Forbidden Zone*, on a data base of more than one thousand case reports of male professionals having sexual relationships with their patients, clients, parishioners, or students.[22] Rutter states flatly that as a result of his study he believes that sexual exploitation of professional relationships is epidemic in our society.[23]

Given the likelihood that the percentage of actual cases is seriously underreported, the frequency with which such inappropriate counselor-client contact occurs is truly alarming. What is even more frightening, however, is the number of therapists admitting such behavior who are also willing to acknowledge sexual contact with more than one client. In one study 5.5 percent of the male respondents admitted engaging in sexual intercourse with their patients, and *eighty percent of the abusers admitted sexual contact with more than one patient.*[24]

One writer has made such statistics stunningly real with the following scenario:

> In 1982 there were 31,300 licensed psychotherapists in California, and if one projects that approximately 7 percent of the total, or 2,200 therapists have sexually abused a patient, and some of those have abused several patients, then one could expect there to be roughly 6,000 patients who have been abused and psychologically damaged. In the same year, l982, in California, records show that at least 12 *but no more than 16 therapists* were disciplined by their licensing boards.[25]

COUNSELOR INDISCRETION IN THE CHRISTIAN COMMUNITY

Lest we think that pastors and Christian counselors are automatically excluded from such chilling statistics, it is instructive to consider the results of a recent survey.[26]

Results indicated that 12 percent of the pastors responding to the survey acknowledged having had sexual intercourse with someone other than their spouse. Eighteen percent of the respondents reported other forms of sexual contact with someone other than their spouse (i.e., passionate kissing, fondling/ mutual masturbation). Those pastors who acknowledged having had intercourse or other forms of sexual contact were asked about who the other person was. In 17 percent of the cases that person was a counselee.[27]

There has been no specific study undertaken to establish the incidence of therapist/client sexual intimacy among Christian counselors.[28] However, the survey among pastors is sufficient to strongly suggest that such a study would reveal disappointingly high results. Collins, in discussing the counselor's sexuality, expected that his readers would have common knowledge of such inappropriate behavior.[29] McBurney reports sexual intimacy with parishioners or counselees a frequent problem of clergy seeking his help.[30]

Denial and refusal to take corrective action may, however, be even greater within the Christian community. Of the pastors admitting sexually inappropriate behavior, 31 percent said it had had *no consequences* in their lives. Only 4 percent said that their churches had found out about what they had done. The survey did not indicate if in that limited 4 percent of cases any disciplinary action by the church had been taken.[31] Lack of knowledge and corrective action on the part of the Christian community in these instances appears to be a dismal parallel to the failure of the California licensing board to deal with abusive psychologists.[32]

CONSEQUENCES FOR ABUSIVE COUNSELORS

In considering possible repercussions for abusive therapists, one writer reviewed action taken against offenders and concluded, "Action is taken in about four percent of the cases where sexual intimacy occurs between patient and therapists, and only half of these are carried to completion. . . . Obviously, offending therapists have little to fear from legal or ethics action."[33]

The church and Christian counselors do not appear to respond in a significantly different fashion. The church's failure to act is described graphically in the tragic case reported by Marie Fortune in which a pastor sexually abused a number of women under his care.[34] Fortune concludes, "The bottom line . . . is a clear recognition that the church is responsible for the professional conduct of its clergy and must act to prevent misconduct from causing harm to its members or the community at large."[35]

Clearly, in a parallel manner, Christian counselors are responsible for the professional conduct of Christian counselors.

We too must act to prevent misconduct from causing harm to clients or to the community at large. Requiring Christian counselors to subscribe to a code of ethics specifically forbidding such behavior is an important first step. Development of reporting procedures, assistance for the victims, and discipline and rehabilitation of the abusing therapists (when possible) must assume higher priority for us as Christian counselors if we are to maintain responsible ministry to women within the Christian community.[36]

There are two additional aspects which must be considered in dealing with the myth of the sexually safe therapy hour. One is the difficult question of how and why such abuse happens. The second is the tragic impact upon women clients, and their need as victims for specialized therapeutic help.

CAUSES OF THE ABUSE

Why does it happen? There is no single reason for such complex destructive behavior, but there are some possible explanations.

First, it appears likely that therapists, regardless of their specific professional discipline, receive insufficient training in recognizing and handling their own sexual feelings. Feelings of sexual attraction on the part of the therapist for the client do happen. In most training programs, such feelings are severely prohibited and are regarded as evidence of psychological disturbance or sin, rather than a normal response that sometimes occurs in the counseling relationship.

Consequently, when individuals experience such feelings during training, the feelings are suppressed or denied by the student in fear of official repercussions rather than being openly recognized and dealt with in supervision. Such patterns of denial and suppression developed during training then continue on into professional practice.

One study reported that 95 percent of the male therapists acknowledged being sexually attracted to their clients.[37] However, only 9 percent of the respondents felt that their training programs had been adequate in assisting them to acknowledge and deal appropriately with such responses. Peter Rutter gives a candid, moving account of his own utter shock when he was

confronted with his powerful and potentially destructive
sexual feelings for a woman client.[38]

In discussing the problems of pastors, Archibald Hart commented, "Too many people are trying to prevent the arousal,
the erotic feeling. That's not where the battle ought to be."[39]
Hart went on to point out that the experience of erotic passion
is in some ways a conditioned response, but that recognition
of the response, and *choice* of how to handle such feelings, lie
under the individual's control. Collins, similarly, expressed
concern about the absence of preparation for pastors to anticipate, recognize, and handle sexual feelings when they occur.[40]

A second major contributor to the problem is the imbalanced
level of interpersonal power which in traditional roles exists
between a woman client and her male therapist. Peter Rutter's
summary of this point merits full quotation.

> It took me nearly a decade to stop believing in the
> myth of the beneficent doctor. I discovered instead
> that sexual exploitation by men of women under their
> care or tutelage is not unusual and in actuality is quite
> common. Furthermore, I found remarkably similar
> patterns of sexual contact not only by male doctors
> and therapists but by male clergy, lawyers, teachers,
> and workplace mentors. These highly eroticized en-
> tanglements can occur, behind closed doors, in any
> relationship in which a woman entrusts important as-
> pects of her physical, spiritual, psychological, or
> material welfare to a man who has power over her.
>
> I also found that the men who have sex with their
> female patients, clients, parishioners, students, and
> protegees are not the obviously disturbed men who
> occasionally show up in the headlines. Instead, they
> are accomplished professionals, admired commu-
> nity leaders, and respectable family men whose
> integrity we tend to take for granted. I can now see
> that sexual violation of trust is an epidemic, main-
> stream problem that reenacts in the professional
> relationship a wider cultural power-imbalance be-
> tween men and women.[41]

Rutter's study makes clear the powerful sexual attraction that can, and frequently does, occur between a man and woman in the secrecy of the therapeutic hour. On the basis of his study, however, Rutter concludes that the failure to handle such sexual attraction ethically does not come from the irresistible biological urge of such impulses. It comes, rather, from unexamined issues of power which encourage the male to act in self-gratification rather than in responsible care of the woman client. Such a view is consistent with the growing clinical understanding that other forms of sexual abuse such as incest and rape are not motivated primarily by male sexual needs in a biological sense but are instead the expression of both anger against women and power over them.

One major denomination is developing a working document outlining procedures for dealing with sexual misconduct by clergy. In this document the issue of power in relationship to sexual misconduct is viewed in a way quite similar to the position taken by Rutter. What is said regarding pastors might equally be said of Christian therapists.

> Not only is the pastoral office a position of great trust and responsibility, it is also, by virtue of the trust persons place in the office and the person of pastor, a position of great authority and power over others.
>
> It is unthinkable that anyone would violate that trust and power for the sake of personal gratification, and yet the experience of the church is that it does happen. Persons in pastoral roles may betray the trust placed in them by misusing power in many ways. These guidelines deal with the specific abuse of power by those who engage in sexual advances toward or contact with those for whose spiritual welfare the pastor is responsible. Any improper or unwanted sexual contact is damaging. The harm is increased many times when the contact comes from a person to whom the victim has every right to look for guidance, protection and care.[42]

The therapist's willingness to abuse the power of his position of trust in order to achieve sexual gratification is evidence of deep, unresolved emotional and spiritual issues in the therapist's life. One therapist who had been sexually involved with a woman client, said in retrospect, "A great deal of what we men struggle for in our sexual behavior is really a quest to heal ourselves and find value in this world."[43]

After having reviewed more than a thousand such instances, Rutter concluded, "Profound needs for healing and self-validation infuse men's sexual fantasy. Although many men who exploit women are in touch with no motivation more complicated than simple sexual desire and opportunism, I believe the search to heal a wounded sense of self is what underlies most destructive sexual behavior in men."[44]

One experienced marriage and family therapist who is also a pastor concludes flatly, "All the safeguards in the world will not help the counselor who has not come to terms with his own sexuality. . . ."[45]

Why does sexually inappropriate behavior between the therapist and client happen? Probably for at least four reasons: (1) insufficient professional training; (2) unresolved sexual issues coupled with lack of spiritual maturity; (3) unexamined issues of power fostering male exploitation of the vulnerable female client; and (4) inadequate, ineffectual policing by professionals. Certainly the sexual dilemmas of the helping professionals remain a largely uncharted, dangerous territory.[46]

IMPACT ON WOMEN CLIENTS

Who gets hurt? Everyone—but the woman client is injured in particularly painful ways.

The woman client learns again through the experience that she is useful as a sexual object and of little worth as a person. She learns that if she offers her body sexually, preservation of her sense of worth and personhood is of less value to the man than satisfaction of his sexual impulse. She is taught again that her role is to meet the man's needs even when doing so is destructive to her psychologically and spiritually. She is given powerful data suggesting that no man is trustworthy, that no relationship with a man is safe. She is pushed toward despair and away from hope. She develops a growing sense of helplessness. She begins to believe that there is no way to make her life better. She has tried, and what has happened is more injury both to herself and to others.

She experiences emotional trauma much like that associated with rape and incest. She has participated in forbidden sex. She believes it is her fault and is often encouraged to believe this by the offending therapist. It is (presumably) her female sexuality that was the source of the problem, the reason for the injury. She often feels she must keep the shameful secret and defend and protect the man; she must endure and deal with her guilt alone. The married woman must deal with the pain, turmoil, and injury to her marriage. The single woman must often deal with her fear that the experience has ruined forever the possibility of a trusting, committed relationship with a man. The woman often experiences herself as alienated from God and immobilized in the practice of her faith.

At the most complex level of identity formation, female sex and feminine gender are destructively enmeshed in the dysfunctional therapeutic experience. The woman is left with the agonizing sense that she cannot value herself as a woman because of her destructive female sexuality. The wound to the woman who experiences sexual exploitation in the therapeutic relationship goes to the soul of her identity as a woman and impacts all aspects of her life.

Rutter reports a previously unidentified damage to women experiencing such injury. None of the women he interviewed had borne a child since her experience of sexual violation in the therapeutic relationship. Rutter does not, of course, suggest that this is necessarily true for every woman having such an experience. His conclusion is, nevertheless, that such sexual violation has a profound and lasting impact on the woman's perception and management of her fertility in ways not yet recognized nor studied.[47]

Help for victims of such sexual exploitation parallels in basic ways the procedures found to be helpful for women who are victims of incest and rape.

The woman must be assisted to deal with four issues:
- Responsibility—Was it my fault?
- Cause and vulnerability—Why didn't I keep it from happening?
- Response—What can I do now with my anger, pain, injury?
- Meaning—Where was God? Can I ever be whole again? What does this mean to me as a woman to have had this experience?

Dealing with each of these issues is difficult, complicated work. It is not the purpose here to provide a substantive guide to therapeutic work with women who have been injured in this way. The point is rather to emphasize that our belief in the myth of the sexually safe therapy hour has led us as counselors to ignore the fact that many women in the church and many of our present women clients have special needs. They need help in recovering from a profound injury they have received in an unsafe therapeutic relationship. Such injury may have occurred with a physician, lawyer, pastor, employer, or former therapist. We as counselors need the courage to explore how many women, including some of our present clients, are the silent walking wounded, survivors of sex in the forbidden zone who have not yet been able to tell us what happened and to acknowledge their deep wound.

THE MYTH OF ECONOMIC IRRELEVANCY

There is another professional myth which should be included in this discussion of the mythology that affects psychotherapy with women. This myth occurs in many forms, but it has at its core the idea that the important problems with which the counselor is called to deal are within the person (intrapsychic), between persons (relational), or with God (spiritual). This myth suggests that all other aspects of the client's life are neither the therapist's responsibility nor concern.

This myth has obscured the important fact that the difficulties that women bring to therapy are often the direct product of the life circumstances in which the woman lives.

For example, if a single mother with two children, working two jobs at minimum wage, comes to therapy because she is depressed, what is the point on which counseling for this woman should focus? The fact that she is a woman? That she is a mother? That she is depressed? What is the therapeutic significance of the fact that she is struggling to survive on an income well below poverty level? In what ways can/should therapy encourage her as a believer to look to God to supply her needs? Is it true for this woman that happiness is simply a choice? In short, in what ways should counseling for this woman relate to the socioeconomic reality of her life?

One nationally known therapist for women recently commented:

> Women are now participating in different realms of life in numbers that seemed almost impossible to imagine ten to fifteen years ago—they attend medical school, law school, and business school and hold positions in professions and corporations previously closed to them. . . [but] the vast majority of working women, 80 percent, hold the lowest-paid and most dead-end jobs in this country.[48]

Data from the 1980 World Conference on Women reported women as 50 percent of the world population, composing 33 percent of the official labor force, but providing 66.6 percent of the working hours. In return, they receive 10 percent of the world's income, and own only 1 percent of the world property.[49]

Poverty is a women's issue, but it is all too frequently ignored as a counseling issue in therapeutic work with women. This may be because for the most part the women with whom counselors are most familiar are the white, relatively affluent middle-class people who can afford counseling fees.

One writer who has specialized in study of women who are poor summarizes the situation bluntly:

> While poor women experience a particularly high incidence of mental health problems, they are often reluctant to use mental health services. Among those who do seek professional help many are so dissatis-

fied that they drop out of treatment. Minority
women particularly are likely to be poor, to find their
opportunities limited by discrimination, and to discover that potential therapists do not share basic
knowledge and values with them.[50]

It is both sad and disconcerting to discover how few Christian counselors are knowledgeable about the mental health
problems of the poor, or are engaged in providing services for
them.

Perhaps one of the most destructive myths about women is
one held about women who are poor. The common attitude is
that these women are poor because of a major character de-
fect. The myth describes these women as either lacking
willpower and the motivation to change their circumstances
or as lazy, enjoying the welfare life and the experience of having others take care of them. Too often we hear the complaint,
"If those women don't like being poor, why don't they get a
(better) job?"

Not all of the poor are found in urban settings. The rural
poor, particularly poor women, often live with only minimal
contact with the outside world, without social or educational
services, with limited transportation, and with little or no
health care.

Women who are poor are not alike. Every counselor who sees
women needs, I think, to spend the equivalent of a week with
the proud women trying to maintain themselves and their families in the deteriorating coal-mining areas in West Virginia, with
the fiercely independent rural women of the Midwest whose
families are losing farms but can find no other employment,
with courageous urban women, struggling to live in the violence
and deterioration of much of our public subsidized housing.

A counselor can acquire a valuable lesson in the struggle of
most poor women to provide health care for their children simply by sitting with a woman for the hours of necessary waiting
in order for an overworked doctor to see a sick child in a city
hospital emergency room. Spending a night learning from the
homeless women in any large urban center is a graphic education in the present emergency in housing which impacts

women and their children in distinctive ways. Poor women are not the same, nor are their stories, but the grinding depression of poverty is.

Minority women face particularly painful dilemmas. Because many of us as Christian counselors live out our days in a comfortably middle-class setting, it is difficult for us to realize the degree to which economic conditions have actually deteriorated for many women over the last two decades, particularly for women of color. As Belle points out, women and their children have come to constitute an increasingly large proportion of America's poor, and the poverty population has also become increasingly minority as it has become more female.[51]

The poverty population is also becoming increasingly elderly. Elderly women are nearly twice as likely as men of the same age to be impoverished.[52] One therapist in discussing the difficulty of poor elderly women has pointed out the often neglected responsibility of the church for these women in regard to both financial assistance and emotional support.[53]

The sheer numbers of poor women is stunning. Basow points out that nearly two-thirds of the people over seventeen years of age who are living below the poverty line are women. She comments, "The most affected are Black women, single mothers, and women over 65. The reasons for the increase in female poverty levels are complex but three factors are important: low salaries, increased longevity, and single parenthood."[54]

In 1980, two out of three poor people were female.[55] It is possible that further feminization of poverty over the decade of the eighties may make the proportion higher when analysis of the 1990 census data is complete. Change in the number of families with a female householder and no spouse present accounted for 83.8 percent of the *net* increase in poor families between 1989 and 1990. However, there has been no statistically signficant change during 1985–1990 in the *proportion* of poor families that are maintained by women with no spouse present.[56]

It is crucial for counselors working with women to recognize that the poor are not those people out there somewhere and to examine some of our stereotypic concepts of poverty.[57] Who is the woman who is poor? Often it is the single mother, who needs help with physical exhaustion, the emotional trauma of her divorce, and the logistical struggle of managing her children alone. It is the single working woman whose salary is limited, without mental health benefits, but who needs a counselor (whom she cannot afford) to help her in her struggle to find healing from incest. It is the young mother in an intact suburban nuclear family whose husband has just been laid off his job, or whose family has lost their home in foreclosure proceedings. It is the elderly woman who does not get out of the house much anymore, but who uses her arthritis as an excuse to disguise her depression. It is the urban woman who comes sporadically to the inner-city church; it is the rural woman who comes to the country church, or stops coming when they lose the farm. These women cannot afford standard fees (sometimes no fees at all), but they have overwhelming needs for help.

To wait for such women to come to the conventional counseling office setting to seek help is itself an approach open to serious criticism from proponents of services for women. But in those circumstances when such women do come for help, then to act as though the stress, anxiety, and depression of these women can be treated medically or therapeutically without reference to the socioeconomic realities of their lives is an extraordinary example of denial of reality. Such a belief is more than a cruel professional myth, although it is that. It is also a belief dangerously close to that attitude so roundly condemned by James when he said, "Suppose a brother or sister is without clothes and daily food. If one of you says to him, 'Go, I wish you well; keep warm and well fed,' but does nothing about his physical needs, what good is it? In the same way, faith by itself, if it is not accompanied by action, is dead."[58]

Therapy with women in socioeconomic need poses some difficult issues and raises hard questions to which there are no easy answers. What is important at this point, however, is our understanding and acknowledgement that as therapists we can be tempted by our professional myth to act as though talk can be substituted for action when it is action that is needed.

For counselors serious about increasing their skill in working with women, it is vital to accept the fact that we cannot do effective therapy with women while disregarding the socio-economic reality of their lives. To believe otherwise is pure myth, and as such it is dangerous to client and counselor alike.

NOTES

1. Miriam Greenspan, *A New Approach to Women and Therapy* (New York: McGraw- Hill, 1983), 28.

2. Betty Carter as cited by Harriet Goldhor Lerner, *Women in Therapy* (New York: Harper and Row, 1988), xvii.

3. Lerner, 110.

4. Ibid., xvii–xxi.

5. Susan Sturdivant, *Therapy with Women* (New York: Springer, 1980), 8–9. See also Sturdivant's discussion of this point in her preface, xi–xiii.

6. Julia A. Sherman, "Therapist Attitudes and Sex-Role Stereotyping," in *Women and Psychotherapy*, ed. Annette M. Brodsky and Rachel Hare-Mustin (New York: Guilford, 1980), 60.

7. Ibid., 45.

8. Lynne Bravo Rosewater, "Feminist Therapy: Implications for Practitioners," in *Women and Mental Health Policy*, ed. Lenore E. Walker, Sage Yearbooks in Women's Policy Studies, vol. 9 (Beverly Hills, Calif.: Sage, 1984), 268–69.

9. David G. Benner, *Psychotherapy and the Spiritual Quest* (Grand Rapids, Mich.: Baker, 1988), 154–64.

10. H. J. Eysenck, " The Effects of Psychotherapy: An Evaluation," *Journal of Consulting Psychology* 16 (1952): 319–24.

11. M. L. Smith, G. V. Glass, and T. I. Miller, *The Benefits of Psychotherapy* (Baltimore: Johns Hopkins University Press, 1980).

12. D. A. Shapiro and D. Shapiro, "Meta-analysis of Comparative Therapy Outcomes Studies: A Replication and Refinement," *Psychological Bulletin* 92 (1982): 581–604.

13. Jeanne Morecek and Marilyn Johnson, "Gender and the Process of Therapy," in *Women and Psychotherapy*, ed. Annette Brodsky and Rachel Hare-Mustin (New York: Guilford, 1980), 67–93.

14. Brodsky and Hare-Mustin, 389–91, 405–9. The discussion by David Orlinsky and Kenneth I. Howard, "Gender and Psychotherapeutic Outcome," in Brodsky and Hare-Mustin, ibid., 3–34, gives a helpful beginning to understanding the complexity of this issue. The discussion of Brodsky and Hare-Mustin, "Psychotherapy and Women: Priorities for Research," ibid., 385–409, similarly gives understanding of the issue as well as recommendations for research.

15. "Principles Concerning the Counseling and Therapy of Women," prepared by the American Psychological Association, Division on Counseling Psychology, Committee on Women, reprinted with permission in *Handbook of Feminist Therapy: Women's Issues in Psychotherapy*, ed. Lynne

Bravo Rosewater and Lenore E. Walker (New York: Springer, 1985), xxix–xxxi.

16. Orlinsky and Howard; see also Brodsky and Hare-Mustin.

17. Diane Marshall, "Current Issues of Women and Therapy, "*Journal of Psychology and Christianity*" 4, no. 1 (Spring 1985): 62–72.

18. Alexandra G. Kaplan, "Female or Male Psychotherapists for Women: New Formulations," *Work in Progress*, no. 83–02 (Wellesley, Mass.: Stone Center, 1984).

19. H. Newton Maloney, "Codes of Ethics: A Comparison," *Journal of Psychology and Theology* 5, no. 3 (Fall 1986): 94–101.

20. Jacqueline C. Bouhoutsos, "Sexual Intimacy Between Psychotherapists and Clients: Policy Implications for the Future," in *Women and Mental Health Policy*, ed. Lenore E. Walker, Sage Yearbooks in Women's Policy Studies, vol. 9 (Beverly Hills, Calif.: Sage, 1984), 209–11.

21. John Shackelford, "Affairs in the Consulting Room: A Review of the Literature on Therapist-Patient Sexual Intimacy," *Journal of Psychology and Theology* 8, no. 4 (Winter 1989): 26–43.

22. Peter Rutter, *Sex in the Forbidden Zone: When Men in Power—Therapists, Doctors, Clergy, Teachers, and Others—Betray Women's Trust* (Los Angeles: Jeremy P. Tarcher, Inc., 1989), 37.

23. Ibid., 12.

24. J. C. Holroyd and A. M. Brodsky, "Psychologists' attitudes and practices regarding erotic and non-erotic physical contact with patients," *American Psychologist* 32 (1977): 843–49. See also Bouhoutsos, 209.

25. J. S. Vinson, "Use of complaint procedures in cases of therapist-patient sexual contact," *Professional Psychology: Research and Practice* 18, no. 2 (1987): 159–64, as cited in Shackelford, 27. Italics mine.

26. "How Common Is Pastoral Indiscretion?", results of a Leadership Survey, *Leadership* 9, no. 1 (Winter 1988): 12–13.

27. Ibid., 12.

28. Shackelford, 40.

29. Gary Collins, *Christian Counseling: A Comprehensive Guide*, rev. ed. (Dallas, Tex.: Word, 1986), 154–57, 263–70.

30. Louis McBurney, *Counseling Christian Workers* (Dallas, Tex.: Word, 1986), 31.

31. "How Common Is Pastoral Indiscretion?", 13.

32. An account of the failure of both the law and the licensing agencies to deal adequately with an abusive therapist is given in Carolyn M. Bates and Annette M. Brodsky, *Sex in the Therapy Hour* (New York: Guilford, 1989).

33. Bouhoutsos, 213.

34. Marie M. Fortune, *Is Nothing Sacred? When Sex Invades the Pastoral Relationship* (New York: Harper and Row, 1989).

35. Ibid., 126.

36. Shackelford, 40–41, discusses general concerns regarding the offending therapist but does not, unfortunately, also consider the needs of the abused women clients.

37. K. S. Pope, P. Keith-Spiegel, and B. G. Tabachnick, "Sexual Attraction to Clients," *American Psychologist* 41, no. 2 (1986): 147-58.
38. Rutter, 2–6.
39. Archibald Hart in "Private Sins of Public Ministry," *Leadership* 9, no. 1 (Winter 1988): 23.
40. Gary Collins in "How Common Is Pastoral Indiscretion?", 12.
41. Rutter, 1–2.
42. "Sexual Misconduct by Clergy within Pastoral Relationships," working document developed by the Northwest District of the American Lutheran Church, 1987, in Marie Fortune, 135–36.
43. Rutter, 61.
44. Ibid.
45. Andre Bustanoby, "Counseling the Seductive Female," *Leadership* 9, no. 1 (Winter 1988): 51. See also Peter Steinke, "Clergy Affairs," *Journal of Psychology and Christianity* 8, no. 4 (Winter 1989): 56–62.
46. Jerry Edelwich and Archie Brodsky, *Sexual Dilemmas for the Helping Professional* (New York: Brunner/Mazel, 1991).
47. Rutter, 89–90.
48. Jean Baker Miller, *Toward a New Psychology of Women*, 2nd ed. (Boston: Beacon Press, 1986), xii–xiii.
49. Helen V. Collier, *Counseling Women* (New York: The Free Press, 1982), 171.
50. Deborah Belle, "Inequality and Mental Health: Low Income and Minority Women," in *Women and Mental Health Policy*, ed. Lenore E. Walker, Sage Yearbooks in Women's Policy Studies, vol. 9 (Beverly Hills, Calif.: Sage, 1984), 135.
51. Ibid., 136.
52. Collier, 230–31.
53. Mary Franzen Clark, *Hiding, Hurting, Healing: Restoration for Today's Woman* (Grand Rapids, Mich.: Zondervan, 1985), 155–60.
54. Susan Basow, *Gender Stereotypes: Traditions and Alternatives*, 2nd ed. (Pacific Grove, Calif.: Brooks/Cole, 1986), 263.
55. Collier, 230.
56. Bureau of the Census, *Poverty in the United States, 1990*, Current Population Reports, Consumer Income, Series P-60, no. 175 (Washington, D. C.: U. S. Department of Commerce, 1991), 6–7.
57. One helpful discussion of stereotypes is found in Sarah J. Couper, "Prelude to Equality: Recognizing Oppression," in *Gender Matters: Women's Studies for the Christian Community*, ed. June Steffensen Hagen (Grand Rapids, Mich.: Zondervan, 1990), 249–56.
58. James 2:15–17, NIV.

Chapter Five

The Complexities of Gender Research

Up to this point, we have focused on the misbeliefs about women which cause the counselor and the woman client difficulty. However, to be effective with women clients, we must do more than identify the myths. We must also establish the truth about gender, similarities *and* differences, as it is presently understood.

Establishing the truth is not easy. There is disagreement regarding the facts themselves and for good reason. Research is not easy in this field. But difficult as it is to know what the facts are, it is even more difficult to know what the facts *mean*.

For example, there is some evidence to indicate that men and women differ in their ability to perform spatial tasks. In a famous early study of sex differences, Maccoby and Jacklin wrote, ". . . boys excel in visual-spatial ability. Male superiority on visual-spatial tasks is fairly consistently found in adolescence and adulthood, but not in childhood."[1]

In 1985, however, another team of researchers published a review of seventy-nine major studies and concluded, "'No, sex differences in spatial abilities do not exist' or at least 'It is by no means clear as yet.'"[2]

Even when there is some consensus about the facts themselves, there is often sharp controversy over the meaning and application of facts in real life. Some individuals may believe that presumed spatial differences reflect lack of encouragement and educational opportunities for women; they argue that women therefore should be given special assistance and opportunity for training and employment in fields such as engineering. Others argue that differences mean that coveted positions in engineering and other technical fields should be reserved for men who have a natural superiority in the required skills. Individuals holding both views are likely to cite science as proving their position.

At the outset it is helpful to think about the significance such debate has for the counselor. As counselors we sometimes assume that questions about sex and gender differences such as those concerning spatial ability have relevance only to researchers and the academic world. This is not so.

For one reason, the counselor's office is the place where such information is translated into real-life decisions of individual women. The counselor's beliefs about women's abilities shape the way in which the counselor encourages, or fails to encourage, a woman to examine her options and strongly influences the woman's belief or distrust in herself. Accurate information is essential for counselor and client as they explore different questions.

If not checked by facts, the cultural myth to which we are all exposed can tempt us as counselors to overlook a woman's gift if it lies in a nontraditional area, for example in the area of mathematics or architecture. As a consequence, we can neglect our responsibility to encourage the woman to explore her gift and to consider what God's leading might be for her in relation to that gift. We can also fail to see and understand the struggle the woman may be experiencing in regard to her gift. Equally important, such information stretches our understanding as counselors so that we are encouraged to see women as a group in less stereotyped ways. It also reminds us to view each woman as an individual who may not demonstrate the characteristics that we commonly associate with women. One prominent researcher commented, "If psychotherapy is to help female patients, therapists must become aware of sex differences where they do exist and refute assumptions about sex differences where they do not exist."[3]

This sounds like a fairly straightforward assignment. The example dealing with spatial abilities demonstrates, however, that it is not.

While I was working on these chapters dealing with gender research, a friend said, "Why is this taking so long? Identify the differences, say simply what they mean, and get on with other things." It was very good advice, but like much good advice it proved quite difficult to take. However much I and my readers might wish it were so, gender differences and similarities cannot be made into a simple list of facts to be learned like the table of atomic weights in a chemistry textbook.

"Why not?" you may be thinking. The complicated truth about gender research is that it is not easy even to explain why such research is difficult to carry out and the results difficult to understand.

UNDERSTANDING THE LANGUAGE OF SCIENCE

One difficulty lies in translating the research language in which gender studies are reported. This translation process requires the reader to do two things: (1) to identify and evaluate the ideas underlying the study (usually referred to as the basic assumptions of the study), and (2) to understand the procedures and statistical conclusions the researcher has drawn. There can be serious problems at either or both points.

UNDERLYING ASSUMPTIONS

In gender studies, as in all other research, the underlying assumptions are of two kinds. There are *stated* assumptions, ideas that the researchers have used and that they explain in the text of the research report. There are also *unstated* assumptions, ideas that the researchers have used but that they did not verbally identify. For the readers to recognize these unstated ideas when they occur is often a tricky business. In addition, basic assumptions, stated and unstated, may be incorrect yet permit the statistical conclusions growing out of the research procedures to be mathematically accurate. Correct statistics do not guarantee correct assumptions. This fact led one wit to note that if you can just lead researchers to make invalid assumptions, you need not pay attention to their correct answers.

An example of this can be seen in an experimental procedure commonly used to measure male/female differences in spatial abilities. The procedure, the Rod and Frame Test, requires the subject to be alone with the experimenter in a totally dark room. The assumption has been that the sex of the subject will affect the test score, but that the sex of the experimenter will make no difference.

Common sense, however, might well raise some questions about this assumption—unstated in every experiment of which I am aware. Think for a moment. Suppose that the woman subject in the pitch dark room is a student (usually the case) and the experimenter is a male graduate student or psychology professor. Is the sex of the experimenter of *no* significance to the subject's response? Additionally, conditions of the test require the woman subject to insist that the experimenter adjust the rod to her satisfaction. Would the woman be more likely to be assertive with a female experimenter or with a male? We do not know. We do know, however, that the assumption that the sex of the experimenter has no effect on the subject's response is likely to be untrue, and the study therefore open to question, no matter what the accuracy of the statistical analysis of the results may be.

In some cases, as we will see in reviewing studies of women and aggression, the basic assumptions underlying gender research may well have been influenced by cultural myths about women in ways that the scientists themselves failed to recognize at the time.

PROBLEMS WITH STATISTICS

Sometimes statistics themselves provide the problem since most of us do not always understand what the statistical conclusions may mean. For example, I can randomly select a hundred men and carefully measure their height. In exactly the same way, I can select and measure a hundred women. Then in the conclusion of my study, I can report that my measurements show that men are taller than women. It is important to understand, however, that I have reported that *on average* men are taller than women. This overlooks the fact that *some women are taller* than some men.

Statistical analysis can be reported in ways that suggest proof for quite different points of emphasis. When I report the results of my study, I can simply say that men are taller than women, placing an emphasis on presumed male superiority. Or I can say that I have discovered a small group of women who are taller than men, placing an emphasis upon presumed female superiority.

However, if I want to be both complete and accurate, I will say that my study indicates that there are both short and tall men and short and tall women. I will add that the differences are greatest between short women and tall men, and short men and tall women, and note that the group of men who are taller than women is larger than the group of women who are taller than men.

I will also measure the difference within the women's group (i.e., between tall and short women) and within the men's group (i.e., between tall and short men) and compare these differences with the average difference *between* men as a group and women as a group. This is called inter/intra group differences in the language of science and helps us place the difference between groups in context. If, for example, the differences between the tallest and shortest men in the men's group is eleven inches, and the average difference between men and women seven inches, careful reporting would note that while there was a significant difference in height *between* the men's and women's groups, this difference was *less* than the difference *within* the men's group.

Inter/intra group differences have particular importance in gender studies. When we are talking about differences between groups of men and women, it is important to be able to compare the size of the difference *between* the groups to the size of the difference *within* each group. Reports of such differences are often omitted or misunderstood.

Something else is clear in this simple example of measuring heights. If you were to select from this study one woman and one man, you would be unable to tell without further measurement whether this specific woman would be taller or shorter than this specific man. As counselors, it is important for us to remember that averages reported about groups cannot give us reliable information about specific individuals.

While many incorrect conclusions are the result of poorly planned or improperly executed research, some problems result from the reader's misunderstanding of the meaning of statistical conclusions and consequent misapplication of them.

Basic statistical procedures are designed to tell us if a difference between selected groups occurs and if that difference should be attributed to chance or to the influence of an experimental factor identified in the study. When a study reports a significant statistical difference, it means that some factor other than chance has most probably influenced the response of the subjects in the study. Measurements of significance are the tests scientists use to tell us about the probability of chance. Such measures do not give us information about the actual size of the difference between the groups, nor do they measure the relationship of the difference *between* groups to the difference *within* the groups. Statistical significance does *not* mean we can apply the findings of the study to an individual client's case without caution. Neither does it indicate that the results of the study have broad social significance at practical levels. All too often the problem lies not in what the researcher said, but rather in what the reader thought the researcher meant and in the resulting misapplication that was made.

Research demonstrates another potential problem which has nothing at all to do with mathematics. This complicating factor is the politics of science. In reviewing gender studies, the reader soon discovers that he or she must try to identify the often unstated value system of the researcher which has shaped the way in which the research has been reported.

UNDERSTANDING THE POLITICS OF GENDER RESEARCH

It is a myth to believe that science is carried out by rational, objective searchers for truth, who are uninfluenced by the world around them. Scientists, like other humans, are deeply influenced by their belief systems and the environment in which they work.

POLITICS AND THE RESEARCH ENVIRONMENT

Freud's concept of penis envy can provide a hypothetical example of how gender research might become entangled with the politics of science. Suppose that at a prestigious university two famous researchers, psychologists named Smith and Jones, measured women subjects for something these researchers identified as penis envy. The measurements were carefully done and analyzed with statistical accuracy.

Now let us suppose an unknown woman researcher, a biologist from a small state college, published a study showing that the very idea of penis envy itself was a theoretical invention with no real substance and that Smith and Jones had been measuring something else, which she has now identified as "Hormonal Variation."

Now what? For one thing, the famous researchers are going to be very unscientifically grumpy (and at pains to keep this hidden—scientists, by definition, do not get grumpy). Nevertheless, Smith and Jones are not going to feel cheerful about the possibility that their famous measures of penis envy, about which they have been writing important papers, may have been demonstrated to be incorrect, if not downright silly. Scientists, being human, have no fondness for looking foolish.

Besides, the famous researchers now face other serious problems. Smith and Jones are friends of the man who developed and marketed the Penis Envy Test. They hold stock in a company that sells the Penis Envy Test and scores it by computer for a fee. They also hold stock in a pharmaceutical company that sells an antianxiety drug frequently prescribed for women suffering from severe forms of penis envy. Smith has a contract for a book on penis envy—its publication will influence his election to tenure. Jones has an application in process for a research grant that will enable him and Smith to study further large numbers of women suffering from penis envy—the grant application includes a new expensive computer for his office. Whatever will happen to their system if it is indeed true that the very concept of penis envy itself may have been proven to be wrong?

It is not difficult for anyone familiar with the competitive nature of university life to imagine Smith and Jones simply deciding that no decent work could come out of a small college like that in the first place. (The idea that no good can come from Nazareth is, unfortunately, not limited to the Scripture.)

Besides, Smith and Jones might reason, is not this woman's resistance to the idea of penis envy proof in itself of the validity of the idea? Anyway, they think, if the truth were fully known (i.e., if this obstinate woman would only let us reanalyze her raw data), it would be clear at once that her statistical analysis was shaky. Women, you know, never have a good head for math. Certainly, Smith and Jones are likely to conclude, there is no reason to be alarmed about Hormonal Variation. It really has not yet been proven. Besides, what could a biologist know about psychology?

Smith and Jones then issue a press release through the university to the local newspaper stating, "Penis envy has been demonstrated in a recent major study to be a significant contributor to women's depression." The editor, who knows nothing and cares less about penis envy, uses the release for a filler. Local subscribers to the paper, including a young mother home alone with three preschoolers and no help, read about this scientific proof. The young mother concludes, "I'm feeling depressed today, but at least I now know what is wrong. I'm suffering from penis envy. Science has discovered what is wrong."

When a skeptical neighbor asks, "Do you really think penis envy causes depression?" the young mother says, "Oh, yes, I'm sure it does. I've experienced it," with no realization of the way in which the politics of science has shaped her interpretation of her life experience.

Meanwhile Drs. Smith and Jones have gone to Washington where they play golf with Sam Greenback, their personal contact for federal funding. They also take Sam to dinner at an expensive restaurant where the three of them discuss Smith and Jones's application for follow-up study of their investigation of penis envy. (They pay the check out of the grant expense account.) Sam Greenback thinks to himself, "These guys do a good job. We've already got the machinery in place for handling grants with them. Besides, I don't know that woman from the state college. Anyway, Smith and Jones's university gave us a bad time about the last appropriations because they thought they didn't get their fair share. Let's keep it sane and simple." The grant is approved, and the scientific proof of penis envy rolls on.

Of course, not all research is subject to such politicized procedures. However, far more often than is commonly recognized, decisions that determine what is studied, how it is studied, and, particularly, how it is reported are shaped by factors that have little if anything to do with scientific study of the question at hand.

INTERNALIZED BELIEF SYSTEM

There is another powerful factor that influences our understanding of gender studies; it is our internalized belief system that leads us to see what we think is there or want to be there. An exercise frequently used in general psychology courses is a good place to begin considering how this difficulty can occur. We will end by considering a real life example.

Many of us can remember when in our first psychology course we were presented with a figure in which two wavy lines extended from the top to the bottom of an otherwise empty page. In looking at the lines we discovered something. Whether we saw two wavy lines, a picture of a vase, or a picture of two faces looking at each other depended on how we looked at the two wavy lines. In most lectures on perception, students are also given a similar figure in which, depending on how the individual looks at it, there is a beautiful young girl or a wrinkled old woman.

We may have been intrigued by the realization that perception is more than the brain's *reception* of light waves—it is also the brain's *translation* of these light waves into meaning. But even more intriguing was the further discovery that the brain's translation was something we could influence by choice. We could see what we decided to see—vase or faces—we had a choice.

Gender research often presents us with something like the perception cards—information about which we have to decide what we see. And at that point of decision, it is not just the researcher's report or the data itself that determines what happens. It is our belief about the nature of things—similarities and differences between women and men, in this instance—that determines what we choose to see.

An excerpt from a book by a well-known evangelical author was recently included in *Male/Female Roles: Opposing Viewpoints*. In this article, entitled "Biology Determines Gender Roles," James Dobson says,

> Careful research is revealing that the basic differences between the sexes are neurological in origin, rather than being purely cultural as ordinarily presumed. . . . Males and females differ anatomically, sexually, emotionally, psychologically, and biochemically. We differ in literally every cell of our bodies, for each sex carries a unique chromosomal pattern . . . . It is my deep conviction that each sex displays unique emotional characteristics that are genetically endowed. . . .[4]

In this article Dobson describes contrasting emotional responses of himself and his wife when the plumber made a mistake in the installation of a gas barbecue unit in their backyard. How did Dobson view this difference in emotional response? Given his "deep conviction that each sex displays unique emotional characteristics that are genetically endowed," no one will be surprised that he viewed this difference in response as evidence of emotional patterns that were determined by his maleness and his wife's femaleness. In a perceptual sense, Dobson chose to see these differing emotional responses as evidence of biologically determined differences.

In contrast, Anne Fausto-Sterling, a distinguished biologist (genetic embryologist) at Brown University, in her book, *Myths of Gender: Biological Theories About Women and Men*, argues instead:

> . . . for a more complex analysis in which an individual's capacities emerge from a web of interactions between the biological being and the social environment. Within this web, connecting threads move in both directions. Biology may in some manner condition behavior, but behavior in turn can alter one's physiology. Furthermore, any particular behavior can have many different causes. This new vision challenges the hunt for fundamental biological causes at its very heart, stating unequivocally that the search itself is based on a false understanding of biology. The question, "What fraction of our behavior is biologically based," is impossible—even in theory—to answer, and unanswerable questions drop out of the realm of science altogether, entering instead that of philosophy and morality.[5]

If Anne Fausto-Sterling had observed with James Dobson the differing emotional reactions of Dobson and his wife to the plumber's mistake, would they have seen the same biological evidence? I do not think so. Their differing beliefs about the significance and nature of biological factors would likely have led them to see the same data as proof of two quite different facts.

Perceptual Bias

This same problem but in the broader context of culture can further complicate our understanding of gender research. Again, the old perceptual exercise from the general psychology class provides a good place to begin to think about this problem.

In my class, I remember the professor saying in his highly directive teaching style, "Now, see a vase; now, change and see the faces," and as a good, obedient sophomore I did as I was told. It was not until I was wandering back to the library that it occurred to me that I had learned *two* things, both of which were important—only one of which, however, had been pointed out by my professor.

First, I had learned that I could decide what I would see. Second, the point my professor neglected to discuss, I had learned that someone could tell me what to see. While thinking about this second discovery, it occurred to me that at the point I was told what to see, I had an additional, crucial choice: I could choose to see as I was told, or choose my own point of view.

Understanding gender research can be difficult because as consumers of research we are quite often told what to see without being aware that this is happening and, consequently, without exercising conscious awareness in our choice of response. Many times the understanding we have of what science says comes from others—the church, television, newspapers, or the pop psychology press, for example, of whose instructions to us we are not consciously aware.

An interesting demonstration of such influence on public perception of sex/gender research occurred recently and focused on a report of work carried out in the laboratory of scientist Doreen Kimura, widely known and respected for her study of brain lateralization.[6]

In the June 1988 issue of *Behavioral Neuroscience*, Kimura and Elizabeth Hampson, one of her doctoral students, reported that they had tested a small group of women and found evidence of fluctuations in motor coordination and spatial abilities linked to changes in hormone levels. The significance of the conclusions, according to Kimura in an interview with *Science News*, was the reciprocal nature of the change—that is, in the specified tests women scored *both* higher on motor coordination and lower on spatial ability during the midluteal, or middle, phase of their menstrual cycles than they did during the menses phase. Kimura, according to *Science News*, commented further that her guess was that such reciprocal hormonal effects also happened in males.

Up to this point Kimura and Hampson's research was progressing through the usual professional channels of journal reports and peer review, with public comments reserved for *Science News*, a small specialty magazine whose staff is specifically

trained to understand scientific findings and to report them to
the general public. In November, however, Kimura and
Hampson participated in a symposium and prearranged press
conference at the Toronto meeting of the Society for
Neuroscience. Life for the researchers and their studies took a
decidedly different turn from this point on.

Beryl Lieff Benderly, a contributing editor of *Psychology Today*, describes graphically what happened next:

> On the 17th, Los Angelenos consumed, with break-
> fast coffee, a *Los Angeles Times* account of the
> "strongest scientific evidence to date that the level
> of sex hormones in the bloodstreams of women can
> affect their thought processes, reasoning ability,
> and muscular coordination." The next morning,
> strap-hanging New Yorkers saw in the *New York
> Times* that "Female Sex Hormone Is Tied to Ability
> to Perform Tasks." For the first time, the article said,
> scientists had found "a relationship between
> monthly fluctuations in female sex hormones and a
> woman's ability to perform certain tasks."[7]

Unfortunately, at that point Kimura and Hampson declined
all interviews and refused further comment on the study for
reasons that we may guess. Their silence, while perhaps understandable, unfortunately contributed to the continuing
misunderstanding and misuse of their data.

However, *Psychology Today* eventually persuaded Kimura to
discuss her work in a public forum. In a November 1989 article in *Psychology Today*, Kimura herself explained in her own
words the background studies, the details of her reported research, and her interpretations of the findings. She did so in
clear nontechnical terms, which enabled the average reader to
grasp easily the procedures that had been utilized and the nature and significance of her work as Kimura herself understood
it.[8] Kimura summarized:

> What do our studies on the apparent fluidity of cer-
> tain abilities mean for the day-to-day functioning of

women? While the fluctuations we find are interesting and significant—they tell us something about how cognitive ability patterns are formed—they are not large. Also, up to now they seem most consistent for the kinds of things women already do well. So *for most women, they aren't an important factor.* Of course, women vary widely in their sensitivity to these influences. For some, the changes may make them feel clumsier at some periods of the month than at others.

It's important to remember that we studied women because it was easy to do. It turns out that men also undergo hormonal fluctuations, both daily and seasonal. We are looking into both types. . . .[9]

Psychology Today then followed Kimura's article with a report by Beryl Lieff Benderly dealing with what *Psychology Today* characterized as the media flap. Benderly carefully examined the various events and actions that resulted, in Benderly's judgment, in newspaper reports that "captured the essential outline of [Kimura and Hampson's] experiments. But . . . got the larger meaning totally wrong."[10]

The message, which by inference was the bottom line in both *The Los Angles Times* and *The New York Times,* indicated that science had proven that women's monthly hormonal fluctuations affected a woman's ability to perform certain tasks and, by clear implication, altered this ability significantly and negatively. Reading Kimura's own summary of her work, as given above, one might well ask, how could such a misunderstanding of the material occur, particularly with a researcher of Kimura's stature?

The answer lies in my sophomore discovery in general psychology class: someone can tell me what to see. In effect, the media instructed the general public to see Kimura and Hampson's research as evidence that women's fluctuating hormones rendered them seriously incapable at least once every month. In this case, the public was instructed to see this biologically based data as information supporting gender stereotype. The clear inference of the newspaper articles was that the "raging hormone" theory of feminine behavior is now supported by science. Such a conclusion was not at all what Kimura saw, nor what she intended the public to see.

Generally, science is slow to accept new ideas or to correct old ones, and not always for the best of reasons. Because of this, it is important to keep in mind that the study of differences between men and women is at present enmeshed in an ideological struggle which makes clear thinking and good science extremely difficult to come by.

What is the nature of the struggle? The answer is again complex, as appears so frequently to be the case in gender studies.

THE UNACKNOWLEDGED AGENDA

In the late 1960s, science and society began to ask similar questions at the same time. Were men and women different? If so, how were they different? And why had these differences occurred? And if they were different, what was to be done about these differences? These questions, as we will see, became highly politicized.

There were advantages at first for all parties in this common concern. Public interest made grants easier for researchers to secure, and the general public felt pleased to have scientists using their tax dollars to work on something that appeared to them to be sensible. For a scientist to study about men and women seemed to the general public more worthwhile than having them study the mating habits of an obscure small fish in the waters off north Australia. Some scientists found it pleasant to have a wider audience for their work.

Few people anticipated, however, what might happen when the results from laboratories began to be reported by journalists in daily papers and newsstand magazines as well as by researchers themselves in professional journals. (The report of Kimura's work is a good example.) While science and society appeared to agree as to the information needed, there was no clear agreement about means of reporting or use of the information. And the unacknowledged issue upon which both scientists and society were focused was a complex and controversial one. They were really concerned about the politicized question: if men and women were different, what were we as a society going to do about those differences? And in a troublesome way, the proposed options began to be cast in the form of a polarized dichotomy.

If gender studies indicated that men and women were different because of biology (genetics, heredity), then it was probable that the differences must be accommodated, for the most part, as irreversible. If, to the contrary, the differences were found to be the result of environment (learning), then the differences must be evaluated and, where needed or desired, changed. To change or not to change society was really the debated question.

It was at this point that institutionalized science, radical elements of the women's movement, the common wisdom of the culture, and components of the institutionalized church entered into a highly politicized debate. And in the service of this ideological struggle, information provided by researchers in gender differences came to be reported and used in curious and dismaying ways, as Kimura and Hampson discovered.

The core of the controversy, of course, centered on the social change sweeping society. In the emotionally and politically intense climate of that time, as well as in the uneasy decades since, people have chosen and strongly held widely divergent points of view. This has tended to further polarize the question.

Individuals advocating change looked for scientific studies to indicate that gender differences result from learning and then argued that gender roles were amenable to change and that change should occur. Those individuals and institutions resistant to change looked for scientific studies to indicate that gender differences result from biology. They then used this data to argue that efforts to bring about social change were not only ill-advised but fruitless since, in a new application of an old idea, anatomy was destiny.

Those individuals arguing for tradition and resistance to change frequently cited as scientific proof the biological determinism flowing from the new academic discipline of sociobiology. Sociobiologists argued flatly that science proved that in the long process of evolution males and females had evolved differently, and that the cultural stereotype and social

double standard of contemporary society are in reality biologically inevitable.

Mary Stewart Van Leeuwen summarizes the traditional argument of the sociobiologist:

> They argue that the males of any species will maxi-
> mize the survival of their own genes by copulating
> with as many females as possible. By contrast, once
> a female is impregnated, further copulations are
> pointless for the increase of her genes' survival. In
> addition, since she so heavily "invests" in carrying
> only a few infants to term, it is in her genes' survival
> interests for her to play "coy" and "hard to get" un-
> til the genetically strongest male wins "copulatory
> rights" with her by defeating all male rivals. Trans-
> lated into modern human terms, this means that
> there is really not much point in trying to change
> patterns such as male promiscuity or female sexual
> subterfuge.[11]

The political agenda of the sociobologists' science has become so clearly overt that one noted biologist titled a chapter
dealing with sociobiologists' work, "Putting Woman in Her
(Evolutionary) Place."[12] Some Christians who cite the natural
revelation of sociobiology in arguing for traditional gender
roles may have failed to realize the danger in this position.

One biologist imagined a look into the future in which the
social impact of biological determinism was reflected in a hypothetical newspaper article headlined "Admitted Rapist
Freed as Jury Buys Biological Defense!" The imagined article
read further:

> Admitted rapist Joe Smith was released today after
> a jury—in a landmark decision—bought the defense
> that sexual assault is biologically natural, and that
> some men—including Smith—have especially
> strong urges to rape. . . . There are precedents for this
> decision. For some years now, women committing
> violent acts during their premenstruum have been

absolved of legal responsibility after testimony that they suffered extremely from the Premenstrual Syndrome, a hormonal imbalance resulting in temporary insanity. . . . Expert witness A attested that "Rape is common among birds and bees and is epidemic among mallard ducks . . . . Rape in humans is by no means so simple. . . . Nevertheless mallard rape . . . may have a degree of relevance to human behavior. Perhaps human rapists, in their own criminally misguided way, are doing the best they can to maximize their fitness."[13]

Fausto-Sterling points out that the use of the word *rape* to describe animal behavior was rare until the mid 1970s when women began to protest the failure of the legal system to apprehend and prosecute rapists. She notes, "The sudden increase in the use of the word in the biological literature, as a response to the furor raised by feminists, was at the very least a non-conscious attempt to establish rape as a widespread natural phenomenon and thus deflect and depoliticize a subject of intense and specific importance to women . . . thus trivializing its effect on women's lives. . . ."[14]

This misuse of both language and science is disconcerting at many levels. The claim that whatever is, is right (as sociobiologists appear to be arguing) is not a position that Christians would be wise to adopt in regard to any issue, including gender differences. Mary Stewart Van Leeuwen noted, "Thus, it is important to realize that Christians who argue for 'traditional' gender roles by appealing to the natural revelation of sociobiology will get more than they bargained for. They will get nothing less than the swallowing up of moral accountability, in both men and women, by the mechanics of biological determinism."[15]

The Problem of Perceptual Mind-Set

Biological determinism is not the only problematic politicized response to gender research. There is, in addition, the familiar response of "I've made up my mind, so don't confuse me with the facts." Melvin Konner, in his 1982 book, *The*

Tangled Wing: Biological Constraints on the Human Spirit, begins
chapter 6, "The Beast With Two Backs," by citing a number of
distinguished women scientists who have devoted their professional lives to the study of human behavior. He notes that
among the difficulties with which they have been forced to
contend are the assaults of feminist critics who in many cases,
Konner suggests, "will not or cannot read their papers."[16]

The criticism that Konner levels at those determined to
minimalize or eliminate gender differences may well be equally
laid at the feet of some who in resisting change seek to maximize such differences. As Christians we may be pleased to join
Konner's criticism of the more radical feminists who disregard
science in pursuit of their political agenda. We may be less
pleased, and less willing, to acknowledge that as evangelicals
we may be all too ready to disregard research that does not support our conservative theological agenda. As evangelicals, in our
response to gender studies, we need to be reminded of the biblical injunction to remove the plank from our own eyes before
attempting to remove the splinter from another's.

Within the conservative arm of the church there has recently
been considerable criticism of psychology.[17] Some of this criticism appears to have been well merited. One influential
Christian counselor has recently called counselors to reexamine their beliefs and professional practices.[18]

Unfortunately, this criticism has also produced some negative effects. One of them has been an attitude that encourages
Christians to discount anything associated with psychology,
including research.

While much of this religious resistance to reading gender
research might be explained by an unwillingness to be associated with anything feminist or psychological, it is possible that
another factor is also at work. While there are notable exceptions, Christian counselors in general do not have a good
reputation either as producers or consumers of research. It is
possible that for some of us, as for some of the feminists whom
Konner criticized, the "will not read" ought to be accompanied by a "cannot read and understand."

When counselors assume that we do not need psychological research because the Bible tells us all we need to know

about human nature, including gender differences, we are putting ourselves in a debatable position.[19] Mastery of special revelation, the Word of God, is crucial for a Christian counselor, including, of course, those who see women clients. Mastery of special revelation cannot, however, substitute for mastery of general revelation, and that requires us to learn to be skillful consumers of research. When counselors neglect to develop or to use the skills necessary to understand and apply gender research in counseling women, we place ourselves in a dangerous position and our clients at risk. It remains a hard fact of professional life for the Christian counselor that personal piety cannot transform ignorance into virtue, nor can it protect our women clients from our failure to learn from gender research what we need to know to better help them.

In the context of the present politicized environment, we must continue to recognize that our understanding and response to research can also be influenced by social pressure. Subtly and powerfully, we are urged to be politically correct, to confirm and support the true point of view adopted by the group of which we are a member. As counselors, we are not immune to peer pressure.

SOCIAL PRESSURE BY ACADEMIC PEERS

An interesting example of the effect of social pressure on professionals is noted by Burton L. White, an internationally known expert in early childhood education. In an article discouraging day-care for infants and young children, White reported his impression that a number of his colleagues agreed with this point of view. In White's opinion, they were reluctant to state their view publicly, however, because it was not politically correct in the emotional climate of his professional world which is largely committed to a different position.[20]

While working on the manuscript for this book, I had a personal experience that demonstrated the same problem but from the contrasting emotional climate of the world in which I work.

While waiting at my church for a meeting to begin, I was reading a professional paper that a colleague had forwarded to me. In rather bold type, it was entitled, "Women and

Power." An individual came in, sat down by me, glanced at the title of the paper, and remarked, "Becoming a women's libber these days?" The accompanying smile did not entirely remove the sting from the remark.

I had the uncomfortable sense that had I been reading a paper entitled "Two-Year-Olds and Their Struggle for Power," I would have been viewed simply as studying, a procedure no more noteworthy for me than that of grading papers for a teacher. Reading a study on "Women and Power," however, suggested, at least to this individual, something quite different, emotionally less neutral, and politically incorrect.

In the following chapters as we begin to review specific sex and gender studies, we will see examples of the difficulties we have discussed here. At several controversial points, we will find scientists themselves in disagreement about both the facts and what they may mean. We will need to remember that the common practice of emphasizing differences at the expense of equal attention to similarities has likely given an artificially inflated significance to those studies that have presumably identified sex and gender differences.

We will also need to remember that the language in which studies are reported provides in itself some serious challenges to the average counselor who attempts to read and understand it. There may be significant errors in the basic assumptions, stated and unstated, underlying the research. It is easy for most of us to miss or misunderstand important information inherent in the statistical conclusions of studies. Researchers often neglect to report this information in a language readily comprehensible to the average counselor seeking to understand the report, and sometimes we confuse what the researcher said with what we want it to mean.

The politics of science and emotional attitudes regarding social change further complicate our understanding of what we read. In often unacknowledged ways, these factors frequently influence what is studied, how it is studied, and, particularly, the emphasis with which the results are reported.

Those who carry out the research, those who report it, those who seek to understand and apply the results of the research— all of us are in turn influenced by the value systems of the environment in which we work and the emotional pressures on us as individuals to conform to the party line of the group of which we are a part.

For many of us, there is an additional challenge. Like Smith and Jones in my hypothetical example of research, we are reluctant to look too closely at any ideas that may challenge us to change. We are not only reluctant to rock the boat; we are particularly reluctant to have our own boat rocked.

Much (although not all) of the current research regarding women does challenge us to change. It challenges women to think differently about themselves, while confirming some things that women have long intuitively believed about themselves. It challenges scientists to think differently about women and about the way in which they study women (but sometimes in surprising ways reconfirms old truth). It challenges all of us to think differently about many of the pressing problems women face in the shifting world of social change, yet affirms, sometimes reluctantly, that much of the old is good and needs to be kept.

For years I have been an admirer of J. R. R. Tolkein, and a devoted friend of Hobbits. When I think of tackling the current research regarding sex and gender differences, I think of the task in somewhat the same way Bilbo regarded an adventure—a wretched uncomfortable thing quite likely to make one late for tea.

But I have come to learn both as a woman and a counselor that if, like Bilbo, I will simply gather up my courage and go (even without a clean handkerchief), something very wonderful comes of it in the end.

NOTES

1. E. E. Maccoby and C. N. Jacklin, *The Psychology of Sex Differences* (Stanford, Calif.: Stanford University Press, 1974), 351.

2. Paula J. Caplan, Gael M. MacPherson, and Patricia Tobin, "Do Sex-Related Differences in Spatial Abilities Exist?", *American Psychologist* 40, no. 7 (July 1985): 786–99 (quote from 797).

3. Rachael T. Hare-Mustin, "An Appraisal of the Relationship Between Women and Psychotherapy: 80 Years After the Case of Dora," *American Psychologist* 38 (May 1983): 593–601 (quote from 599).

4. James C. Dobson, "Biology Determines Gender Roles," in *Male/Female Roles: Opposing Viewpoints*, ed. Neal Bernard and Terry O'Neill, Opposing Viewpoints Series (San Diego, Calif.: Greenhaven Press, 1989), 17–23 (quote from 18–19).

5. Anne Fausto-Sterling, *Myths of Gender: Biological Theories about Women and Men* (New York: Basic Books, 1985), 8.

6. The following account of the controversial reporting of Kimura's work is based upon the report by Beryl Lieff Benderly, "Don't Believe Everything You Read," *Psychology Today* (November 1989), 67–69.

7. Ibid., 67.

8. Doreen Kimura, "How Sex Hormones Boost—or Cut—Intellectual Ability," *Psychology Today* (November 1989), 62–66.

9. Ibid. 66, italics mine.

10. Benderly, 68.

11. Mary Stewart Van Leeuwen, *Gender and Grace: Love, Work and Parenting in a Changing World* (Downers Grove, Ill.: InterVarsity, 1990), 92.

12. Fausto-Sterling, 156–204.

13. Ibid., 156–57.

14. Ibid., 162.

15. Van Leeuwen, 92. Van Leeuwen's discussion of sociobiology in the context of gender studies is helpful; see Van Leeuwen, 90–92, 127–28. Her critique of Christians' too-easy acceptance of some forms of sociobiology is found in "Selective Sociobiology, and Other Follies," *Reformed Journal* 38, no. 2 (February 1988): 24–28. Fausto-Sterling's *Myths of Gender* is particularly well worth reading carefully and in full, since her critique is founded upon objections as a scientist, both as a biologist and geneticist, apart from religious values.

16. Melvin Konner, *The Tangled Wing: Biological Constraints on the Human Spirit* (New York: Harper and Row, 1983), 106–7.

17. For examples see Martin and Deidre Bobgan, *Psychoheresy: The Psychological Seduction of Christianity* (Santa Barbara, Calif.: Eastgate, 1987), and Dave Hunt and T. A. McMahon, *The Seduction of Christianity* (Eugene, Oreg.: Harvest House, 1985).

18. Gary R. Collins, "A Letter to Christian Counselors," *Journal of Psychology and Christianity* 9, no. 1 (Spring 1990): 37–39.

19. See Gary R. Collins, *Can You Trust Psychology? Exploring the Facts and the Fictions* (Downers Grove, Ill.: InterVarsity, 1988), 21–25, 93–97.

20. Burton L. White, "Should You Stay Home With Your Baby?" in *The Psychology of Women: Ongoing Debates*, ed. Mary Roth Walsh (New Haven, Conn.: Yale University Press, 1987), 358–66 (quote from 358).

Chapter Six

Sex Differences

 THE FIRST SEX AND GENDER STUDY which most of us remember is
in *Mother Goose*—it reports distinct differences between boys
and girls.

"What are little girls made of?" asks the old nursery rhyme.
The answer is quite positive: "Sugar and spice and everything
nice, that's what little girls are made of." In contrast, the description of little boys reflects a clearly gender-biased view:
"Frogs and snails and puppy dog tails, that's what little boys
are made of."

Present research both confirms and denies the old nursery
rhyme. The answer to the question, "Are men and women different?" appears to be, "Yes, but . . . ," not as much as we once
thought, and often in ways quite different than we once assumed.

In considering these differences it is important to distinguish between *sex differences* and *gender differences*. The terms
sex and *gender* are sometimes used interchangeably, occasionally by scientists themselves. Nevertheless, in most instances

it is helpful to retain a functional distinction between the two terms.

In preferred usage, *sex* is defined as a biological construct, and reserved for reference to differences in reproductive structures, chromosomes, hormones, and physical features. Even these factors cannot always be easily organized into exclusive categories labeled *male* and *female*.[1]

In contrast, *gender* is used to refer to the social, cultural, and psychological components associated with *masculinity* and *femininity*. Sex is assumed to be biologically determined; gender is assumed to be socially learned.

In keeping with this distinction, it is more accurate to refer to *gender roles* rather than sex roles, since roles are learned patterns of behavior rather than biologically determined responses. The term *sex roles*, as Sherif has noted, "uncritically couples a biological concept (sex) with a sociological concept (role). Thus, the concept suffers double jeopardy from myths about sex smuggled in uncritically and from denotative confusions in the sociological concept of roles."[2]

A note of caution is necessary at this point, however. Although the sex/gender distinction is useful, in some ways it is an artificially imposed dichotomy that does not represent reality accurately. Scientists disagree or do not know exactly how biological sex and psychological gender interact, although it is clear that they do so, sometimes in powerful and puzzling ways. Few, if any, scientists now think that the two factors can be separated in the way the old nature vs. nurture controversy once suggested. There are at least two reasons for this.

First, environment, including learned gender roles, and heredity, including sexual identity, occur together; they cannot be fully separated. As variables, they are confounded in the language of research. One psychologist put the dilemma this way:

> Parents who read books tend to have children who read books. Parents who are athletic tend to have children who are athletic. Parents who eat bagels and lox tend to produce children who eat bagels and lox.

> The point is, that since we pass our *environments*
> on to our children along with our *genes*, there is no
> way of saying for sure which of these factors is
> producing a certain behavior in a certain child, or
> by how much it outweighs the other factor.[3]

Second, an additional complication is becoming more apparent as biological research progresses. Some evidence suggests structural differences between the brains of males and females. Some studies describe differences in the cognitive processes of men and women which appear to be hormonally influenced. The problem in applying the results of such studies is that the simple, one-way theoretical model suggesting biology as the cause and behavior as the result has proven to be seriously inadequate. We know that behavior influences biology even as biology influences behavior. This complex two-way interaction in which the body influences the mind and the mind, in turn, influences the body is difficult to study and describe.

An influential researcher, highly respected for her study of sex and gender differences, cautioned bluntly in a recent paper:

> The simple models of hormone-behavior relationships that were developed from animal research are not adequate to explain the data from normal human populations. . . . Correlations between hormones and behavior are typically interpreted as cases in which the biological causes the psychological. It fits our predispositions to assume that hormones cause behavioral outcomes. The hormone system is an open system. Much more empirical work is needed before the direction of the causal arrows are understood.[4]

To illustrate from daily life: if a boy chooses building blocks as a toy and a girl chooses a doll, we cannot describe precisely the mixture of socialization and biology that influenced these choices for either child.

In adults we might ask, does a woman act in a learned sexually seductive manner and in consequence evoke physical arousal in herself and in her partner? Or is the learned sexually seductive social behavior a response to a hormonally mediated physical arousal which preceded it? Current research suggests that sometimes biological factors stimulate gendered behaviors; at other times gendered behaviors stimulate biological responses, and often both occur simultaneously in a complex combination. Counselors see daily evidence that men and women act in response to their bodies, but that, in turn, men's and women's bodies respond to how they act (and think and feel). In studying sex/gender issues we rarely if ever can consider biology or gender totally independent of the other.[5]

DIFFERENCES WE CAN IDENTIFY

In the early 1970s, two scientists attempted to summarize what had already been established about differences between boys and girls. They spent about three years compiling, reviewing, and interpreting a very large body of research—over two thousand books and articles.

At the end of this exhaustive study, they described those beliefs about sex differences that they viewed as supported by evidence, those beliefs that had no scientific support, and those for which there was as yet no conclusive answer.

Over the past twenty years this work by Eleanor Maccoby and Carol Jacklin has powerfully influenced our thinking about sex/gender differences. Table 1 summarizes the conclusions Maccoby and Jacklin drew at that time.

As one would expect, Maccoby and Jacklin's conclusions have been challenged. One study argued that they had seriously *understated* the case for sex differences.[6] Another study argued that they had *overstated* the case, at least in regard to aggression.[7]

In 1989, fifteen years after the publication of *The Psychology of Sex Differences*, Maccoby was granted a Distinguished Scientific Contributions Award by the American Psychological Association. In a paper based on her award address, Maccoby

Table 1
Summary of Maccoby and Jacklin's Findings
on Sex Differences

Unfounded Beliefs About Sex Differences	Open Questions of Differences	Fairly Well Established Sex Differences
Girls are more social than boys.	Tactile sensitivity.	Girls have greater verbal ability.
Girls are more suggestible than boys.	Fear, timidity, and anxiety.	Boys excel in visual-spatial ability.
Girls have lower self-esteem than boys.	Activity level. Competitiveness. Dominance.	Boys excel in mathematical ability.
Girls are better at rote learning and simple repetitive tasks; boys are better at higher level cognitive processing.	Compliance. Nurturance and maternal behavior.	Boys are more aggressive.
Boys are more analytic than girls.		
Girls are more affected by heredity; boys are more affected by environment.		
Girls lack achievement motivation.		
Girls are more inclined toward the auditory; boys are more inclined toward the visual.		

Source: Eleanor Maccoby and Carol Nagy Jacklin, *The Psychology of Sex Differences* (Stanford, Calif.: Stanford University Press, 1974).
Table reproduced with permission from A. Fausto-Sterling, *Myths of Gender* (New York: Basic Books, 1985), 25.

looked back to the original work and commented, "We [Maccoby and Jacklin] felt at that time that the yield was thin. That is, there were very few attributes on which the average values for the two sexes differed consistently. Furthermore, even when consistent differences were found, the amount of variance accounted for by sex was small, relative to the amount of variation within each sex."[8]

Maccoby noted that work on sex differences has become methodologically more sophisticated in the last fifteen years. She pointed out that statistical analyses are now more sensitive in indicating both the direction of differences and quantitative estimates of their size. Maccoby viewed aggression studies as continuing to support the original finding that men are more aggressive than women. She cited Eagly's 1987 work[9] indicating women may be more easily influenced than men and men more altruistic than women, findings somewhat at variance with the 1974 report. She then concluded:

> In my judgment, the conclusions are still quite similar to those Jacklin and I arrived at in 1974: There are still some replicable sex differences, of moderate magnitude, in performance on tests of mathematical and spatial abilities, although sex differences in verbal abilities have faded. Other aspects of intellectual performance continue to show gender equality. When it comes to attributes in the personality-social domain, results are particularly sparse and inconsistent. . . . In general, however, personality traits measured as characteristics of individuals do not appear to differ systematically by sex. . . . [10]

In short, in Maccoby's judgment, fifteen years of increasingly sophisticated research has not yielded significantly different results: there are sex differences, but they are minimal, particularly when viewed in relationship to the amount of variation within each sex. In those areas most clearly influenced by gender (the personality-social domain), the results of studies of difference continue to be "particularly sparse and inconsistent."

The Significance of Difference

At this point it may be helpful to remember some of the issues raised earlier regarding the complexities of sex/gender research. Differences that Maccoby identified were "of moderate magnitude," but they appeared small when compared with the differences that occurred *within* groups of males and females. This is an example of a careful researcher paying attention to the significance of the within/between group differences that we discussed in chapter 5.

In noting current puzzling indications that sex differences in verbal performance appeared to be fading, Maccoby indirectly raised the issue of assumptions, also discussed in chapter 5. Verbal differences, like visual-spatial differences, have commonly been assumed to be sex-based (i.e., biological). If, however, verbal differences have in fact shown change over the relatively short time of fifteen years, the assumption of sex as the basis for the difference is clearly open to question. Biologically speaking, no gene can travel that fast.

Maccoby noted the shift in verbal scores briefly and in passing, since this change was not the focus of her paper. However, this shift merits attention here as a warning. In 1974, who would have been brave (or foolish) enough to have suggested that female verbal superiority might look quite different in so short a time as fifteen years? Further research may explain this shift as an anomaly of measurement and/or experience. At the present time, however, this shift is a clear reminder that some current research findings that appear to be absolutely certain may yet in our lifetime come to look quite different. Caution about the significance of differences is both good science and good sense.

Maccoby, however, was interested in a different issue, one that also suggests caution regarding our present understanding of differences.

Having noted that, in her judgment, evidence supporting sex differences continues to be minimal, Maccoby went on to argue for a somewhat surprising conclusion:

> Nevertheless, I believe that the null findings coming out of comparisons of male and female individuals

on personality measures are partly illusory. That is,
they are an artifact of our historical reliance on an
individual differences perspective. Social behavior,
as many have pointed out, is never a function of the
individual alone. It is a function of the interaction
between two or more persons. Individuals behave
differently with different partners. There are certain
important ways in which gender is implicated in social behavior—ways that may be obscured or missed
altogether when behavior is summed across all categories of social partners.[11]

Having started out looking for sexual differences, Maccoby
and other researchers have indeed found some. But after fifteen years in which she pursued her own research and
carefully reviewed the work of others, Maccoby chose this
prestigious moment to call for increased attention not to biology itself, but to biology *and* gender in a way which recognizes
the confounded relationships of the two. Maccoby argues that
the major sex differences emerge primarily in social situations,
and their nature varies between men and women with the gender composition of the dyad or the group.

A personal experience may illustrate the point Maccoby
wishes to make.

I grew up in a remote rural area in which transportation of
children to school was a challenge for most families. Many
parents solved the problem by encouraging each child to acquire a school-only driver's license at age thirteen—with the
state's approval. They then provided an ancient vehicle of
limited value, and limited potential for speed, and made the
adolescent responsible to transport himself or herself to
school.

My car was an ancient 1934 Ford with a top speed of forty-
five miles per hour, unreliable brakes, a radiator that both
leaked and boiled, and a tendency for the fuel pump suddenly
to cease functioning on the most remote stretch of country road
I traveled.

One busy autumn, my father overheard the car give a suspicious hiccup as I rattled into the yard one evening. On the

basis of this evidence and previous experience, my father placed a fuel pump he had previously purchased in the trunk of the car. He explained to me how to replace it in case I needed to do so before he had completed the fall grain harvest and had time to do so himself.

As he had wisely anticipated, the next afternoon on the most remote section of my trip home, the car coughed, ran an erratic half-mile, then stopped dead. My dilemma was clear: walk or repair the car.

I might have chosen to walk if it had not been that particular Friday. It happened that I had a date with the captain of the football team, an overwhelmingly handsome individual ardently pursued by most of my female classmates. Additionally, I had chores to do and was forbidden by family rules to leave until my chores were completed. There was clearly no alternative but to change the fuel pump, speed for home, persuade my sister to help with my chores, hoping meanwhile that my date would be late.

I did so and managed to get home, finish chores, and, totally out of breath, be ready by the time my date arrived. My long hair was curled, my white blouse starched and ironed, my skirt carefully pressed. I waited sedately while he opened the car door and helped me in. During the evening, he helped me climb the bleachers, took the cap off my bottle of soda pop, helped me with my sweater, helped me back down the bleachers, into his car, and, at the end of the evening, out of his car and back into my house. Had the fuel pump in his car expired anytime during the trip, I am sure that I would have sat properly in the car, looking helplessly feminine, and acting as though I had no earthly idea what a fuel pump was.

Looking at this story, Maccoby would point out the impact of the social context on my behavior. How dependent was I? How instrumental? How relational? How, Maccoby might ask, can you measure any presumably sex-based behaviors without taking into account the social context and the gendered behaviors through which they will inevitably be expressed? How was this female's behavior different when alone and grappling with a fuel pump, when seeking to persuade her younger sister, when with the young man whose company provided her both with the physical excitement of courting behaviors and the prestige of social rank?

Measurement of behavior in any of the three differing social environments would likely have given a quite different picture of what being female and being feminine was.

Men and women are different. Some of these differences are sex-based, and they are important. But the idea that we can study or understand these differences in isolation from issues of gender is a very bad idea, one which, as we will see, has led to considerable confusion.

What happens when we consider sex differences in the context of the sex/gender interface? While it does not alter the *fact* of a sex-based difference, it profoundly alters our understanding of the fact. Aggression studies are a good place to begin to think about this.

DIFFERENCES IN AGGRESSION

Traditionally, aggression studies have shown males to be more aggressive than females, as Maccoby and Jacklin summarized.[12] Can we be certain about this? Maccoby continues to think that we can.[13] It is helpful, however, to look at some questions about this conclusion, because the controversy itself underscores Maccoby's point about the significance of social context.

To begin with, there are serious problems in defining aggression. Researchers have defined and measured aggression in ways that vary widely, with the result that we may well be comparing apples with eggs with little awareness that we are doing so. One study identified at least eight different types of aggression, at least one of which appears to be more common in females.[14]

Boys tend to express aggression in physical and destructive ways; girls tend to utilize verbal responses and disobedience.[15] Many studies are weighed toward defining aggression in terms of physical acts such as pushing, hitting, kicking, or destruction of property—stereotypically male methods of expressing aggression. By these measures, which assume a male norm for defining aggression, boys do indeed appear more aggressive than girls, as one would expect. If the aggression measures include verbal means of aggression such as, "You're ugly. You can't be in our club, and nobody is going to play with you," the differences between boys and girls in aggression begin to look quite different. Not surprisingly, gender differences are largest in physical aggression.[16]

This methodological problem in definition incorporates a faulty assumption which has caused serious problems in other areas as well as in aggression studies. This faulty assumption has grown out of an unconscious gender-biased point of view rather than a misunderstanding of biology. The assumption, stated rather baldly, is the belief that masculine experience is a valid measure of *all* human experience—that is, if something is true for men, then it can safely be assumed to be true in general for the human race. In early aggression studies, it was assumed that aggression was expressed in the same way by boys and girls; that aggression was not present if it did not appear in the male form. To say that boys and girls act out aggression differently now seems self-evident, but researchers have not always been clear about this. Consequently, the old idea that girls were aggressive only if they demonstrated aggression in ways identical to those used by boys seems likely to have skewed our definition and measurement of sex-based differences in aggression. As a result, conclusions of much of the early research are open to question.

Aggression research has often presupposed the male experience in another way. It has been widely assumed that males and females experience equal permission to be aggressive under identical experimental conditions or in natural observational settings such as playgrounds.

This assumption has led observers and researchers to overlook the fact that little girls have been taught a very different message about hitting, for example, than have little boys. (Boys hit; girls are nice; this is the Mother Goose Syndrome.) This assumption also demonstrates Maccoby's point; in presuming male experience, the researchers also presupposed that sex could be separated from gender. In many studies, the researchers appear to have believed that the only difference they were testing was sex-based aggression, when in reality they were testing *both* sex-based aggression *and* the gender-based messages the children had been taught.

It is easy to visualize the impact of this confusion once we see the problem. Imagine a mother getting a daughter ready to go to the university to "play" with Dr. Smith, a research psychologist. The mother's expectation (verbalized or nonverbalized) is that the girl will be a *nice* girl while she is with Dr. Smith. The daughter understands this. Imagine another mother getting a son ready to go to the university to "play" with Dr. Smith. The mother's expectation (verbalized or nonverbalized) is that the boy will *behave* himself. The boy understands this. But the socially approved behaviors authorized under the mother's instruction to the girl (be nice) and the mother's instruction to the boy (behave yourself) clearly do not contain the same permission for the girl to act out aggression, particularly in physical forms. The testing situation or observation site cannot be considered gender-neutral by any means. Consequently, in most aggression studies we cannot be clear if we are measuring sex, gender, or both confounded (as is most likely the case) when differences in aggressive behavior occur.

Some recent studies, recognizing this, have sought to reflect these differences in socialization in providing opportunity for girls to demonstrate aggression. When girls were rewarded for behaving aggressively, or when they were in circumstances where they thought no one was watching, females were just as aggressive as males. When rewards gave girls tangible evidence that gender-based rules had been temporarily suspended, or when girls were certain that violation of gender-based rules would not evoke negative consequences for them, then levels of aggression changed.[17] On the basis of such results, we cannot yet say that there are no sex-based differences in aggression. What we can and must say is that there is no gender-free measure of these differences.

Another gender-relevant factor which may affect reported differences in aggression is the issue of safety. Most researchers assume, again, the male experience—that a woman will feel as safe acting aggressively as does a man. Once identified, this assumption appears clearly untrue. Most women believe, and feel emotionally, that they are likely to be injured, physically or psychologically, if they behave in an aggressive fashion. Consequently they may inhibit aggression in the service of safety, particularly when they perceive the likelihood of retaliation to be high.[18] Some studies may reflect artificially low aggression scores for women because of this.

The tasks and circumstances in which aggression is measured frequently appear to mirror the male experience without the conscious awareness of the researcher. Often the methods used in aggression studies require arousing strong feelings in people or exposing them to a hostile act. One study asked researchers why they used only males in their aggression studies; they replied that they did not want to use methods physically harmful to women![19] Other investigators discovered that in order to avoid such methods researchers shifted to passive, indirect measures such as reading a story about aggression when testing women.[20] Such procedures illustrate the gender-biased social context often unwittingly established in the experimental setting.

Consider those studies noted above in which, by the researchers' own admission, the procedures incorporated activities judged by the researchers to be appropriate for men, but unsuitable for women. Responses that were hostile and potentially injurious were judged acceptable for men and not for women *in the researcher's value system*, and the experiment was structured to conform to the researcher's stereotyped view of gender-permissible behavior. (This is an example of the issue of the researcher's unacknowledged assumption discussed in chapter 5.)

It should be emphasized that studies using only men or women as subjects can be well designed and provide valuable information. The problem in these studies is not the use of men only as subjects, but rather the gender-biased choice of experimental tasks which led to the elimination of women. These studies, by excluding women as subjects, obviously eliminated even the option of women choosing the male-permitted response.

Such studies do not measure sex-based differences; they measure instead how many men will perform those behaviors the *researchers* expect that men, and men only, can be expected to perform.

In other experiments that include both men and women, it is possible that the structure of the experiment biases the responses in yet another unrecognized way. Since aggression is stereotypically considered to be a gender-congruent response for males and an incongruent response for females, an incongruent experimental task combined with an incongruent experimental response can influence the performance of women with a double-barreled impact. In those instances in which women's scores are inhibited, it is possible that the women failed to act aggressively not because they were female, but because they were being asked to feel what nice girls do not feel (i.e., aggressive) *and* do what nice girls do not do, even if they are asked (hit, for instance). It is possible in such cases that the deck is doubly stacked to inhibit women's aggressive responses. If so, it is stacked by gender, not by sex. Mother Goose, rather than testosterone, is likely to be the crucial variable.

One interesting study lends some credibility to this suppostition. In this study, in response to stereotypical situations (both masculine and feminine), men were more aggressive than women. However, *both* men and women were most aggressive in what they perceived to be gender-congruent situations dealing with gender-congruent tasks.[21]

Aggression studies using children as subjects cannot give us reliable information about adults both because of biological changes that occur between adolescence and adulthood and because gender-roles differ for adults and children.

Recognizing this, some researchers reviewed seventy-two previous studies comparing the aggressiveness of adult females and males.[22] Their findings clearly support Maccoby's emphasis upon the significance of social context.

These researchers found that in 61 percent of the cases, adult men were *not* more aggressive than adult women. Differences between men and women in aggressive behaviors were influenced by factors such as the sex of the investigator, the sex of hypothetical victims, empathy with hypothetical victims, guilt feelings, anonymity of the victim, justification for behavior, and similar gender-based factors. Men are more aggressive than women in many situations. Always? No. Further, gender is as important as biology, or more so, in understanding differences, in either direction, when they occur between adults.

The actual amount of differences in aggression among adult men and women appears to be quite small. One sophisticated statistical analysis of a large number of studies reported "less than one-third of a standard deviation in the direction of greater aggression by men than women."[23]

It is important to remember that this conclusion reflects analysis of *between-group* differences. Measures of differences in aggression *within-groups* of men or women or between individuals may, of course, yield larger scores in given social contexts. Counselors are likely to think both of individuals who fit the stereotypical picture of the aggressive male and the passive female and of others who do not. Group differences may or may not describe a given individual. Unfortunately, the counselor cannot predict from the sex of an individual much about that person's aggressive behavior. The point remains, however, that between-group differences in aggression in adult men and women appear to be smaller than we once thought, and that gender and social context plays a greater role in the expression of aggressive behaviors than is commonly believed.

DIFFERENCES IN SPATIAL ABILITIES

Differences in aggression is one of the two most consistent findings in gender/sex differences. The second is male advantage in visual-spatial abilities. However, the present controversy regarding presumably sex-based differences in visual-spatial ability reflects problems which parallel the difficulties in aggression studies.

Much like aggression studies, problems in the study of visual-spatial abilities focus on definitions of terms, design of studies, failure to recognize and account for gender-biased testing instruments and experimental settings; and the politicized context in which research findings are interpreted and used.

As a result of these difficulties, there is continuing disagreement about the presumed facts of the matter. Do males have better spatial abilities? "Decidedly," argues Harris.[24] "Moderately so," concludes Maccoby cautiously.[25] "Yes, but only if . . ." Linn and Peterson qualify with careful attention to gender-influenced factors.[26] "No—or at least it certainly is not yet proven," conclude Caplan, MacPherson, and Tobin on the basis of a scathing analysis of the flaws in the experimental design and procedures which mark most studies of visual-spatial differences.[27]

What are visual-spatial abilities? Generally, visual-spatial abilities refer to the skills required to see objects or figures in relationship to space *and* to each other. Tasks entailing use of visual-spatial skills frequently require the individual to turn objects mentally so that they are seen in a different way or from a different point of view in his/her mind. Reading or drawing blueprints or following a map, for example, are tasks requiring these kinds of skills.

Men have been commonly reported to have more of this kind of ability than do women. It has been frequently assumed that men have more of this ability because of biological differences between the sexes.

However, when people began to reexamine studies to see if presumed male superiority in visual-spatial abilities was in fact true, they discovered that under the umbrella term *visual-spatial abilities* researchers were studying a number of quite different behaviors.[28] One study examined the major research performed since Maccoby and Jacklin's 1974 review and concluded that in practice visual-spatial studies cover investigation of three distinct subtypes of spatial ability, only one of which—mental rotation of pictures—shows clear gender differences.[29] Like aggression, spatial abilities does *not* refer to a unitary factor, and the size of the gender effect depends on the specific type of spatial skill that is assessed.[30]

As in aggression studies, the size of gender effect also depends upon the circumstances and procedures through which data is gathered and tests are administered. Both appear in many cases to be gender-biased, or gender-incongruent. In one study utilizing the Rod and Frame Test, sex differences disappeared when the rod used was presented as a human figure, and the test was described as measuring empathy.[31] As in aggression studies, the assumption of the male experience often appears to underlie this unwitting failure of researchers to incorporate gender-congruent tasks in studying visual-spatial skills.

I recently observed two women in a fabric store. They were examining a piece of expensive wool fabric on sale at the remnant table. They were holding a pattern, looking at the sketch on the envelope showing how the pieces of the pattern were shaped, and how to place them on the fabric to cut them out.

"There's not enough," the young woman said. "No, wait," said the older woman. "Look, if you turn this . . . no, like this . . . over, and the other way . . . see, like this. . . . You have to do it opposite of what they show you there, but turned like this or it will be wrong side out when you cut it. See . . . this will work."

This woman was demonstrating a very high level of visual-spatial skills. The actual sewing process is even more complicated. Patterns must be turned, flipped, inverted, and worked on while the user visualizes how they will look when returned, re-inverted, and re-flipped.

What would happen to male superiority on visual-spatial scores if tests incorporated *only* complex sewing tasks? Such tasks would be gender-congruent for women, but not for men, and would represent a task at which many women, but few men, have had training and experience, and at which more women than men would expect themselves to succeed. We do not know what the specific results of such testing would produce, but we know enough to expect that under such circumstances some group differences in visual-spatial scores would likely be significantly reduced, if not eliminated. In fact, under such conditions, findings might support that women are superior on visual-spatial tasks.

Most men would certainly object to having their *male* visual-spatial skills measured only by their performance on a *female* sewing task. Thinking about this probable reaction helps us to understand the degree to which the gender-incongruent nature of many of the testing tasks may have influenced women's responses in visual-spatial testing.

As with aggression studies, the conditions under which visual-spatial tests are given are sometimes gender-biased. The usual procedure for administering the Rod and Frame Test is an example. Procedure for the test requires the subject to be alone with the experimenter in a pitch dark room. For a man to be alone in the dark with a male experimenter is a quite different experience than for a woman to be alone in identical circumstances. Further, in one form of the test, the subject is required to insist that the experimenter adjust the rod to his or her satisfaction. In the case of a woman subject, are we measuring the woman's perception, or her ability and willingness to be assertive with a male stranger in the dark? Once we think realistically about this test procedure, it is not difficult to imagine circumstances in which issues of gender rather than perception might influence the woman subject, as Fausto-Sterling noted, to decide that "close" was good enough.[32]

When we talk about visual-spatial abilities, how big is the alleged between-group difference? Again, as with the aggression studies, the presumably sex-based difference is surprising for its smallness, not its size. This is, however, consistent with what appears to be the relatively small size of other sex differences.[33] One researcher reanalyzed the studies upon which Maccoby and Jacklin had based their conclusions and reported that the difference between means is only about one-fourth to one-half a standard deviation.[34] However, the fact remains that small reliable gender difference in visual-spatial abilities are found at about seven or eight years of age, increase at age eighteen, and continue throughout the life span, with the size of the gender effect dependent on the type of spatial task that is assessed.[35]

What does this mean? It is difficult to say. It does *not* mean that women cannot perform well in the so-called hard sciences. Contrary to common wisdom, at the present time there is no conclusive evidence that high levels of visual-spatial skills are a prerequisite for high achievement in mathematics or a number of other scientific pursuits.[36] Differences do *not* imply that education and experience are irrelevant. Jacklin noted that when the number of mathematics courses taken by high school students is parceled out, some sex-related differences in visual-spatial ability fade.[37] There is some evidence that certain subtypes of spatial abilities are affected by training.[38] While visual-spatial studies continue to indicate the presence of presumably sex-based differences, those differences are smaller than we once thought and are influenced by gender in ways more powerful and subtle than we generally understand.[39]

DIFFERENCES IN VERBAL ABILITIES

While female superiority in verbal abilities has also been commonly reported as one of the facts of sex differences, such presumably sex-based differences are now viewed as smaller and less significant than earlier studies indicated.[40] In current studies, differences in verbal abilities are reported to be fading.[41] Conclusions regarding differences in verbal abilities from earlier studies are open to question for many of the same reasons studies of aggression and of visual-spatial abilities are questioned.

There are serious problems in definition. *Verbal ability* has been used to mean responses varying from quality of speech in two-year-olds, performance on the Peabody Picture Vocabulary Test by five-year-olds, essay writing by high school students, to solutions of anagrams and analogies by adults of differing ages, physical health, and levels of education.[42] There are problems in design of studies. Additionally, as is true in studies of aggression and visual-spatial abilities, there is difficulty in controlling for factors other than sex which may have influenced the outcomes of the studies.[43]

How big are the presumed differences? In 1988 two researchers reported the results of a complex statistical analysis of the findings from 165 major studies, including those cited by Maccoby and Jacklin in 1974. The authors concluded, "Our meta-analysis provides strong evidence that the magnitude of the gender difference in verbal ability is currently so small that it can effectively be considered to be zero."[44]

Others are unwilling, however, to accept these results.

Halpern, for example, continues to find evidence supporting female superiority in verbal abilities and male superiority in visual-spatial and mathematical abilities.[45] She argues that the alleged fading of female verbal superiority reported by Feingold[46] is primarily an artifact of the interaction between testing procedures and current high school dropout patterns.[47] If differences in verbal abilities do in fact exist, it appears likely that between-group differences are small, particularly in comparison to within-group variability.

Differences in Mathematical Ability

Problems in measuring presumed differences in mathematical functioning reflect the same issues complicating our understanding of differences in aggression, visual-spatial skills, and verbal ability. In dealing with mathematics, the gender-role bias against female proficiency in math obviously confounds any measurement of sex-based differences. However, studies of differences in mathematical abilities commonly report conclusive evidence having made little or no effort to deal with the confounding of gender/sex variables within the study, and with no acknowledgement of this crucial omission in the discussion of the conclusions of the study.

In the early 1980s, Benbow and Stanley published a series of articles that described the performance of a large population of bright boys and girls on a standardized test of mathematical ability.[48] In every study, the boys scored higher than the girls. In discussing the results of their studies, Benbow and Stanley speculated at length, both in the studies and to the avidly interested press, about biological causes for their results, *although they had collected no biological data in the course of their studies.* Benbow and Stanley's studies were criticized professionally on other grounds as well.[49]

At the time the results of Benbow and Stanley's studies were published and the resulting media circus occurred, Eccles and her colleagues were collecting data for a large-scale study of mathematics course-taking and mathematical achievement of seventh through ninth graders. By this happy chance, Eccles and her colleagues had opportunity to study the way in which the media's interpretation of Benbow and Stanley's study influenced the attitudes of people directly concerned with the subject matter of the study—the students and their parents involved in the Eccles math study, in this case.[50]

On the basis of their primary study, Eccles and her colleagues believe that math anxiety, gender-stereotyped beliefs of parents, and the perceived value of math to the student account for the major portion of sex differences in mathematical achievement.[51]

According to Eccles and her colleagues, students' attitudes about mathematics are most strongly related to their mothers' beliefs concerning the difficulty of mathematics for their children. When the media reports that science has proven that males are inevitably superior in math, and mothers read and believe this to be so, it is not difficult to see that it will take more than enrolling their daughters in a math course to provide a level playing field for girls in math achievement. When differences in math achievement are reported as sex-based without reference to gender-based factors such as those identified by Eccles and her associates, such reporting loses all relationship to science and is reduced to propaganda in the gender wars.

However, it is also important to remember that major studies, such as that carried out by Eccles and her associates, have not proven that there are no sex-based differences in mathematical ability. What these studies clearly demonstrate is that we have no gender-free expression of these abilities and no gender-neutral measurement of them.

Between-group differences in mathematics achievement remain puzzling and appear likely to be influenced by complex gender-based factors. But as counselors, it is important that we keep in mind the degree to which between-group differences can obscure the significance of individual differences and the ability of any given woman.

Science News recently reported a young woman's achievement in a way that demonstrates the significance of such individual differences.

Inspired by a high school course on fractal geometry, Ashley Melia Reiter, 17, captured first place this week in the 50th Annual Westinghouse Science Talent Search. A senior at the North Carolina School of Science and Mathematics in Durham, Reiter won a $40,000 scholarship for finding the dimensions of fractals generated by Pascal's triangle and its higher analogs.[52]

CONCLUSIONS

When we consider sex-based differences, at least as they are presently measured, we find that there appear to be some replicable differences in aggression (especially physical aggression), in mathematical and spatial abilities (especially mental rotation of objects), and probably, although less certainly, in verbal abilities. The size of between-group differences in these variables is small, particularly when compared to within-group differences. Their expression is influenced powerfully by gender-based factors, including the social context in which they are expressed. In areas of difference most clearly influenced by gender (the personality-social domain), the results of studies of difference continue, to borrow Maccoby's phrase, "particularly sparse and inconsistent." In 1981, following a meta-analysis of Maccoby and Jacklin's original data base, Janet Hyde concluded that gender differences (i.e., sex differences, in the more restricted usage followed here) accounted for no more than 1–5 percent of the population variance.[53] Her conclusion has not been seriously challenged in the decade since.

If the between-group differences are small, influenced by gender-based factors, and account for less than 5 percent of human variance, it is reasonable to wonder what the fuss is all about. Why does the issue of sex-gender differences have the power to raise the social temperature of almost any group into which the subject is introduced?

The controversy revolves less around known facts than around what we *want* the facts to be and what we want them to mean. Sex differences, because they are commonly believed to be biologically controlled, give promise of data that can be used to support arguments for and against social change. For this reason it is important to retain considerable caution about the certainty of sex differences, at least as they are popularly reported.

NOTES

1. Beryl Lief Benderly sensitively tells a hypothetical story of a "girl" who discovers she is a "boy" in the first chapter of *The Myth of Two Minds: What Gender Means and Doesn't Mean* (New York: Doubleday, 1987). Benderly's account is a complicated biology lesson told simply in a moving, human context. More formal studies of chromosomal and hormonal anomalies are found in: J. Money and A. Ehrhardt, *Man and Woman, Boy and Girl* (Baltimore: Johns Hopkins Press, 1972). J. Money and P. Tucker, *Sexual Signatures: On Being a Man or a Woman* (Boston: Little, Brown and Co., 1975). J. Money, *Love and Love Sickness: The Science of Sex, Gender Difference and Pair Bonding* (Baltimore: Johns Hopkins Press, 1980).

2. C. Sherif, "Needed Concepts in the Study of Gender Identity," *Psychology of Women Quarterly* 6 (1982): 375–98 (quote from 392).

3. Leon Kamin, as cited by Mary Stewart Van Leeuwen, *Gender and Grace: Love, Work and Parenting in a Changing World* (Downers Grove, Ill.: InterVarsity, 1990), 18–19.

4. C. N. Jacklin, "Female and Male: Issues of Gender," *American Psychologist* 44, no. 2 (February 1989): 127–33 (quote from 130).

5. For a readable account of basic aspects of this complex issue, see Melvin Konner, *The Tangled Wing: Biological Constraints on the Human Spirit* (New York: Holt, Rinehart and Winston, 1982), and R. Bleier, *Science and Gender: A Critique of Biology and Its Theories on Women* (New York: Pergamon, 1984).

6. J. H. Block, "Debatable Conclusions about Sex Differences," *Contemporary Psychology* 21 (1976): 517–22.

7. T. Tieger, "On the Biological Basis of Sex Differences in Aggression," *Child Development* 51 (1980): 943–63.

8. E. E. Maccoby, "Gender and Relationships," *American Psychologist* 45, no. 4 (April 1990): 513–20.

9. A. H. Eagly, *Sex Differences in Social Behavior: A Social Role Interpretation* (Hillsdale, N.J.: Erlbaum, 1987).

10. Maccoby, "Gender and Relationships," 513.

11. Ibid.

12. E. E. Maccoby and C. N. Jacklin, *The Psychology of Sex Differences* (Stanford, Calif.: Stanford University Press, 1974), 110.

13. Maccoby, "Gender and Relationships," 513. Studies cited by Maccoby showing men more frequently the agents of aggression than are women in-

cluded: Eagly, *Sex Differences in Social "Behavior"*; A. C. Huston, "The Development of Sex-Typing: Themes from Recent Research," *Developmental Review* 5 (1985): 1–17; and E. E. Maccoby and C. N. Jacklin, "Sex Differences in Aggression: A Rejoinder and Reprise," *Child Development* 51 (1980): 964–80.

14. K. E. Moyer, "Sex Differences in Aggression," in *Sex Differences in Behavior*, ed. R. C. Friedman et al. (New York: Wiley, 1974) 149–63.

15. J. S. Hyde, "How Large Are Gender Differences in Aggression? A Developmental Meta-Analysis," *Developmental Psychology* 20 (1984): 722–36.

16. Ibid.

17. Ibid. See also I. H. Frieze et al., *Women and Sex Roles* (New York: Norton, 1978).

18. Eagly. See also A. H. Eagly and V. J. Steffen, "Gender and Aggressive Behavior: A Meta-Analytic Review of the Social Psychological Literature," *Psychological Bulletin* 100 (1986): 309–30.

19. S. Prescott, "Why Researchers Don't Study Women: The Responses of Sixty-two Researchers," *Sex Roles* 4 (1978): 899–905.

20. W. McKenna and S. J. Kessler, "Experimental Design as a Source of Sex Bias in Social Psychology," *Sex Roles* 3 (1977): 117–28.

21. S. M. J. Towson and M. P. Zanna, "Toward a Situational Analysis of Gender Differences in Aggression," *Sex Roles* 8 (1982): 903–14.

22. A. Frodi, J. Macaulay, and P. P. Thome, "Are Women Always Less Aggressive than Men? A Review of the Experimental Literature," *Psychological Bulletin* 84 (1977): 634–60.

23. Eagly and Steffen, 309–30.

24. L. J. Harris, "Sex Differences in Spatial Ability: Possible Environmental, Genetic, and Neurological Factors," in *Asymmetrical Function of the Brain*, ed. M. Kinsbourne (New York: Cambridge University Press, 1987), 405–522.

25. Maccoby, "Gender and Relationships," 513.

26. M. C. Linn and A. Peterson, "A Meta-Analysis of Gender Differences in Spatial Ability: Implication for Mathematics and Science Achievement," in *The Psychology of Gender: Advances through Meta-Analysis*, ed. J. S. Hyde and M. C. Linn (Baltimore: Johns Hopkins University Press, 1986), 67–101.

27. P. J. Caplan, G. M. MacPherson, and P. Tobin, "Do Sex-Related Differences in Spatial Abilities Exist? A Multilevel Critique with New Data," *American Psychologist* 40, no. 7 (July 1985): 786–99.

28. Ibid.

29. Linn and Peterson, "Meta-Analysis of Gender Differences."

30. D. F. Halpern, *Sex Differences in Cognitive Abilities* (Hillsdale, N.J.: Erlbaum, 1986).

31. S. F. Naditch, "Sex Differences in Field Dependence: The Role of Social Influence" (Paper presented at the meeting of the American Psychological Association, Washington, D.C., September 1976), as cited in Caplan, MacPherson, and Tobin, 788.

32. Anne Fausto-Sterling, *Myths of Gender: Biological Theories about Women and Men* (New York: Basic Books, 1985), 32.

33. Maccoby, "Gender and Relationships," 513.

34. J. S. Hyde, "How Large Are Cognitive Gender Differences? A Meta-Analysis," *American Psychologist* 36 (1981): 892–901.

35. M. C. Linn and A. C. Petersen, "Emergence and Characterization of Sex Differences in Spatial Ability: A Meta-Analysis," *Child Development* 56 (1985): 1479–98.

36. Linn and Petersen, "Meta-Analysis of Gender Differences," 67–101.

37. C. N. Jacklin, "Epilogue" in *Sex Related Differences in Cognitive Functions*, ed. M. A. Wittig and A. C. Petersen (New York: Academic Press, 1979), 357–71, as cited in Caplan, MacPherson, and Tobin, 787.

38. A. Stericker and S. LeVesconte, "Effect of Brief Training on Sex-Related Differences in Visual-Spatial Skill," *Journal of Personality and Social Psychology* 43 (1982): 1018–29. See also P. Tobin, "The Effects of Practice and Training on Sex Differences in Performance on a Spatial Task" (Master's thesis, University of Toronto, 1982).

39. Fausto-Sterling, 30–36.

40. Maccoby, "Gender and Relationships," 513.

41. A. Feingold, "Cognitive Gender Differences Are Disappearing," *American Psychologist* 43 (1988): 95–103. See also Fausto-Sterling, 26–30.

42. J. Hyde and M. Linn, "Gender Differences in Verbal Ability: A Meta-Analysis," *Psychological Bulletin* 104, no. 1 (1988): 53–69.

43. R. Plomin and T. Foch, "Sex Differences and Individual Differences," *Child Development* 52 (1981): 383–85.

44. Hyde and Linn, 53–69.

45. D. F. Halpern, *Sex Differences in Cognitive Abilities* (Hillsdale, N.J.: Erlbaum, 1986).

46. Feingold.

47. D. F. Halpern, "The Disappearance of Cognitive Gender Differences: What You See Depends on Where You look," *American Psychologist* (August 1989), 1156–58.

48. C. P. Benbow and J. C. Stanley, "Sex Differences in Mathematics Ability: Fact or Artifact?" *Science* 210 (1980): 1262–64. C. P. Benbow and J. C. Stanley, "Consequences in High School and College of Sex Differences in Mathematical Reasoning Ability: A Longitudinal Perspective," *American Educational Research Journal* 19 (1982): 598–622. C. P. Benbow and J. C. Stanley, "Sex Differences in Mathematical Reasoning Ability: More Facts," *Science* 222 (1983): 1029–31.

49. See Carol Jacklin, "Female and Male: Issues of Gender," *American Psychologist* 44, no. 2 (February 1989): 127–33.

50. J. S. Eccles and J. E. Jacobs, "Social Forces Shape Math Attitudes and Performance," *Signs* 11 (1986): 367–89. J. E. Jacobs and J. S. Eccles, "Gender Differences in Math Ability: The Impact of Media Reports on Parents," *Educational Researcher* 14 (1985): 20–25.

51. J. S. Eccles, T. F. Adler, and C. M. Kaczala, "Socialization of Achievement Attitudes and Beliefs: Parental Influences," *Child Development* 53 (1982): 310–21. J. S. Eccles, C. M. Kaczala, and J. L. Meece, "Socialization of Achievement Attitudes and Beliefs: Classroom Influences," *Child Development* 53

(1982): 322–39. J. S. Eccles et al., "Expectations, Values, and Academic Behaviors," in *Achievement and Achievement Motivation*, ed. J. T. Spence (San Francisco: Freeman, 1983), 75–146. J. S. Eccles and J. E. Jacobs, "Social Forces Shape Math Attitudes and Performance," *Signs* 11 (1986): 367–89.

52. "Student Researchers Win Top STS Awards," *Science News* 139, no. 10 (March 9, 1991): 150.

53. Hyde, 892–901.

Chapter Seven

Gender and Developmental Differences

SUPPOSE THAT WHILE YOU WERE DINING in a favorite restaurant an individual near you began to scream and throw food. Would you be annoyed? Or alarmed? What would determine your response?

Your immediate response would probably be that screaming and throwing food is undesirable behavior. But your emotional response, annoyance or alarm, would be influenced more by the age of the offending individual than by the behavior itself.

While screaming and food throwing may be an embarrassment to parents and an annoyance to nearby diners, no one becomes overly concerned if such behavior is demonstrated by a frustrated two-year-old. However undesirable such behavior may be, most adults understand that tired, emotionally healthy two-year-olds sometimes act this way.

In contrast, if a twenty-two-year-old abruptly begins to scream and throw food, nearby diners are more than annoyed.

They quickly become alarmed; they understand that something is seriously wrong. Such behavior by a twenty-two-year-old is more than undesirable. It is not normal—even though we may not be able to define *normal* to our precise satisfaction.

Suppose further that the incident occurred at a table at which a twenty-two-year-old male and a twenty-two-year-old female were seated. Throwing food and screaming would be inappropriate for either of these people, but if we asked nearby diners *how* inappropriate or abnormal the behavior was, we might discover an interesting difference in their evaluations of the woman and the man.

Culturally, in this setting the women has the advantage. If she screams at her companion and throws spaghetti on him, fellow diners are not likely to approve of her behavior. Some diners, however, may view her behavior less negatively because she is female. They may think, in effect, "Here is a *woman* being angry and impulsive, hardly desirable behaviors in any case, but understandable given her sex. Women are emotional creatures by nature and often get upset; besides, it may be that time of the month."

If the man, in contrast, screams at the woman and throws spaghetti on her, diners may evaluate him differently. The cultural expectation is that under provocation he (being male) will remain rational and logical and retain control over his impulses. Consequently, if he does scream and throw food, his behavior, while equally inappropriate socially, may be viewed as psychologically more serious and evoke greater concern and anxiety in nearby diners.

Such assumptions are both developmentally and gender-based. Observers generally assume that adults (female or male) ought not to act in this fashion. But observers who believe that women are more emotional than men because they are female are more likely to hold the woman to a less stringent standard of impulse control.

Sometimes a similar argument is used to excuse the seriousness of sexually inappropriate behaviors of men. Let us assume that this troubled couple went to an apartment (his or hers) in order to remove the remains of the spaghetti, and the evening culminated in what the woman later reported as date rape.

At this point, the so-called advantage might shift to the man. Some individuals—and sometimes, tragically, the judicial system as well[1]—may suggest that it was the man's uncontrollable hormones which precipitated his aggressive sexual behavior. They reason that since his hormones presumably coerced him to do it, it is therefore unfair for the man to be punished for the crime of rape. Some may reason further that the woman must have wanted the sexual encounter to occur, or she would not have gone to the man's apartment or permitted him to visit hers.

Whether we are functioning as individuals out to dinner or as counselors, gender and developmental level strongly influence our judgment of human behavior. The example also demonstrates the importance of facts and the danger of myths. Is rape the result of a male's uncontrollable sexual urges? Are women more emotional than men? Are women uniquely vulnerable to emotional binges premenstrually? How does age affect these factors? What are the facts?

The counselor cannot avoid considering gender differences and developmental levels in evaluating client behaviors. However, acquiring facts about gender and development and then applying them in counseling women is far more difficult than the example suggests.

ADULT DEVELOPMENT

Determining the level of adult development is not easy. While chronological age is helpful as a quick and easy index, age is certainly no guaranteed measure of maturity. Twos are indeed different from twenties, and twenties different from forties. However, most of us can easily recall individuals (male and female) who are in their forties but whose behaviors have consistently over the years seemed more appropriate for someone in their early twenties. Conversely, most of us can also recall individuals (male and female) who appear to have skipped over their early adulthood and to have been "old" forever.

Further, most counselors can readily call to mind an instance in which a woman coming for assistance communicated nonverbally, "I'm a little girl who has come to you for help, but don't ask me to grow up." In these circumstances, it is sometimes difficult to describe precisely what there is in the woman's behavior that leads us to write *immature* in the case notes. It is even more difficult to describe the shadowy standard of maturity against which, in our minds, we have measured such women and found them wanting. Defining emotional maturity clearly (for women or men) is one of psychology's unfinished tasks.

There is growing troublesome evidence that we do not yet understand the developmental pattern of women and may have attempted unwisely to use the presumed pattern of male growth on which to plot women's progress through their adult life span. Sheehy suggested in *Passages* that men and women pass each other in the middle years traveling in opposite directions developmentally; he is restructuring his life for increased relationships and emotional intimacy while she is restructuring her life for increased achievement and involvement in the larger world beyond her home.[2] Is this true? No one yet knows for certain how the developmental path for women goes. Early adult developmental studies focused primarily, although not exclusively, on men.[3]

How can counselors determine where a woman is in her developmental span? As a simple point of beginning, age tells us something, but almost always less than we need to know. Chronological age alone can give us information that can mislead us if we are not cautious about the context in which we interpret its meaning. Recently I had two women clients, both of whom were forty years of age but whose age told little of their stories. One was celebrating her first pregnancy; the other was celebrating her first grandchild. Men's development is commonly mapped in relation to career/work history; women are categorized according to the functioning of their reproductive systems.

While as counselors we may feel confident that a forty-year-old woman and a sixty-year-old woman are at different stages of life, lack of established developmental data makes us less certain about the precise nature of the differences that separate them. And, as counselors, having seen no two sixty-year-old women who were alike, we are even less certain about the impact of individual differences in the adult developmental process. There is some indication that variability (i.e., the range of individual differences) increases with age.

Lack of developmental data can lead to another error. We can classify the problems the client brings as evidence of psychopathology when in reality the problems are the normal tension and conflicts of adult life processes. Laura, the unhappy client in chapter 2 who "had it all," was struggling with a major developmental crisis with which she needed professional help. She was not, however, in any clinical sense of the word, emotionally disturbed or mentally ill.

Similarly, gender information is difficult to manage not only because of the complexity and confusion surrounding gender research but also because cultural stereotypes can so easily and unconsciously influence our thinking.

In the example of the spaghetti-throwing couple, the belief that women are more emotional than men is a stereotyped assumption that gender research does not support. There is no scientific reason to view failure to maintain adequate impulse control as a less serious behavior in females than in males. Similarly, the stereotyped belief that males are unable to control sexual impulses is a misbelief that has no basis in fact and must not be used to excuse the seriousness of sexually aggressive behaviors.

Scientists hold divided opinions about what has come to be called Premenstrual Syndrome (PMS).[4] Some believe that it is a biologically based phenomena to which all women are subject to lesser or greater degrees. Others question this, pointing out that there are no controlled studies that provide a scientifically precise definition of PMS, account for its cause, or identify with certainty any form of intervention that eases its symptoms.

The lack of knowledge about gender and women's adult life span may appear odd, since study of human development historically has been a major focus of psychological research. Until the 1970s, however, developmental psychology by definition meant the study of the human from conception to early adulthood. Research examining gendered patterns of adult behavior and the developmental processes of adult life did not begin in earnest until the late 1960s. University courses in adult life-span psychology began in the 1970s and did not become a part of the established curriculum in most institutions until the 1980s.[5] As a result, many counselors undertake work with both men and women with little reliable information about developmental patterns of adult life and even less information about gender and the complex processes through which it is learned and expressed.

The commercial success of Gail Sheehy's book, *Passages*, indicates that information about adult development is of serious interest to most men and women, not only to therapists. What made *Passages* a bestseller was Sheehy's attempt to answer at the popular level questions that had also begun to interest psychologists. If adults do in fact change over the adult life span, do men and women change differently? If there are clearly definable differences, what are they? And (a question we have met before) which of these differences are due to biology, and which are due to learning? What do we know about women's experiences across their adult life span?

As with sex differences, once we began to ask questions about gendered behaviors and the adult developmental span of women, we quickly discovered how little we knew, and, disconcertingly, how much of what we thought we knew was likely to be quite wrong. For example, one early researcher asked, "How do women experience menopause? Do women in fact grieve the empty nest?" In seeking answers to these questions, Bernice Neugarten discovered that, contrary to Freudian theory and the common wisdom of the day, the overwhelming majority of women do *not* perceive menopause as the end of meaningful life sexually or emotionally, and women, for the most part, are glad when their adult children move out and establish homes of their own.[6]

In the beginning stages of adult life-span psychology, early developmental studies were reviewed by researchers looking for clues about adult development and the processes—psychological and physical—through which little girls grew up into women. In reviewing these early studies, two major problems became apparent.

Little girls had been studied, of course, but it became clear that early developmental research (e.g., early aggression research) had often lumped little girls in with little boys in ways that resulted in misleading data and conclusions that could not be fully trusted.

Additionally, as had occurred in early study of sex differences, researchers had often assumed that what was true developmentally for males was also true for females. In those cases in which the facts could not be made to fit this assumption, female development was often explained in terms of deficiency. Distinctively female behaviors or processes were regarded as significant primarily for the absence of that which was present in the male.

Kohlberg's frequently cited study of moral development is an example of this assumption. Kohlberg's initial study was based on the responses of eighty-four boys whose development Kohlberg followed over a period of twenty years.[7] Using the responses of these selected males, Kohlberg devised a system of stages of moral development which he presented as universal human responses. Women then were measured on this scale and judged deficient in moral maturity *as women* because they responded at lower levels than did the males in Kohlberg's original study. Such inappropriate generalization might be viewed simply as unfortunate if it were not for the amount of unquestioning acceptance that greeted Kohlberg's work and the presumed evidence it provided for the woman-as-deficient school of thought.[8]

Assumption of the male experience also underlaid an influential developmental theory proposed by Freud. According to Freud, women's development pivoted around the little girl's discovery of her lack of a penis and her presumably lifelong efforts to compensate for the absence of this essential organ.

For a male child, being born without a penis would indeed be a serious deficiency and a great emotional trauma, one that might well influence his entire life. However, to presume that a healthy female child would experience the absence of a penis (*normal* female body) with the same emotions with which a male child would experience the absence of a penis (*abnormal* or *defective* male body) reflects an assumption in which the experience of the male is the norm by which female development was to be understood and explained.

In the last two decades an enormous amount of material relating to gender and developmental issues has been published. In this chapter we can do no more than identify important issues, summarize major theories and research findings, and briefly review responsible differences of opinion at crucial points. In this material two issues have immediate practical importance to counselors: (1) the nature of the developmental path women follow, and (2) the distinctive patterns of behavior that characterize adult women. Our knowledge of these two factors shapes our general understanding of what *normal* is for women.

THE DEVELOPMENTAL JOURNEY: LEARNING TO BE A WOMAN

When we see a woman client sitting in the reception area awaiting her appointment, we usually notice that the client is a woman, but it does not usually occur to us as counselors to wonder how she became one. We assume, for the most part, that being born female is sufficient to insure that an individual will grow up to be a woman.

Biologists and developmental psychologists, however, are less certain about the inevitability of this process and increasingly curious about the way in which it occurs. How do those tiny females with pink ribbons on their cribs grow up to be adult women anyway? And once they have become adult women, then what happens? By what processes does the tennis player who today is sending a powerful volley across the net become the middle-aged woman who still plays tennis, but at a slower pace, and then, at the end, become the silver-haired senior who is able only to remember those bygone summer days and the feel of the racket in her hand? And how, as her body changed, has she changed as a woman? Are young women and old women different in ways that body changes alone cannot explain?

THE BIOLOGICAL PROCESS

There are, of course, powerful biological processes at work throughout the life span for both women and men. Maturation from conception to adulthood is a complex process for both sexes, one which does not always proceed smoothly for the female (or for the male, who, biologically speaking, remains the more vulnerable sex).[9] And biology propels us, men and women alike, through adulthood toward death despite our resistance to the aging process.

A woman's adult life span is marked by physiological events associated with reproduction that have no counterpart in male experience—menarche and the consequent rhythm of menstruation; breast development; pregnancy; parturition; lactation; and menopause. However, the counselor needs to understand these events not only as biological processes but also as body events that are an integral part of women's *emotional* lives.

Many women are uninformed or misinformed about their bodies. In such circumstances, women profit emotionally from reading and discussing informational material with a supportive therapist.[10]

Counselors need, of course, to integrate biological information into the counseling process in a way that keeps the focus upon the emotional, relational issues with which the client is struggling. For example, talking about the facts of body functioning is often an effective bridge to exploring the myths about their bodies that some women believe (see chapter 2). Body issues for women are often directly connected to issues of competence, self-worth, and sexuality. To attempt to deal with such issues without dealing directly with the body image and processes with which these feelings are associated often leads to an impasse for both client and counselor.

There continues to be insufficient and incomplete information about biological processes as well as lack of information about the direct effect, if any, of these biological events on the emotional lives of women. These body events are clearly emotionally important experiences in the lives of women. However, present information indicates that the effects of these events is for the most part indirect, linked, as Williams noted, to the consequences of these events and to the meanings they have for the woman and for those individuals with whom her life is connected.[11]

Research regarding women's health and physical functioning has focused heavily on securing information about reproductive processes. In other areas, we know considerably less. For example, most people know that heart disease represents the number-one killer of men in the United States, but most people do not realize that it is the number-one killer of women as well.[12] Osteoporosis-related problems kill as many women every year as breast cancer does and leave thousands of women dependent on the care of others. Yet this "woman's disease" gets less than half the government funds allocated for breast cancer, and scientists still know relatively little about its prevention and treatment.[13]

Is estrogen replacement therapy wise after menopause? Why has the number of cesarian procedures and hysterectomies increased so dramatically over recent decades? How safe is a "late" pregnancy? Why do some women suffer postpartum depression and others do not? What is a safe program for cardiovascular conditioning for women sixty-five to seventy-five years of age? Does intelligence decrease with age? It would be difficult to list all the important questions about women's health and aging to which we do not yet have reliable answers.

Failure to include women as subjects in basic research continues to limit our information about women and tempts us to apply the results of male-only research to women without adequate testing and proper safeguards. Mary Lake Polan is head of the Department of Gynecology and Obstetrics at Stanford University School of Medicine and a member of the Board of Directors of the Society for the Advancement of Women's Health Research. Her professional concern regarding women's health research was recently expressed in a widely syndicated column in which she noted the following facts.[14]

- A widely publicized study concluded that taking an aspirin every other day may reduce the risk of heart disease; this conclusion was based on observation of 22,071 men—no women.
- A famous long-term study of lifestyle factors related to cholesterol levels and the development of heart disease was carried out by twenty-two major health research centers, and included observation of 15,000 men—no women.

- A study released by the Harvard School of Public Health in 1990 concluded that coffee consumption did not encourage the development of heart disease. The research was based on a study population of 45,589 men—no women.
- A definitive longitudinal study on aging, financed by the National Institute on Aging, was initiated in 1958. It did not include women until 1978, twenty years after the initial collection of data. This means that long-term data on women and the aging process are unavailable from this important study.
- In December 1991, researchers from the University of California, Los Angeles, and Harvard reported two studies of the effects of aging on mental faculties. Subjects? Men only, even though women routinely live longer than men.
- Since 1980 breast cancer has produced nearly eight times as many fatalities among women as AIDS has produced among the population at large—men, women, and children. Yet forty-four times as much money was spent by the National Institutes of Health on basic AIDS research in 1989 as was spent on breast-cancer research. Such statistics do not argue for diminishing AIDS research but rather for increased attention to basic developmental research that seeks to understand women's health needs and define the sex and gender parameters of women's adult lives.

A woman's average life span today is seventy-eight years, so she can expect to live nearly half of her adult life postmenopausally. Life expectancy of this length for women is now occurring for the first time. Despite this unique moment in human history, we have been slow to implement systematic investigation of this special generation of women. A slow beginning is only part of the problem, however. Initiation of current studies only emphasizes the lack of longitudinal data needed for comparison. For example, the first major government-funded study on menopause was undertaken in 1990. There is no reliable information from past studies to anticipate what these women may expect in their approximately thirty postmenopausal years or to provide a context in which to understand their unique experiences.

There are more than a few of these women. By the year 2000 there will be more than 50 million American women fifty years and older, many of whom will live into their eighties, well beyond the present average life span.

Some of these women already have begun to find their way to the counselor's office with midlife problems. When these women ask, "Is this normal for a woman at this stage of my life?" counselors must acknowledge the fact that we have too little information to permit us to answer the question definitively.

It is important for counselors to understand the biological development and function of adult women—at least what we know of it. What is of particular interest to counselors, however, is the parallel growth and development in gender that accompanies biological change. While a female infant is developing into an adult female, a little girl is becoming a woman.

DEFINING GENDER

Since the interactive effect of biology and learning is central to our understanding of gender, it is perhaps wise to remind ourselves of Kamin's point as we begin to think about the processes through which gender identity and role develop. Kamin noted that since "we pass our *environments* on to our children along with our *genes*, there is no way of saying for sure which of these factors is producing a certain behavior in a certain child, or by how much it outweighs the other factor."[15]

Ruth Bleier also emphasized this point:

> Biology can be said to define possibilities but not determine them; it is never irrelevant but it is also not determinant. For each person, brain-body-mind-behavior-environment form a complex entity the parts of which are inextricable from each other; the parts and the whole are ceaselessly interacting and changing and carry within themselves the entire history of their interactions.[16]

In thinking about the developmental processes through which gender is acquired, we will use the term *gender* carefully.

Gender is those ways of thinking, feeling, and behaving that express femininity and masculinity in culturally established patterns. Such patterns are built upon biological parameters and are influenced by biological factors; indeed, they cannot be fully separated from them, in men and women alike. However, gender is more than a predetermined product of chromosomes, hormones, and physiological factors. Gender is a complex pattern of attitudes and behaviors that men and women acquire through a lifetime of learning and interacting with one another in various social environments. In turn, these complex patterns are suppressed or expressed in various forms in differing social environments, often in response to factors that are not yet fully identified.

It is wise to keep in mind both how comprehensive and how complex the gender acquisition process is. For little girls to grow into adult women requires them to acquire culturally defined, sex-appropriate preferences, skills, personality attributes, behaviors, and self-concepts.[17] They must then express these gendered behaviors over a lifetime of differing relationships, changing social contexts, and shifting roles.

Culturally defined, sex-appropriate patterns of behavior vary widely in reference to given ethnic and economic factors. It is insensitive and seriously misleading to assume that the experience of the white, middle-class woman reflects in whole the gender-role reality of a Black, Hispanic, or Asian woman, or to assume that the gender-role requirements for the rich and the poor are identical.

As a further part of the complexity of gender-role learning, adult women, in whatever ethnic or economic environment, must continue to revise original gender learning over their adult life span and acquire new learning as the aging process occurs. For example, sexual needs are considered gender role appropriate and desirable for a forty-year-old woman. In contrast, sexual needs experienced by a seventy-year-old woman must be hidden in most settings, particularly nursing homes, or become a source of shame.

Counselors are all too aware of the painful ways in which the gender acquisition process can go wrong. Every counselor has women clients whose problems are rooted in the process through which these individuals learned to be women. Many women who are troubled about their value and identity as women received emotionally significant information about gender from a father who was relationally incompetent, emotionally dysfunctional, or perhaps physically and/or sexually abusive, but whose definition of womanhood continues, nevertheless, to control his daughter's life.[18]

THE GENDER JOURNEY

By the time most little girls are four years old, they are already acting in ways that foreshadow the gender patterns of adult women. A little girl is born female, but by the age of four she has learned that she is both female and a little girl (*gender identity*). Additionally, she is beginning to understand that girls cannot change into boys, although she is not yet absolutely certain of this under all circumstances.[19] Acquiring this knowledge that girls cannot turn into boys, or boys into girls, is referred to as the child's development of *gender constancy*. Consistent with this developing world view, the little girl is also beginning to understand that girls grow up to be women, not men. She has also begun to learn that girls do things differently than do boys (*gender-role*), and that some objects, events, and other factors have different meanings for girls than for boys. This process of classifying behaviors, clothing, objects, attitudes, and other factors according to their gender significance is referred to as *sex-typing*.

Because gender acquisition occurs early and consistently in the developmental cycle, it has been traditionally assumed that it is biologically controlled. We now know that biology is only one of the factors influencing the acquisition of gendered behavior, although it is an important one. Explanations of how and why gender learning occurs vary significantly.

DEVELOPMENTAL THEORIES: FREUD

Freud believed that infant females become adult females as a result of biological processes, which is true, of course. However, he also believed that females became women (i.e., acquired gendered behavior) through emotional processes centered around what he believed to be their lifelong task of mastering appropriate emotional responses to the biological absence (loss) of a penis. In Freud's theory, beginning at about the age of four, girls realize their absence of a penis and "feel seriously wronged, often declare that they want to 'have something like it too,' and fall a victim to 'envy for the penis' which will leave ineradicable traces on their development and the formation of their character and which will not be surmounted in even the most favorable cases without a severe expenditure of psychical energy."[20]

In Freudian theory, a mature woman is passive, narcissistic, masochistic, and resigned to the biologically imposed "deficiency" which as a female shapes the parameters of her woman's life. Life satisfaction for the mature woman is vicarious and flows through her role as wife and mother, which provides attachment to the powerful active male. Williams noted, "Freud believed that the mother-son relationship is the most perfect and most free of ambivalence of all human relationships. She [the mature woman] can realize through her son all the ambition she had had to suppress in herself, and through him she can satisfy all that was left of her old masculine strivings."[21]

Because Freudian theory has been so influential in shaping cultural concepts of women, and has shaped the belief system of many therapists as well, it has received increasingly sharp criticism as women's development has become more clearly understood.[22]

DEVELOPMENTAL THEORIES: ERIKSON

Perhaps the most familiar theory of human development is that of Erik Erikson. Erikson has proposed "eight ages of man," each with a characteristic social/emotional task, to describe stages of identity development beginning in infancy and culminating in old age.[23] Erikson presumably believed these stages and their associated life tasks were applicable to women as well.

Erikson's work, like Freud's, has strongly influenced the way we think about adult development. However, Erikson's work, again like Freud's, has serious deficits in helping us think about women's development. In *Childhood and Society*[24] all of the children and youths Erikson studied are male; women are discussed only as mothers, and then only in terms of the ways in which they influenced the boys' development. For Erikson the male experience was the human experience, and women merited specific attention only in their role as mothers. Erikson, again like Freud, did not turn his attention to the development of women as women until late in life—his seventh decade, and then primarily in response to the criticism of his earlier work by women scholars.[25]

In his paper, "Inner and Outer Space: Reflections on Womanhood," Erikson proposed that it was the design of the female body, the "inner space" of its womb and vagina, that determines the developmental experience and identity formation of women. Erikson believed that the history of a woman's life and her potential for fulfillment lies in her disposition of this "inner space." Consequently, Erikson thought that a woman's mature identity as a woman achieved closure only after she had taken the crucial step of choosing a husband. By this choice she "relinquishes the care received from the paternal family in order to commit herself to the love of a stranger and to the care to be given to his and her offspring."[26]

How, asks Erikson in effect, can a woman possibly know who she is until she is married? How can she be fully a woman until she is a mother?

Erikson's developmental theory represents old, familiar problems. There is the use of the male experience as though it were human experience, with women to be explained as exceptions to the rule. There is the focus upon biology as the source and explanation for *all* gendered behavior. There is also an arbitrary, limited identification of the mature, psychologically healthy woman with the mother role. There is, additionally, the presence of questionable data used uncritically as the basis of theory and conclusions.

It is not widely known that Erikson's concept of the "inner space" orientation of females and the "outer space" orientation of males was based on an uncontrolled study of preadolescents (eleven to thirteen years of age). These children were asked one at a time to build an exciting scene from an imaginary motion picture using a random selection of toys.

Erikson reported that the girls tended to build interior scenes that were serene and peaceful, with enclosures of low walls, or vestibules with gates and doors. In contrast, boys built towers or buildings and often knocked them down, or provided other excitement through aggressive behaviors. Erikson thought these behaviors reflected sexual anatomy, with the males emphasizing "erectile, projectile, and active motifs," and the females emphasizing "enclosure, protection, and receptivity." Erikson also thought that females characteristically demonstrated a defensive posture against the "ever-present threat" of forceful intrusion into their serene, peaceful world by boys, men, or animals.[27]

A recent study has indicated, however, that the way in which children choose to play is influenced by the nature of the toys available, not simply by the sex/gender identity of the child.[28]

In an application of these findings, some researchers replicated Erikson's study but structured it so that the children used the same toys. They discovered that, in this situation, children—girls and boys—built the same constructions *when given the same toys.*[29]

Does girls' play indicate that their development displays an orientation toward inner space? Clearly, it depends. As Basow noted, "Children of both sexes make 'feminine' constructions with 'girl' toys such as dolls, and 'masculine' constructions with 'boy' toys such as trucks."[30] Gendered behaviors in this instance are the result not only of what is *in* the individual genes (biology), but also of what is *in* the individual in interaction with the environment (the sex-typed toys, in this instance).[31]

Further, who can estimate the degree to which Erikson's thinking was influenced by the exploration of outer space that was occurring internationally at the time Erikson first developed this inner space/outer space concept? Certainly in the real world of outer space exploration, at that time still in its early stages, outer space was exclusively and vigorously a males-only domain. No one yet knew Sally Ride. Again it is helpful to remember that scientists are not immune to the influence of the environment in which they work or to the *zeitgeist* of their times.

DEVELOPMENTAL THEORIES: KAGAN

Jerome Kagan is a Harvard psychologist whose study of child development spans more than three decades. Unlike Freud or Erikson, Kagan does not believe that the girl's biology controls her development of gender, but he does believe that it influences it in a profound and interesting way.

> Every girl knows, somewhere between the ages of 5 and 10, that she is different from boys and that she will have a child—something that everyone, including children, understands as quintessentially natural. . . . If in our society nature stands for the giving of life, nurturance, help, affection, then the girl will conclude unconsciously that those are the qualities she should strive to attain. And the boy won't. And that's exactly what happens.[32]

Kagan calls such gender differences "inevitable but not genetic," reflecting the point made earlier that in women's development (and men's as well) biology does indeed count, but at some points counts more heavily than at others and in different ways than we commonly suppose. Early developmental theories, however, viewed biology as the *only* thing that counted. Erikson, for example, even though he emphasized the social/historical context in which human development occurs, nevertheless ended his theory building by defining a woman's development in terms of her body and its reproductive functions.[33]

Kagan, while respecting the powerful influence of biology, suggests something else as an important correlate—a choice that the girl herself makes about how she develops, a kind of "emotional logic," so to speak, that leads her to choose behaviors because they fit with her understanding of who she is.

If indeed gender is something about which the girl/woman learns and chooses in her development, how does this learning come about?

DEVELOPMENTAL THEORIES: GENDER SCHEMA

One of the early explanations of gender learning was based on ideas stemming from Skinner and other behaviorists. Reinforcement theory suggested that the girl learned to display gender appropriate behaviors as the result of the rewards she received for "girl" behavior and the aversive response she received when she displayed "boy" behavior.

The process of social reward does indeed shape some aspects of gendered behavior. Watching a father with his daughter or son in a clothing or toy store will provide a quick example. However, while reinforcement theory explains some aspects of gender learning, it does not answer an important question: How does the little girl learn "I am a girl," and "There are girl behaviors," so that she can perform in a way for which she can receive positive reward?

A second theory, based upon the work of Albert Bandura and others, explained this complex learning about gender as social learning, the result of observational learning, or imitation. According to this theory, the little girl learns by observing and imitating adult females in her social environment, particularly her same-sexed parent. An example of the effect of social modeling is also easy to find: watching a small daughter play dress-up with her mother's discarded clothing and cosmetics provides a clear demonstration of the power of social learning. However, while very helpful in explaining some aspects of gender learning, this theory could not answer another important question: What leads the child to choose to imitate some of the behaviors of the adult women she observes and not others? What is the basis of the selective imitation of gender-congruent behaviors?

In an effort to explain how gender identity and gender-role are learned, a third theory, gender schema theory, began to evolve.

In 1966, Kohlberg wrote an important paper proposing a cognitive basis for the development of gender identity and gender constancy.[34] Maccoby, who is not known for poetic exaggeration in her professional papers, recently called this early work of Kohlberg "remarkable" and "revolutionary" for its time and noted the debt that current research in the field owes to the concepts developed by Kohlberg in this important paper.[35]

In this early paper, Kohlberg proposed that children's concepts of gender are constructed, not directly taught.[36] In saying this, Kohlberg was suggesting that the child develops a concept of gender identity ("I'm a girl") in somewhat the same fashion that she learns to categorize other parts of her environment ("That's a dog, not a horse"). Development of such cognitive maps is a complicated process and appears to be strongly influenced by the developmental level of the child, as Piaget had previously demonstrated. In the decades since Kohlberg's paper, researchers[37] have amassed considerable evidence that gender identity and the girl's learning of the rules of her culture for girl-appropriate behavior are indeed the result of cognitive/developmental processes. There is now general agreement that the cognitive map for gender—a gender schema—is developed in somewhat the same way that other cognitive constructs are acquired.

However, developing a cognitive map for *girl* and girl-behaviors is particularly complicated. It entails defining and categorizing *self*, then developing and modifying the social behaviors of the self across the changes age brings, and doing this in relation to other individuals in a shifting social environment.

For the child to learn to use her cognitive map (gender schema) as a framework for self-knowledge and to find her way safely through complex social relationships is a challenge. Mistakes can be made in this process, as every counselor knows, particularly if the child is faced with working out this developmental task in the context of a dysfunctional family. If choosing girl behaviors satisfies the child's need to express authentic gender identity but results in depreciating labels from important adults"girls are stupid," for example), gender development becomes a painful as well as a complex process. It is in this way that the misbeliefs or myths, as we have called them here, can become incorporated into the schema of some of our women clients.

The process of gender acquisition is fascinating as well as complex. A little girl must learn that she is female and that she is a little girl. She must also learn that this is different from being male and being a little boy. If she is logical, and most children are, she will conclude that since she is a little girl, she should do little girl things and must figure out what these are. This requires a high level of discrimination since some little girl things and some little boy things are the same—boys and girls both brush their teeth and both wear boots on a snowy day, for example—and some are not. Kagan, as noted earlier, believes that girls learn at an early age, through modeling, reward, and other complex ways, that taking care of babies is one important distinctive way of being a girl, not a boy. Gender schema theory, reflecting Kagan's point of view, would explain a three-year-old girl's doll play as the child's practice of the supremely important business of being distinctively a girl, rather than the expression of some early biological urge toward motherhood.

Because it is challenging to identify on the gender map what is girl, what is boy, and what is acceptably either girl or boy, children do not welcome any more confusion than is already present in their social world, particularly in the early stages of gender development. Complicated options or confusing alternatives are not helpful. Keeping the emotionally essential task of learning to be a girl simple and consistent becomes a matter of practical good sense as well as social survival for the child. In this way, gender schema helps us understand why young children display highly sex-typed behaviors and are resistant to nonconventional expressions of male/female roles even in those circumstances when modeled by significant adults.

A speaker at a conference I recently attended told an amusing story that illustrates this point. A woman who was a physician overheard her four-year-old daughter explaining to a male playmate that girls were nurses and boys were doctors. "But, Sally," protested the woman, "you know that I am a doctor." "No," retorted her small red-headed expert on gender studies. "I know what you are—you're a mommy."

Sally's gender schema did not yet accommodate girls as doctors, even though her mother as an adult woman modeled that option. This does not mean that Sally's gender schema will not at a later time expand to include women as doctors. In fact, her mother's modeling makes that a strong probability at a relatively early age. However, Sally's gender schema at age four included women as mommies and women as nurses; the inclusion of women as doctors as well was a complication she was unwilling to consider.

Most of us have had an experience that helps us understand this phenomena. Few things in life are more exasperating than to be struggling to master a complicated task and have an instructor say, "But you don't have to do it that way," and then offer another way to do the task. I recently gave a rather firm rejection of an instructor's offer to demonstrate alternative procedures for word processing on my computer. At that moment I just wanted to know *one* way to move a paragraph and be able to do it that way correctly.

For Christians, and for counselors, gender schema theory has an additional broad appeal. It regards the individual's choice as an essential part of the developmental process. Counselors, I think, are particularly aware that a theory adequate to explain human development (women's or men's) must acknowledge the power of choice. Counselors are made aware daily in particularly vivid ways that at many essential points individuals have become who they have chosen to be. A given woman client has no choice about being female; however, she has rich, exciting options available to her in her choice of expressing her identity and role as a woman. Since that is so, as counselors we often puzzle why a woman client has chosen what appears to be a self-destructive pattern, and why, in some instances, she appears unwilling to choose differently.

GENDER SCHEMA: COUNSELING IMPLICATIONS

In my opinion, when the mythology or misbeliefs we discussed earlier become integrated into the woman's gender schema, our women clients experience a limitation in choice somewhat like Sally's. The misbeliefs integrated into the gender schema prevent them from choosing differently regardless of the alternatives modeled for them or the options the counselor may help them identify. If the counselor helps the woman client identify an option that is not on her gender map, then no matter how reasonable it may appear to the counselor, it is not an option to the client.

For example, as counselors we may suggest to an exhausted woman client that she set some appropriate limits upon her efforts to care for others. However, we cannot expect the client to be able or willing to comply if her gender schema for good woman continues to require that she exhibit unlimited, uncompensated acts of caring.

How do women develop their sense of gender identity and gender-role? Gender schema theory presently appears to provide the most helpful explanation: a complex, lifelong interaction between biological and cognitive processes that produces culturally prescribed patterns of behavior, learned through complex social interaction.

The good news is, of course, that change in dysfunctional concepts can occur. The bad news, as counselors know all too well, is that change often comes only after long, difficult therapeutic struggle to alter the woman's deepest sense of self.

Gender schema also changes naturally across the individual's normal life-span. The gender schema that a woman holds as a map for herself at eighteen will differ markedly from the one she holds for herself as a woman at eighty.

The crucial point therapeutically and developmentally, however, is the counselor's awareness of the importance and content of the gender schema of the client. Counselors cannot attempt to elicit a response that is marked "undesirable" or "inappropriate" on the client's gender map and have any hope for successful intervention. In many instances the counselor's first task is to help the client understand, evaluate, and, where desired and/or necessary, alter her gender map. Healing is impossible in those instances in which the gender schema requires repetition of the old wound.

DEVELOPMENTAL THEORIES: THE DIFFERENT VOICE

Currently, one of the most debated theories of women's development focuses upon women as distinctly different from men in their life process. This approach proposes that the core of this difference lies in developmental processes for women that center around attachment and affiliation with others. This female pattern is viewed as contrasting sharply with the developmental processes of separation and independence commonly presumed to be central for males. These processes of attachment and affiliation produce throughout women's life span gender-specific patterns of living and relationships, and a gender-distinctive world view, the "different voice," as Gilligan has identified it.[38]

In 1976 in *Toward a New Psychology of Women*, Jean Baker Miller expressed this new approach to studying women.[39] She challenged common wisdom regarding women on a number of important points. Miller began her developmental model by viewing women in a biosocial context. Women's development, Miller argued, cannot be understood apart from recognition that women live out their lives as the subordinate or the unequal ones. While Miller believes that this social context for women's development can and should be changed, she believes that we must begin studying women by recognizing women's present social reality—to be born female is to be assigned to the gender-role of the subordinate, unequal one.

Women's experience of inequality is unique, however, according to Miller; while subordinate and unequal, women have simultaneously played a crucial, irreplaceable role. They have been "entwined with men in intimate and intense relationships, creating the milieu—the family—in which the human mind as we know it has been formed."[40] Further, in the culture at large, as well as in the family, women are the designated servers, those whose life task is serving others' needs, doing for others, functioning as the essential caretakers without whose service society in its present form cannot survive.[41]

In Miller's view, the problem is not the serving process itself. "Obviously people have to serve each others' needs, since human beings have needs. Who will serve them if not other people?" Miller asks. Neither does the problem lie in *women* serving. From Miller's view, the problem lies in women as *uniquely designated* servers, those expected to meet the needs of others as if they had no needs of their own, or assigned to serve others' needs because "it is the 'only thing women are good for.'"[42]

This powerful social context of subordination and service, argues Miller, shapes women's developmental paths in a way which contrasts sharply with men's.

The second unique aspect of women's development, according to Miller, stems from the fact that women develop a sense of self by a quite different process than do men. Granting that women are shut out of the male experience, Miller believes nevertheless that:

> . . . women's development *is* proceeding, but on another basis. One central feature is that women stay with, build on, and develop in a context of connections with others. Indeed, women's sense of self becomes very much organized around being able to make and then to maintain affiliations and relationships. Eventually, for many women, the threat of disruption of connections is perceived not as just a loss of relationships but as something closer to a total loss of self.[43]

Building on connections with others, according to Miller, leads not only to a distinctive development of the self but to women's distinctive patterns of living and relational functioning in which affiliation is valued as highly as, or more highly than, self-enhancement or power.[44]

In Miller's opinion, the developmental patterns of women are not only foreign to male development, such patterns are seen as weak and inexplicable to the male whose developmental pathway has focused upon separation, domination, and power. Miller believes that men, nevertheless, remain concerned about relationships and have deep yearnings for affiliation. Consequently, she thinks that study and understanding of women's relational patterns hold promise not only for women but also for men in developing new patterns of connection and community. There are, of course, aspects of relationship that are of particular value to Christians.[45]

The developmental pathway that women follow produces certain challenges for women, in Miller's view. Women need to learn to maintain their life organization around relationships but to do so from a position of cooperative equality rather than subordination. Therapists need to assist women in working out issues of creativity, authenticity, self-determination, and power, including the necessity for engaging in conflict in relationship. Relationship at the cost of identity, self-respect, and justice has little more appeal to Miller than to Van Leeuwen.[46] However, in Miller's view, therapists need to help women accomplish these tasks within the context of their distinctive pattern of developmental processes. For women to seek to become men, or like men, seems a disastrous alternative to Miller.[47]

Miller and her colleagues have produced a steady stream of studies based on this concept of women's development.[48] The basic developmental model growing out of the Stone Center studies has been described by Miller[49] and by Janet Surrey.[50]

Surrey begins with the basic premise common to the Stone Center studies—the idea that for women the self is organized and developed in the context of affiliation and relationships, rather than in separation and individuation:

> The values of individuation have permeated our cultural ideals as well as our clinical theories and practice. In psychological theory the concepts and descriptions of relationship appear to be cast in this model, and much of current theory wrestles with the problem of developing a model of "object relations" from a basic assumption of narcissism and human separateness. The notion of the self-in-relation makes an important shift in emphasis from separation to relationship as the basis for self-experience and development. Further, relationship is seen as the basic goal of development, i.e., the deepening capacity for relationship and relational competence.[51]

In this theory of relational development, empathy is a central process and the mother-daughter relationship serves as a model of the self-in-relation developmental pathway. Additional processes such as mutual empowerment, reciprocity, and resulting mutual self-esteem are also essential aspects of development. "Continuity, the holding of the other as part of the self," is viewed as a basic component of all authentic relationships.[52]

Starting from the premise of the centrality of relationship to women's development, Stone Center studies regard processes of mutuality, empathy, and maintenance of self boundaries as having special significance for women.[53]

Anger and power are believed to assume distinctive importance for women in the context of their relational development. Relational competence becomes an essential developmental goal.[54] Given the essential function of relationships to self, violence within intimate relationships is viewed as posing particularly problematic issues for women.[55]

While the self-in-relation premise raises some exciting possibilities for understanding women's development, it also raises some questions of particular interest to counselors. In the self-in-relation developmental pathway, what is the significance of work and achievement for women?[56] In the processes of mutual empowerment and empathy, how are we to understand women's experiences of guilt, envy, and shame?[57] Some aspects of the self-in-relation theory presently being applied to women appear to have potential significance for men and for men and women in relationship.[58] Some initial effort has been made to deal with these questions, but theoretical work and collection of clinical data is still in early stages.

Effort has also been made to consider the implications of this relational developmental model for therapy with women. Given that women's adult reality is the outgrowth of a developmental history of self-in-relation, for optimal effectiveness the therapeutic relationship needs to reflect this fact.[59]

Women's developmental history also will interact with the gender of the therapist—male or female[60]—and this needs to be recognized as one factor in the client therapist relationship.

Others have also proposed a developmental model for women emphasizing gender differences. Chodorow analyzed differences in the maternal relationship experienced by sons and daughters and proposed that differences in the separation processes for boys and girls accounted for many of the differences in the behaviors of adult women and men.[61]

Little girls have it easier, at least in the short run, according to Chodorow. Since the primary caretaker (mother) provides a same-sex model, little girls need not separate from this powerful caregiver with the same intensity and defensiveness required of their opposite-sex brothers. (In adolescence and early adulthood, however, it becomes more difficult for girls to establish a separate identity from their mothers; boys, of necessity, are further along with this task.) In women, this distinctive pattern of connection with the same-sexed parent results in a lifelong concern with relationships, with both the costs and benefits such an orientation provides.

Chodorow's explanations of this process place her firmly in the psychoanalytic camp. Nevertheless, she argues for an account of gender differences that, while rooted in sexual differences, is shaped and perpetuated primarily by the social processes of parenting rather than by biology. Chodorow analyzes these social forces in economic terms. For example, in a section subtitled "Mothering, Masculinity, and Capitalism" she notes:

> An increasingly father-absent, mother-involved family produces in men a personality that both corresponds to masculinity and male dominance as these are currently constituted in the sex-gender system, and fits appropriately with participation in capitalist relations of production. Men continue to enforce the sexual division of spheres as a defense against powerlessness in the labor market. . . . Women's and men's personality traits and orientations mesh with the sexual and familial division of labor . . . and shape . . . a structure of production and reproduction in which women are in the first instance mothers and wives and men are workers.[62]

Carol Gilligan is well-known for her focus on women's distinctive life patterns. In Kohlberg's study of moral development, women tended to be stuck at stage three, making decisions on the basis of pleasing and helping others, rather than on the basis of abstract rights and universal impersonal principles. This behavior earned women low marks on Kohlberg's scale and resulted in his judgment that women were developmentally backward in moral reasoning.

Kohlberg's scale was developed in a study using all male subjects. Gilligan, a former student of Kohlberg, undertook study of women's moral reasoning and came to a quite different conclusion.[63] Women reason differently than men about moral issues, Gilligan argued. Women are equally morally competent, but they operate out of a different priority system than do men in making moral judgments and formulating life choices. Women do indeed reach moral maturity, but as women they think and speak to moral issues in a distinctive way. The moral reasoning of men, according to Kohlberg, centers around application of impersonal universal principles. The moral reasoning of women, according to Gilligan, centers around responsibility and conflicting human relationships.

Given that women's reality centers around experiences of attachment and affiliation, their sense of integrity becomes entwined with an ethic of care and responsibility, expressed over their life span. In Gilligan's view, men are centered in separation and achievement; they operate out of an ethic of justice that reflects the priority that everyone should be treated the same. Women, in contrast, operate out of an ethic of care that reflects their contrasting priority that no one should be hurt. From Gilligan's view, the developmental path for women, from late adolescence to old age, is shaped by their embeddedness in lives of relationship; women's major transitions (i.e. midlife, old age) entail alterations in their understanding and activities of care.[64] Gilligan is a prolific writer.[65] Her ideas have far-reaching implications, many with rich potential value for those seeking to build a concept of women's development consistent with science and a biblical world view.[66]

Gilligan's idea that women and men possess different moral sensibilities has evoked serious criticism. Some critics have focused on the potential for Gilligan's work to support continuing stereotypical responses and further discrimination in the workplace and in society at large. Gilligan herself has deplored this use of her work. Gilligan's thinking has also been criticized for her failure to incorporate a broader understanding of women's history and of ethnic issues.

Researchers have not yet established experimental evidence of Gilligan's alleged differences in moral reasoning. A number of researchers have objected to the methodology used both by Gilligan and by her critics. No one is certain about the degree to which other factors, such as personality, socialization, and personal consequences of the given choice may interact with gender to produce such differences (if they do in fact exist).

Despite serious differences of opinion regarding Gilligan's thesis, her idea about gender-biased distinctives in moral decision-making has evoked wide interest and popularity. Many women have an intuitive sense that Gilligan has described their experience accurately. What is not yet clear is the basis of women's experience. If women do in fact operate out of an ethic of care, it has not yet been established by Gilligan or by others if this alleged orientation rests on a woman's biology, her gender, or, as now appears probable, a complex interactive effect between the two.

Gilligan's most recent work deals with the alleged turning point in self-esteem adolescent girls experience.[67] According to Gilligan and her co-workers, in their midteens girls experience a crisis in self-confidence with a resulting sharp downturn in self-esteem, associated with their inner conflict when faced with simultaneously caring for others and exerting responsible care of themselves. A survey of elementary and secondary students released in 1991 by the American Association of University Women corroborates Gilligan's findings and indicates that adolescent girls experience genuine, substantial drops in self-esteem that far outpace those reported by boys.[68]

Miller, Surrey, Gilligan, and others have argued persuasively that the distinctive female developmental path is characterized by relational embeddedness. Does this then mean that at the threshold of adulthood girls experience such conflict within an achievement, performance-oriented culture that they enter adulthood with a significantly impaired sense of self-worth? If the identity crisis in the female developmental path is indeed formed in this fashion, what are the implications of this conflict for teenage pregnancy, for women's confidence in their academic abilities, and for their performances in math and science? What is the relationship of this early trauma to women's traditionally higher rates of depression? It appears probable that as we begin to investigate women's experience *as women*, and their distinctive developmental cycle, information about gender and sex will bring both new questions and new answers to old ones.[69]

Such developmental study is also likely to bring renewed awareness of human variability. A recent longitudinal study looked for significant differences within a group of women in the ways they developed values, formed relationships, reared children, and managed work.[70] This study identified four divergent pathways among this group of women, each with its distinctive choices, challenges, and struggles. Stories of ordinary women form the basis of this study and remind us graphically that a viable model for women's development must make provision for a wide range of individual differences. It must also provide for new definition of life tasks and developmental stages that are gender congruent for women. For example, to limit generativity to a late adult task as does Erikson's model, makes no sense at all in understanding women.[71]

SEX, GENDER, AND DEVELOPMENT: AN OVERVIEW

What are the sex-distinctive, gendered behaviors that emerge in women and men over the developmental life span? One writer has suggested that the studies on sex and gender published in the 1970s would make a stack six feet high.[72] Additional studies published in the 1980s would likely add another stack of comparable height.

Table 2 indicates the general conclusions about which there is currently a reasonably strong consensus.[73]

With the general conclusions from this large mass of materials organized in this fashion, it is easy to see that there are fewer established differences between males and females than are commonly supposed. Those differences most reliably identified as arising in the developmental cycle are those most

Table 2
SUMMARY OF GENDER COMPARISONS

PHYSICAL

Anatomy: Females have a uterus, ovaries, a clitoris, and a vagina. Males have testes, a penis, and a scrotum. Males tend to be bigger and more muscular.

Processes: Females mature faster, have slower metabolism. Differences in sensation are unclear; females may be more sensitive to touch, pain, and visual stimuli. Hormonal production is cyclic in females after puberty (ovulation and menstruation); it is mostly continuous in males.[1]

Brain organization: Females may have greater hemispheric flexibility.[2]

Vulnerability: Males are more vulnerable to disease, physical disorders, and early death.

Activity level: No differences in the amount of activity, although differences in type of movements and activities are found.

COGNITIVE

Learning and memory: No differences.

Intelligence: No difference in level of intelligence.

Verbal: Females tend to excel up to age three and after age eleven.[3]
   Quantitative—males tend to excel after age twelve.
   Visual-spatial—Males tend to excel after age eight.[4]
   Analytic—No difference.

Concept mastery: No difference.

Cognitive style: Differences are unclear.

Creativity: No difference with nonverbal material; females tend to excel with verbal material.

PERSONALITY AND TEMPERAMENT

Self-description: Females are more people-oriented; males are more achievement-oriented.

Emotionality: No difference during childhood.

Fears: The evidence is contradictory; females report more fears.

SOCIAL BEHAVIOR

Communication patterns:
   Verbal—Males dominate; depends on situational and sex-typing factors.
   Nonverbal—Males dominate; females may be more sensitive to cues; depends on situational factors.

PERSON-CENTERED INTERACTIONS

Dependency: Depends on the definition used and situational factors.

Affiliation: No difference during childhood. After adolescence, females tend to be more interested in people.

Empathy: Depends on situational and sex-typing factors.

Nurturance: Depends on experience, situational, and sex-typing factors.

Altruism: Depends on situational and sex-typing factors.

Morality: Females seem more concerned with "responsibilities," males with "rights."

Equity/equality: Males seem more concerned with equity, females with equality.

POWER-CENTERED INTERACTIONS

Aggression: Males tend to be more physically aggressive after age two; depends on definitions used and situational factors.

Assertiveness: Depends on situational and sex-typing factors.

Dominance: Depends on situational and definitional factors.

Competition/cooperation: Depends on situational and sex-typing factors.

Compliance: Depends on situational and sex-typing factors.

SEXUAL BEHAVIOR

Response: No difference; females are capable of multiple orgasms.

Interest: Males express more and have more experiences. Meaning of sex may be different for the two sexes.

Response to erotica: No difference.

Homosexuality: Reported more in males.

Masturbation: Reported more in males.

SOURCE: Susan Basow, *Gender Stereotypes: Tradition and Alternatives,* 2nd ed. (Pacific Grove, Calif.: Brooks/Cole, 1986), 94–95. Used with permission.

1. The work of Kimura and others on hormonal fluctuation in males makes this conclusion presently less certain than it was once assumed to be.

2. This conclusion requires cautious understanding and application. See D. Kimura, "Are Men's and Women's Brains Really Different?" *Canadian Psychology* 28 (1987): 133–47.

3. Caution is indicated here as well. See J. S. Hyde and M. C. Linn, "Gender Differences in Verbal Ability: A Meta-Analysis," *Psychological Bulletin* 104, no. 1 (1988): 53–69.

4. Again, caution is indicated. See P. J. Caplan, G. M. MacPherson, and P. Tobin, "Do Sex-Related Differences in Spatial Abilities Exist?" *American Psychologist* 40, no.7 (1985): 786–99. See also M. C. Linn and A. C. Petersen, "Emergence and Characterization of Sex Differences in Spatial Ability: A Meta-Analysis," *Child Development* 56 (1985): 1479–98.

strongly influenced by biological factors. Understanding what this means, however, requires careful thinking.

It is necessary, as always, to keep in mind the ever present reality of the confounded nature of the sex/gender variables and, further, to distinguish carefully throughout the developmental cycle between the power of biology to influence in contrast to its power to control. For example, for a woman, biology controls menstruation and influences aggression (to what degree and in what ways we are not sure), but it has only an indirect correlational relationship to speech patterns. It is a fact that in this culture women develop patterns of weak verbal communication, including use of tag questions, avoidance of certain slang terms, along with higher levels of listening and disclosure of intimate information than are found in the speech patterns of males.[74] There is a high correlation between femaleness (biology) and this pattern of verbal communication (gendered speech). Most if not all females do in fact learn to speak in this way. There are severe social repercussions if they do not. However, it is a serious misreading of the facts to assume that the femaleness (biology) causes or controls the gendered speech. This is only one example of the wide range of gendered behaviors that most females learn in which biology is a correlate but clearly not a cause.

Keeping this distinction in mind, Table 2 presents a helpful summary of the large amounts of information provided by studies undertaken for the most part in the experimental tradition. Conclusions regarding verbal skills, visual-spatial skills, and hormonal variation in males should be held cautiously, however. As noted, current ongoing studies are raising questions at these points.

When on the basis of this information we say that there are very few clearly established differences between males and females, *this does not mean that men and women do not act differently.* Neither does it prove that efforts should be undertaken either to enhance or to extinguish differences. Such a value judgment falls more properly into the domain of theology or philosophy, not science; such issues must be approached consciously by counselors with great care. The conclusion, "Few clearly established differences between males and females," means that in those ways in which men and women do in fact think, feel, and behave differently, there are relatively few of these differences that are compelled or controlled by the biological identity of the individual.

For example, notice in the summary chart the number of points at which differences or similarities are marked as, "Depends. . . ." In those cases the determining factor is related to self-reporting, sex-typing, definitions, or social situations rather than biology. Notice too that "depends . . ." occurs most frequently in those categories dealing with personality, interpersonal interactions, and social behaviors. What this means, in effect, is that women and men are likely to demonstrate many differences, some of which may vary widely, but the greatest proportion of these differences, while they may be biologically influenced, are clearly socially controlled.

The implications of this for the counselor are highly significant. As noted in our description of women's stories,[75] the most common problems women bring to therapy are problems in living and relationships, along with depression and anxiety.[76] Women struggle with their lives *as women*, with their woman's sense of self and worth, relationships, social tensions and conflicts, roles, and expectations (personal and group). It is, in most instances, not her biology but her gender—including at times her assigned role within the church community—that brings a woman client to counseling. This fact does not make counseling easier, but it does aid us in clarifying the focus of our efforts as we seek to bring about healing and change.

For the counselor working in a religious community in which women are socialized into strong belief in traditional gendered behavior and roles, it is important to realize that for these women gender issues are enmeshed in issues of faith in ways that provide consistent challenge to the counselor's sensitivity, integrity, and skill. It reminds us again that behavior—and human pain—is a product not just of the individual but of the individual in interaction with the world in which she lives. Presently, the world in which women are working out their lives as women is a world marked by transition and dramatic change.

NOTES

1. For a chilling description of the fate of battered women in the judicial system, see Lenore E. Walker, *Terrifying Love* (New York: Harper and Row, 1989).

2. Gail Sheehy, *Passages: Predictable Crises of Adult Life* (New York: Dutton, 1974).

3. D. J. Levinson et al., *The Seasons of a Man's Life* (New York: Knopf, 1978); R. L. Gould, *Transformation: Growth and Change in Adult Life* (New York: Simon and Schuster, 1978); G. Vaillant, *Adaptation to Life* (Boston: Little, Brown and Co., 1977); all are major studies that provide helpful information regarding men but give us little if any information regarding women's adult life span history.

4. A particularly helpful presentation of this issue is found in Mary Roth Walsh, ed., *The Psychology of Women: Ongoing Debates* (New Haven, Conn.: York University Press, 1987), 127–46. This section, "Question 4: Are Menstruating Women at the Mercy of Raging Hormones?" includes a brief paper by Walsh defining the issue; a paper by Katharina Dalton arguing for the biological basis and reality of PMS, and a paper by Randi Koeske, Research Psychologist at the University of Pittsburgh, reviewing the available research and examining the highly doubtful assumptions that currently form the common wisdom regarding PMS. Substantial bibliographies of relevant studies accompany each paper and make this a particularly useful reference.

5. P. B. Baltes, "Life-span Developmental Psychology: Some Converging Observations on History and Theory," in *Life-Span Development and Behavior*, ed. P. B. Baltes and O. G. Brim, vol. 2 (New York: Academic Press, 1979).

6. B. L. Neugarten, "Summary and Implication," in *Personality in Middle and Late Life,* ed. B. L. Neugarten et al. (New York: Atherton, 1964). See also B. L. Neugarten, "A New Look at Menopause," in *The Female Experience*, ed. C. Tavris (Del Mar, Calif.: Communications/Research/Machines, 1973), and B. L. Neugarten, ed., *Middle Age and Aging* (Chicago: University of Chicago Press, 1968).

7. L. Kohlberg, "The Development of Children's Orientation Toward a Moral Order: I. Sequences in the Development of Human Thought," *Vita Humana* 6 (1963): 11–33. L. Kohlberg, *The Philosophy of Moral Development: Moral Stages and the Idea of Justice: Essays on Moral Development* 1 (San Francisco: Harper and Row, 1981). L. Kohlberg, *The Psychology of Moral Development: Moral Stages and the Idea of Justice: Essays on Moral Development* 2 (San Francisco: Harper and Row, 1984).

8. In addition to women, others who were not represented in Kohlberg's original group have also scored at lower levels on his (presumably) universal stages. See Constance Halstein, "Development of Moral Judgement: A Longitudinal Study of Males and Females," *Child Development* 47 (1976): 51–56; Carolyn P. Edwards, "Societal Complexity and Moral Development: A Kenyan Study," *Ethos* 3 (1975): 505–27; and Elizabeth L. Simpson, "Moral

Development Research: A Case Study of Scientific Cultural Bias," *Human Development* 17 (1974): 81–106. See also "Woman's Place in Man's Life Cycle," in Carol Gilligan, *In A Different Voice* (Cambridge, Mass.: Harvard University Press, 1982), 5–23.

9. As noted earlier, the work of John Money remains definitive in this area. See J. Money and A. Ehrhardt, *Man and Woman, Boy and Girl* (Baltimore: Johns Hopkins Press, 1972). See also J. Money and P. Tucker, *Sexual Signatures: On Being a Man or a Woman* (Boston: Little, Brown and Co., 1975), and J. Money, *Love and Love Sickness: The Science of Sex, Gender Difference and Pair Bonding* (Baltimore: Johns Hopkins Press, 1980). A helpful overview is found in J. Money and C. Wiedeking, "Gender Identity/Role: Normal Differentiation and Its Transpositions," in *Handbook of Human Sexuality*, ed. B. Wolman and J. Money (Englewood Cliffs, N.J.: Prentice Hall, 1980), 268–84.

10. See, for example, Boston Women's Health Collective, *The New Our Bodies, Our Selves* (New York: Simon and Schuster, 1984). This book is clear and explicit, and deals in very direct language with the menstrual process and the questions that even experienced women may have. Another very helpful book for women and their counselors is Wulf Utian, *Managing Your Menopause* (Englewood Cliffs, N.J.: Prentice Hall, 1990). For more general body issues, see M. C. Hutchinson, *Transforming Body Image: Learning to Love the Body You Have* (Freedom, Calif.: The Crossing Press, 1985).

11. Juanita H. Williams, *Psychology of Women: Behavior in a Biosocial Context*, 3rd ed. (New York: Norton, 1987), 22.

12. Kathy Fackelmann, "The Safer Sex? Probing a Cardiac Gender Gap," *Science News* 139, no. 3 (January 19, 1991): 40–41. See also Patricia Long, "A Woman's Heart," *In Health* 5, no. 2 (March/April 1991): 52–58.

13. "Our Bodies, Their Selves: Bias Against Women in Health Research," *Newsweek*, 17 December 1990, 60.

14. Mary Lake Polan, "Gender Bias in Medical Research is Putting Women's Health at Risk," *The Denver Post*, 2 March 1991.

15. Leon Kamin, as cited by Mary Stewart Van Leeuwan, *Gender and Grace: Love, Work and Parenting in a Changing World* (Downers Grove, Ill.: InterVarsity, 1990), 18–19.

16. Ruth Bleier, as quoted in Juanita Williams, *Psychology of Women: Behavior in a Biosocial Context*, 3rd ed. (New York: Norton, 1987), 97.

17. Sandra Bem, "Gender Schema Theory and Its Implications for Child Development—Raising Gender-Aschematic Children in a Gender-Schematic Society" *Signs* 8 (1983): 598–616. See also Sandra Bem, "Androgyny and Gender Schema Theory: A Conceptual and Empirical Integration," in *Nebraska Symposium on Motivation, 1984: Psychology and Gender*, ed. T. B. Sonderegger (Lincoln, Neb.: University of Nebraska Press, 1985), 179–226.

18. H. Norman Wright, *Always Daddy's Girl* (Ventura, Calif.: Regal Books, 1989). See also J. A. Bannon and M. L. Southern, "Father-Absent Women: Self-Concept and Modes of Relating to Men," *Sex Roles* 6 (1980): 75–84; H. B. Biller, "The Father and Sex Role Development," in *The Role of the Father in Child Development*, ed. M. Lamb, 2nd ed. (New York: Wiley, 1986); W. H.

McBroom, "Parental Relationships, Socioeconomic Status, and Sex Role Expectations," *Sex Roles* 7 (1981): 1027–33.

19. Eleanor Maccoby, "The Role of Gender Identity and Gender Constancy in Sex-Differentiated Development," *New Directions for Child Development* 47 (Spring 1990): 5–20.

20. Sigmund Freud, "New Introductory Lectures on Psychoanalysis" (1933), as quoted in M. Matlin, *The Psychology of Women* (Fort Worth, Tex.: Holt, Rinehart and Winston, 1987), 47.

21. Williams, 37. Williams provides a useful nontechnical summary of Freudian theory regarding women's development, 34–50.

22. See Hannah Lerman, "From Freud to Feminist Personality Theory: Getting Here from There," *Psychology of Women Quarterly* 10 (1986): 1–18. Lerman's paper is her Presidential Address of the Division of the Psychology of Women presented at the American Psychological Association Convention, August 1985. Lerman suggests eight criteria by which a theory of women's development and personality can be evaluated and analyzes Freud and psychoanalytic theory using these criteria. For fuller development of her analysis of Freudian theory see Hannah Lerman, *A Mote in Freud's Eye: From Psychoanalysis to the Psychology of Women* (New York: Springer, 1986). J. Mitchell, in *Psychoanalysis and Feminism* (New York: Grossman, 1974), provides a balancing argument for the value of psychoanalytic concepts.

23. For a useful summary of Erikson's work on identity formation in terms of his concept of women's development see Williams, 57–70.

24. Erik Erikson, *Childhood and Society*, 2nd ed. (New York: Norton, 1963). Original copyright, 1950.

25. Erik Erikson, "Inner and Outer Space: Reflections on Womanhood," *Daedalus* 93 (1964): 582–606.

26. Erik Erikson, as quoted in Williams, 65.

27. Williams, 63.

28. K. P. Darpoe and R. L. Olney, "The Effect of Boys' or Girls' Toys on Sex-Typed Play in Preadolescents," *Sex Roles* 9 (1983): 507–18.

29. B. E. Budd, P. R. Clance, and D. E. Simerly, "Spatial Configurations: Erikson Reexamined," *Sex Roles* 12 (1985): 571–77.

30. Susan Basow, *Gender Stereotypes: Traditions and Alternatives*, 2nd ed. (Pacific Grove, Calif.: Brooks/Cole, 1986), 111.

31. This is, of course, one more example of Maccoby's point regarding the significance of social context in evaluating gendered behavior. See Eleanor Maccoby, "Gender and Relationships: A Developmental Account," *American Psychologist* 45, no. 4 (April 1990): 513–20.

32. Jerome Kagan as quoted in Laura Shapiro, "Guns and Dolls," *Newsweek*, 22 May 1990, 81.

33. E. H. Erikson, "Once More the Inner Space," in *Life History and the Historical Moment* (New York: Norton, 1975).

34. L. Kohlberg, "A Cognitive-Developmental Analysis of Children's Sex-Role Concepts and Attitudes," in *The Development of Sex Differences*, ed. E. E. Maccoby (Stanford, Calif.: Stanford University Press, 1966).

35. Maccoby, "The Role of Gender Identity," 5–20.

36. The following discussion is heavily indebted to Maccoby's analysis of Kohlberg's paper in Maccoby, ibid.

37. See, for example, Sandra Bem, "Gender Schema Theory: A Cognitive Account of Sex Typing," *Psychological Review* 88 (1981): 354–64. See also Bem, "Androgyny and Gender Schema Theory." For a nontechnical description of gender schema theory, see Matlin, *The Psychology of Women*, 53–56.

38. For an early presentation of Gilligan's position see Carol Gilligan, "In a Different Voice: Women's Conceptions of Self and Morality," *Harvard Educational Review* 47 (1977): 481–517. For her more fully developed work see Carol Gilligan, *In a Different Voice: Psychological Theory and Women's Development* (Cambridge, Mass.: Harvard University Press, 1982).

39. Jean Baker Miller, *Toward a New Psychology of Women* (Boston: Beacon Press, 1976). A second edition was issued in1986.

40. Miller, *New Psychology*, 2nd ed., 1.

41. Ibid., 61–80.

42. Ibid., 61–62.

43. Ibid., 83.

44. Ibid., 83–97.

45. Jean Baker Miller, "The Development of Women's Sense of Self," *Work in Progress*, no. 12 (Wellesley, Mass.: Stone Center, 1984).

46. Van Leeuwen, 44–48.

47. Miller, *New Psychology*, 2nd ed., x–xi, 81–140.

48. Miller is affiliated with the Stone Center for Developmental Services and Studies, Wellesley College. Principal participating scholars, Jean Baker Miller, June Jordan, Janet Surrey, Alexandra Kaplan, and Irene Stiver, also hold a variety of professional appointments at institutions such as Boston University School of Medicine, Harvard Medical School, and its affiliated teaching hospital, McLean Hospital, as well as appointments at the Stone Center and Wellesley College. Visiting researchers and scholars have made significant contributions; however, the work of Miller, Jordan, Surrey, Kaplan, and Stiver has provided the core of the theoretical, clinical material underpinning this developmental model. Information and a list of the Stone Center Working Papers may be obtained by writing to the Editor, *Work in Progress*, Stone Center, Wellesley College, Wellesley, MA 02181.

49. Miller, "The Development of Women's Sense of Self."

50. Janet L. Surrey, "Self-in-Relation: A Theory of Women's Development," *Work in Progress*, no. 13 (Wellesley, Mass.: Stone Center, 1985).

51. Ibid., 2. See also the current review of the model the Jean Baker Miller et al., "Some Misconceptions and Reconceptions of a Relational Approach," *Work in Progress*, no. 49 (Wellesley, Mass.: Stone Center, 1991).

52. Ibid. See also Janet Surrey, "Relationship and Empowerment," *Work in Progress*, no. 30 (Wellesley, Mass.: Stone Center, 1987).

53. Judith Jordan, "The Meaning of Mutuality," *Work in Progress*, no. 23 (Wellesley, Mass.: Stone Center, 1986). Judith Jordan, Alexandra Kaplan, and

Janet Surrey, "Empathy Revisited," *Work in Progress*, no. 40 (Wellesley, Mass.: Stone Center, 1990). Judith Jordan, "Empathy and Self Boundaries," *Work in Progress*, no. 16 (Wellesley, Mass.: Stone Center, 1984).

54. Jean Baker Miller, "The Construction of Anger in Women and Men," *Work in Progress*, no. 4 (Wellesley, Mass.: Stone Center, 1983). Teresa Bernardez, "Women and Anger—Cultural Prohibitions and the Feminine Ideal," *Work in Progress*, no. 31 (Wellesley, Mass.: Stone Center, 1988); Jean Baker Miller, "Women and Power: Some Psychological Dimensions," *Work in Progress*, no. 1 (Wellesley, Mass.: Stone Center, 1982). Jean Baker Miller, "What Do We Mean by Relationships?" *Work in Progress*, no. 22 (Wellesley, Mass.: Stone Center, 1986). Jean Baker Miller, "Connections, Disconnections and Violations," *Work in Progress*, no. 33 (Wellesley, Mass.: Stone Center, 1988).

55. Carolyn Swift, "Women and Violence: Breaking the Connection," *Work in Progress*, no. 27 (Wellesley, Mass.: Stone Center, 1987).

56. Irene Stiver, "Work Inhibitions in Women: Clinical Considerations, " *Work in Progress*, no. 3 (Wellesley, Mass.: Stone Center, 1983); Brunetta Wolfman, "Women and Their Many Roles," *Work in Progress*, no. 7 (Wellesley, Mass.: Stone Center, 1984).

57. Judith Jordan, "Relational Development: Therapeutic Implications of Empathy and Shame," *Work in Progress*, no. 39 (Wellesley, Mass.: Stone Center, 1989).

58. Stephen Bergman, "Men's Psychological Development: A Relational Perspective," *Work in Progress*, no. 48 (Wellesley, Mass.: Stone Center, 1991).

59. Alexandra Kaplan, "Dichotomous Thought and Relational Processes in Therapy," *Work in Progress*, no. 35 (Wellesley, Mass.: Stone Center, 1988).

60. Alexandra Kaplan, "Female or Male Therapists for Women: New Formulations," *Work in Progress*, no. 5 (Wellesley, Mass.: Stone Center, 1984).

61. Nancy Chodorow, *The Reproduction of Mothering: Psychoanalysis and the Sociology of Gender* (Berkeley, Calif.: University of California Press, 1978).

62. Ibid., 190.

63. Gilligan, *In a Different Voice*. See also Carol Gilligan, "Remapping the Moral Domain: New Images of the Self in Relationship," in *Mapping the Moral Domain*, ed. C. Gilligan, J. V. Ward, and J. M. Taylor (Cambridge, Mass.: Harvard University Press, 1988), 3–19; Carol Gilligan, "Moral Orientation and Moral Development," in *Women and Moral Theory*, ed. E. F. Kittay and D. T. Meyers (Savage, Md.: Rowman and Littlefield, 1987).

64. Gilligan, *Different Voice*, 174.

65. Gilligan and her associates have produced a series of books and papers through the Center for the Study of Gender, Education, and Human Development. Information and materials can be secured by writing to the Study Center, Harvard Graduate School of Education, 503 Larsen Hall, 14 Appian Way, Cambridge, MA 02138.

66. Mary Stewart Van Leeuwen, "The Female Reconstructs Psychology," *Journal of Psychology and Christianity* 3, no. 2 (Summer 1984): 20–32.

67. Carol Gilligan, *Making Connections: The Relational Worlds of Adolescent Girls at Emma Willard School* (Cambridge, Mass.: Harvard University Press, 1990).

68. Bruce Bower,"Teenage Turning Points," *Science News* (March 23, 1991), 184–86.

69. Emily Hancock, a former student of Gilligan's, has reported a study of twenty women in which this turning point in adolescent identity is examined. See Emily Hancock, *The Girl Within* (New York: Ballantine Books, 1989).

70. Ruthellen Josselson, *Finding Herself: Pathways to Identity Development in Women* (San Francisco: Jossey-Bass, 1987).

71. See Jean Baker Miller, "The Development of Women's Sense of Self," *Work in Progress*, no. 2 (Wellesley, Mass.: Stone Center, 1984), for a careful analysis of the limitations of Erikson's model in explaining women's growth. See also Mary E. Boyce, "Female Psychosocial Development: A Model and Implications for Counselors and Educators," *Counseling and Human Development*, no. 6 (February 1985): 1–12, for a model that views generativity as a continuous aspect of a female's life, a process much larger than reproduction, although childbearing is an expression of it. S. Conarton and L. K. Silverman, "Feminine Development through the Life Cycle," in *Feminist Psychotherapies: Integration of Therapeutic and Feminist Systems*, ed. M. A. Douglas and L. E. Walker (Norwood, N.J.: Ablex, 1989), 37–67, propose an eight-stage theory for women which includes spiritual development, although their definition of spiritual development would not be acceptable to many Christian counselors. Conarton and Silverman also give specific attention to the unique developmental problems encountered by gifted women.

72. Cullen Murphy, "Men and Women: How Different Are They?" *The Saturday Evening Post* (October 1983), 211–15 (quote from 211).

73. Susan Basow, *Gender Stereotypes: Traditions and Alternatives*, 2nd ed. (Pacific Grove, Calif.: Brooks/Cole, 1986), 94–95.

74. Barrie Thorne, Cheris Kramarae, and Nancy Henley, "Language, Gender and Society: Opening a Second Decade of Research," in *Language, Gender and Society*, ed. B. Thorne, C. Kramarae, and N. Henley (Rowley, Mass.: Newbury House, 1983), 7–24. Also D. Tannen, *That's Not What I Meant: How Conversational Style Makes or Breaks Your Relations with Others* (New York: Morrow, 1986); D. Tannen, *You Don't Understand: Women and Men in Conversation* (New York: Ballantine Books, 1990).

75. See chapter 1, page 8–10.

76. Rachael T. Hare-Mustin, "An Appraisal of the Relationship Between Women and Psychotherapy: 80 Years After the Case of Dora," *American Psychologist* 38 (May 1983): 593–601.

Chapter Eight

Women in Transition

E‌LIZABETH ARRIVED FOR HER APPOINTMENT carrying two heavily loaded shopping bags. "Today is show-and-tell," she told me, spreading out on the desk and table a gallery of pictures showing five generations of women from whom her life had sprung.

The personal history of some of the women had been lost. Like other generations before them, some of these women were identified in family genealogy only as wives of designated men and mothers of their children. There were other women, however, whose names and stories had survived.

There was Sarah, who as a young widow had chosen to stay on a Nebraska homestead, working the land, and somehow feeding and clothing seven children, all of whom survived to adulthood. There was Liza (an earlier Elizabeth), who had died in childbirth with her ninth child. Then there was Lucy, who in a great family scandal had defied her father and run away to live with her aunt (her mother's sister). The dispute, of all things, was over Lucy's determination to finish high school. Another story about Lucy reported that in her old age she had again made a family scandal: she had publicly demonstrated for women's right to vote.

And there was Hannah, who had been beaten first by her alcoholic father and then by the brutal husband whom she had run away to marry at age sixteen. Katherine, Elizabeth's grandmother, knew the end of this dark and hidden family story: Hannah had killed herself soon after her last daughter left home. The tragedy had been hushed up by her family, embarrassed by the presumed disgrace.

There was Julia, whose branch of the family had moved west to California during the Great Depression. Julia was a teacher and the first woman in the family to initiate a divorce and enter a second marriage. There was Ruth, who had been an Army nurse and was decorated for bravery. There was Mary, who had married happily the week of her high school graduation. Mary's recipes were family treasures; her quilts and roses had won ribbons at the fair. And there was Leona, Elizabeth's mother, who had finished college, then went to work in the family bank. She had delayed marriage and family until late in her thirties—the first woman in the family to follow this pattern—and continued throughout her adult life to work, retiring at seventy as the bank's vice president.

Elizabeth and I sat, looking at the faces of these women, sharing their histories, wondering aloud about the unremembered stories lost to us. Then, after a while, Elizabeth leaned forward and moved her picture, making a wider space between the picture of herself and her mother. Sensing the question I was thinking, Elizabeth smiled.

"Now don't make this into some Freudian statement of oedipal issues," she said. "It's just that sitting here thinking about all of them, they seem close—yet—somehow—my world seems so different, to have moved so far away."

As this century draws to a close, many women are like Elizabeth—aware in new ways of their identification as women and their connections as women, but aware also of the world of change in which they, their mothers, their daughters, and their granddaughters are living out their lives.

As Elizabeth and I looked at the pictures of those women who had lived before her, we could see some common threads that bound their lives and ours. We were a long line of women, struggling as women with relationships—friendships, marriage, family—struggling with issues—civil rights, domestic violence, education, work—and struggling with a world in dizzying transition. It is indeed a long way from the Homestead Act to the Nineteenth Amendment to Title VII; from death in childbirth, to the pill, to Roe vs. Wade; from high-buttoned shoes to Nikes; from high school diplomas to M.B.A.s and Ph.D.s; from campfires and Indians to microwaves and muggers.

Most women recognize that change is an inevitable part of life in every generation. However, like Elizabeth most women sense that there is something particularly significant for them as women in the changes that have occurred since 1940. Contemporary women often respond with strong ambivalence to the transition in their present world. They have good reason to do so. Like the old Roman god Janus, current patterns of change show these women two distinct faces, each of which looks in an opposing direction.

One face of change is change the destroyer. In this guise change brings loss, grief, and the anxiety and disorientation we feel when the old ways of life dissolve. The opposing face of change is change the great creator and transformer. In this guise change brings the hope of new beginnings and the excitement and challenge of new opportunity and new experience.

Counselors see some women who are grieving the loss of old ways and trying to hold fast a world that is slipping away. Counselors see other women who are experiencing the exhilaration, hope, and promise that lie in new opportunities and who are trying to hurry the abolishment of the old restrictions. Most women, however, find themselves confronted by both aspects of change, often simultaneously. In many life experiences—sending the last child to school, passing a fortieth birthday, entering or leaving the labor force, or becoming a grandmother—women often feel strongly both the loss of the old life and anticipation of the new.

To complicate the issue further, many women discover that other individuals with whom they have significant relationships are experiencing change with an emotional focus quite different from their own. Change in a woman's life often means one thing to her and something quite different to another individual with whom her life is closely tied.

For example, one of my clients, Lois, is a wife and mother who recently returned to work. In doing so, she grieved deeply over the loss of the at-home pattern of life she had cherished, and she grieved for the loss her children would feel as well. In contrast Dennis, her husband, felt relief that his economic load was lightened and his opportunity for family time presumably increased. At the same time another client, Helen, also a wife and mother, returned to work. In contrast to Lois, Helen felt the excitement of new experiences and eager anticipation of personal growth. But in this family, Kenneth, Helen's husband, grieved for the traditional life pattern that he had cherished and had now lost. Sharp conflict can arise at those times when one member of a couple is celebrating change and the other is grieving a loss that change has brought.

To borrow Jessie Bernard's apt phrase, in times of transition it is always the best of times for some and the worst of times for others.[1] If as counselors we view individuals' responses to change solely as matters of personal adjustment or interpersonal conflict, we will have missed the emotional impact of transition itself in the lives and relationships of our clients and, for that matter, in our own lives as well.

As counselors dealing with women in transition, it is important to remember that the impact of change falls differentially not only on individuals but also on various segments of women as a population. Age groups, races, ethnic groups, occupations, and, within each of these groups, differing social classes experience times of transition in distinctive ways with differing experiences of benefit or loss. The resulting impact of change upon the mental health of women is, in turn, varied.[2]

The current accelerated forces of social change are producing the best and worst for women in strange mixture. Over the last fifty years, women's worlds have been dramatically and irrevocably altered both for better and for worse. There has been no lack of advisors (women and men) telling women how to feel and behave in this changing world. However, few of these exhortations have proven particularly helpful to women in managing real life. Women continue to feel uncertain about the frustrating mix of gain and loss that they experience and ambivalent about both the opportunities and limitations that change has brought.

However, whether women welcome change or fear it, whether they are prepared to deal with it or deny it, the world of transition in which they now live presents women with sharp dilemmas of choice. In many ways it is a time of exodus in which women must select what to keep and what to leave behind. They must find new ways to integrate old values and learn to build new forms of relationships that retain old strengths and satisfactions. They must develop new patterns of gendered behaviors that express femininity differently but without destructive compromise of the basic distinctives of womanhood.

In such a time of change, deciding what is significant is sometimes confusing. It is not always easy to determine what *new* and *different* mean. While *new* does not invariably mean improvement, *old* does not necessarily embody truth. Many women, particularly evangelical women, are struggling to maintain old values in a world where they often feel that much of the merchandise and most of the price tags have been changed.

In this time of transition, the emotional cost of living for women is high in relation both to the losses and benefits that change has brought. This cost, and the tension and dilemmas of choice women face, is often an important part of the material they bring to the counseling process. For the counselor working with women clients, issues of change and transition appear to cluster around work, education, and family, with the resulting role shifts that have occurred in each.

CHANGE IN THE WORLD OF WORK AND EDUCATION

The question "Do you work?" evokes exasperation from most women. With rare exception, *all* women are working women. There are, however, some questions about women and work that provide a window through which we can see the changing world of women's lives.

WHERE DO WOMEN WORK?

The description of the honored lady in Proverbs 31 indicates that she worked both within the confines of her home and outside her home within the public arena. Having a dual work setting is not something new for women. However, when we ask the question "Where do women work?" about contemporary women, we discover a major transition. Over the last fifty years there has been a massive shift in the number of women working a large proportion of their time in paid employment within the public setting.[3]

In 1940 the large majority of women (approximately 75 percent) worked primarily within their homes, participating in community work on a limited basis as unpaid volunteers. At that time only approximately one out of four women fourteen years of age and older was included in the labor force. These working women were principally young, single, temporary workers who planned to work only until they married. Less than one-third of this small, female labor pool were married women.[4]

In the decades following 1940, the proportion of women working outside their homes in the general labor force increased dramatically. By 1987 it had doubled. At the present time well over half (56 percent) of women sixteen years of age and over are part of the labor pool.[5] This large increase in numbers of women working outside their homes tells only part of the story of change, however.

Change in the world of work has been paralleled by changes in women's education, their views of themselves, their expectations, goals, and achievements, as well as their direct contributions to the economic life of the nation and to their families. This change has also been accompanied by anxiety, tension, uncertainty, and, in some circumstances, the anger and hostility (among both women and men) that such a massive, relatively rapid social shift has inevitably evoked. Neither women (single or married), men, or families will be the same again.

In the two decades between 1940 and 1960, the proportion of married women in the female working force increased nearly 25 percent. Since 1960, the participation rate of older married women has continued to rise, indicating that significant numbers of married women who had entered the work force as young women have continued to stay.[6]

However, the most dramatic increase of married women in the labor force has been among younger women. In the last thirty years, the labor force participation rate of all women twenty-five to thirty-four years of age has *doubled* (36 to 72 percent).[7] These women are, of course, those women most likely to have small children at home.

Information supplied by the U.S. Bureau of Labor Statistics gives a vivid picture of this change. Between 1960 and 1987, the labor force participation rate of married women with pre-school children nearly *tripled* (19 to 57 percent).[8] At the present time, slightly more than half of women with infants one year of age or less are in the labor market.[9] In a recent report, the U.S. Department of Labor noted that six out of ten American children under eighteen have mothers who work outside the home.[10]

The 1990 annual Profile of Working Women, prepared by a large national association of working women, reported that there are 56 million women in the work force, an increase of 1.3 million since 1987.[11]

This report notes further that the fastest growing segment of the work force is married mothers with children under two years of age, 3.1 million at the present time, an increase of 129 percent since 1970.[12] Large numbers of these young women who have entered the work force have done so with the expectation that they will work throughout their adult lives.

This report also provided some additional interesting glimpses into the lives of women in the labor force. Few of them are driving a Mercedes or skiing in Aspen. Over half (54 percent) of all women in the work force have incomes of less than $10,000 a year.[13] Nearly two out of three (65 percent) of minimum wage earners are women. Fifty-eight percent of the women in the labor force are either single, divorced, widowed, separated, or have husbands who earn less than $15,000 annually. Of the single working mothers who work full-time all year, approximately 10 percent are still trapped below the poverty level with inadequate or nonexistent health care for themselves and their children and no counseling services to assist them in dealing with the stress and danger of their lives.

Additionally, many women who are full-time employees struggling to keep afloat economically are also in the sandwich position of trying to balance work with elder care and family care.[14] According to a recent report, more than half the women who care for elderly relatives also work outside the home. Nearly 40 percent are still raising children of their own.[15]

A 1988 U.S. House of Representatives report indicates that the average American woman will spend seventeen years raising children and eighteen years helping aged parents.[16] This means that thousands of women, while feeling the emotional and economic stress of trying to nurture two generations at once, are trying additionally to deal with the demands of a job and a world still structured in some ways as though women's lives were unchanged from the 1950s.

A client, Ruth, recently provided an example of the reality of the struggle. When I asked her how her week had gone, she said,

> Well, the Social Security office was only open weekdays, so I had to leave work early to do some paperwork for Mom. The washing machine broke and the repairman would only promise to come "sometime between 1 and 5," so I had to take a half day off work for that. With Mom like she is, I have to wash every day. The car's not working right, and I have to figure how to get it to the shop and pick it up and do it without taking any more time off work. I have to save what vacation time I have left so that if the kids or Mom get sick I can take time off without losing pay.
>
> The school tries to help. Jason's teacher scheduled his parent conference late so I could come right after work. Carrie [her teenage daughter] had a rehearsal

with her jazz group that night, but Jane [mother of another member of the group] picked her up and brought
her home, so that worked out. But it was hard to find
someone to check on Mom until I could get home. She
can't be alone all day and evening too anymore.

I think it's just trying to manage everything, when
it's so hard, that makes me feel depressed. This
hasn't been one of my better weeks, but I guess it
was just more of the usual.

The massive shift of women into the paid labor force has
had such far-reaching social implications that it has been called
"the subtle revolution."[17] There is ample evidence to suggest
that we do not yet understand this revolution or its impact on
women's lives, nor do we have a clear understanding of what
working women do.

WHAT DO WORKING WOMEN DO?

Unfortunately, the common concept of the working woman
is a stereotype. For the most part, the media and the advertis-
ing world portrays the working woman as an expensively-
suited, briefcase-carrying executive whose life is less stressful
and more satisfying when she purchases the luxury and labor-
saving items they are seeking to sell. This is a less than subtle
addition to the more familiar stereotypical picture of the baby-
and-house-obsessed suburban housewife to whom these same
advertisers have long attempted to sell diapers, detergent, and
floor wax on afternoon soap operas. Neither stereotype reflects
the reality of women's lives nor the subtle revolution of which
they are a part.

When women work outside their homes, what are they most
likely to be doing? It is now possible for women to enter the
corporate and professional world, and women are choosing to
do so in steadily increasing numbers.[18] However, as Jean Miller
has pointed out, "The vast majority of working women, 80 percent, holds the lowest-paid and most dead-end jobs in this
country."[19]

Many of these jobs are in the clerical field. In 1987, 14.6 million women were engaged in clerical work; well over one-third

(36.2 percent) of all employed women were in this category. As Glenn and Feldberg point out, clerical work is absolutely and proportionally the largest single occupation for women.[20]

With rare exceptions, clerical jobs do not link up to professional or managerial ladders, and many women find themselves to have reached the ceiling of possible advancement relatively early in their work history.[21] Job security in the clerical field is precarious and wages comparably low. Job benefits are limited and are decreasing as employers use subcontracted services to supply clerical help rather than enrolling individuals as part of their regular benefit-endowed work force.

In the trend toward automated offices, stress is increasingly high and personal rewards are low. Such negative job conditions make it difficult for many women to find meaning in their work. Most women in clerical positions are nevertheless committed to working—although often not committed to a specific job—since their income is essential to their survival as single women or, as married women or single parents, to the survival of their families. Current sophisticated electronic monitoring of the individual worker's performance allied with increasing pressure for productivity often result in tension that women experience as insomnia and headaches.

A recent survey found that while women in managerial positions often reported their positions as producing high levels of stress, it was the lower-level workers, primarily women clerical workers, who were more likely to report actual symptoms of stress and stress-related illnesses.[22] Another major study reported that secretaries have the second-highest incidence of stress-related diseases among workers in 130 different occupations studied by the National Institute of Occupational Safety and Health (NIOSH). According to the NIOSH study, the highest level of stress was not found in air traffic controllers but in data-entry clerks whose jobs involve the full-time use of video display terminals.[23] Renzetti and Curran have summarized the problem, "The vast majority of data-entry clerks are women. Jobs such as these provide workers with minimal opportunities for creativity and autonomy and require them to complete tasks under pressure within a limited period of time with minimal errors. But these are jobs that offer few rewards in the forms of compensation, mobility, benefits, or prestige."[24] Counselors seeing depressed women clients who are clerical workers would do well to explore the conditions of the woman's world of work.

Women are employed in other than clerical occupations, of course. However, of the five hundred occupations listed by the U.S. Census Bureau, in 1985 women were primarily concentrated in the twenty-two lowest paid job classifications.[25] The top ten occupations for women are secretaries, elementary teachers, bookkeepers, cashiers, office clerks, managers, waitresses, sales workers, registered nurses, and nursing aides.[26] Women have made some inroads into the skilled trades—carpenters, electricians, auto mechanics, and painters, for example—but remain less than 5 percent of the total number employed in these trades. In June 1991, a report summarizing 1990 U.S. Department of Labor statistics showed that women comprised 98 percent of all secretaries, stenographers, and typists; 94 percent of registered nurses; 90 percent of nursing aides, orderlies, and attendants; 85 percent of elementary teachers; and 73 percent of food servers.[27] So much for the picture of the working woman as a glamorous, well-paid attorney who ends her exciting day with dinner out at an expensive restaurant and an evening at the symphony. While such a picture may play well on television, it is a seriously misleading fiction for those seeking to understand and help women with the reality of their working lives.[28]

However, the number of women in the so-called prestige professions—law, medicine, post-secondary education, science, and engineering—and in corporate management has increased significantly over the past ten years.[29]

In 1985–86 approximately one out of three medical degrees was awarded to a woman; in 1987 women were approximately 20 percent of practicing physicians and 27 percent of medical residents in America.[30] Women have made significant progress in the legal profession. Women receiving law degrees increased from 21 percent in 1976–77 to 38 percent in 1984–85. In 1987 approximately 20 percent of practicing lawyers and judges were women.[31]

In 1986 women accounted for 15 percent of the science and engineering work force, up from 9 percent in 1976. Within science and engineering, women continue to be unevenly distributed, however. Kaufman notes that more than one in four scientists is a woman, but only one in twenty-five engineers is a woman. Among the women scientists, only 5.5 percent are in the hard physical sciences and only 4.9 percent are in mathematics. Women in science and math fare particularly poorly in the academic world. Women are twice as likely as men to be on a nontenure track.[32]

The lower proportion of women in engineering and hard sciences is sometimes attributed to lack of competitive drive, the testosterone theory, and to their supposed genetically based inability, the infamous visual-spatial deficit. It is interesting to note, as Fausto-Sterling has pointed out, that even if, for sake of argument, one accepted a ratio of 2:1 of males to females with the same high levels of visual-spatial skills, one would still statistically expect to find women in about one-third of engineering jobs.[33] One in twenty-five falls considerably short of this. Clearly something other than ability is influencing women's participation in these fields.

Analysis of responsibilities, privileges, and opportunities indicate that women's gains in the professional world are more apparent than real in some respects, however. Kaufman's analysis of the limitations inherent in women's actual status in professional practice is insightful, detailed, documented, and discouraging. For most counselors, Kaufman's description of the difficulties and barriers these privileged women face provides a new and disconcerting glimpse of the pressures and injustices faced by their clients who are professional women. Kaufman's summary is sobering:

> What women are allowed to do [i.e., within the professions] remains limited, and barriers still restrict their mobility in the professional world. In professions that are as male-dominated today as they were a decade ago, women are still likely to be over represented in low-paid and low-prestige subspecialties. . . .

How can we explain women's continuing secondary status within the professions? As we have seen,
the prestige professions are defined primarily in
terms of men and the lives they lead. The processes
that maintain this male model are usually well beyond a woman's control, however committed or
dedicated she may be. No matter what her personal
characteristics, a woman is often assigned the stereotypical characteristics of her sex, and despite her
efforts to transcend these stereotypes, certain structural features of the professions work against her
upward mobility. . . .

Even when women have been able to achieve high-
pay, high-prestige positions within the professions, the
costs for such success have been high. . . . [34]

In increasing numbers women have also been securing
master's degrees in business administration (M.B.A.s) from
prestigious institutions such as Stanford, Harvard, or the University of Pennsylvania's Wharton School of Business. The
majority of these women expected that such degrees would
open for them opportunities in the corporate world that had
been largely reserved for men. However, despite both impec-
cable professional credentials and track records of
demonstrated ability, these women too have faced difficulties
and barriers they did not anticipate and for which business
school did little if anything to prepare them. The majority of
these women discovered that their route to the top was blocked
by what has come to be called the "glass ceiling," subtle patterns of legal discrimination that limit women's participation
and promotion to the highest levels in the professions and in
the corporate world.[35]

Working Woman recently surveyed the 243 women who were
graduates of Wharton's 1980 class (731 total members). Consistent with their expectations, a decade after their graduation,
these women were highly paid: the median income was
$102,938. Corporate executives earned the most (median in-
come, $115,333), compared with entrepreneurs, consultants,
and those employed by small companies (median income,

$99,000). Most of these women plan to work for their entire adult lives; nearly 60 percent have switched careers at least once since graduation.

However, even these women, among the best, brightest, and most well-educated, see themselves as having bumped up against the glass ceiling. "Women have to meet much more stringent criteria than men do to be promoted," commented one former Fortune 500 management consultant. "We had a lot of high, and probably unrealistic, expectations when we graduated from Wharton," wrote one Atlanta executive.

More than half of these women are mothers and are highly critical of the reluctance, or refusal, of corporations to accommodate working mothers. However, many of these educationally and economically privileged women have not waited around for the corporate bureaucracies to change. Almost 25 percent have left the corporate world to open their own businesses, 10 percent work only part-time, and about 14 percent are taking time off temporarily to rear children.[36]

It is important for counselors to keep clearly in mind the enormous variability incorporated in working women. In my community, a local women's news magazine recently published a photo essay that was a tribute to working women. The women pictured included a photo lab saleswoman, film developer, mountain climber and tour guide, florist, attorney, lawn services person, dentist, veterinarian, seamstress, professor, physician's receptionist, artist and goldsmith, small appliance repair person, TV news anchor, journalist, photographer, police officer, computer operator, bank teller, member of a streetlight repair crew, wedding counselor, and translator at a local consulate.[37]

In the news magazine itself were stories and advertisements that showed women selling cosmetics, selling cars, selling insurance, selling real estate, acting as real estate brokers, and working as nannies, therapists, certified financial planners, maids, models, dance instructors, retail clerks, dietitians, teachers, and flight instructors. Stories and advertisements also showed women who were owners/executive directors of their own businesses: cleaning services, real estate, shopping services, tax services, a car dealership, recording studio, book-store, catering services, cookie company, ranch, temporary office and clerical services, printer, public accountant, management consultant, restaurant, auto services for women, mailing/ packaging services, bicycle shop, and other businesses. There was a service directory that listed women in medical practice, dental practice, in practice of psychotherapy/counseling, and in law.

Women continue to work as volunteers. Meetings were announced for women interested in the League of Women Voters and The American Association of University Women. There was a brief article about Big Sisters, an agency that matches adult women volunteers with girls who need attention and nurturing their families cannot provide. There was an appeal for funds and volunteer help for a woman's co-op being organized to support women and children in a rural, economically depressed area.

Women work in government. The Federal government's Western Regional Executive Seminar announced a training meeting for managers that would focus on the increasing number of women and minorities anticipated to be in the federal government labor force by the year 2000. There was notice of a substantial number of appointments of women to local chambers of commerce and to state and federal boards and commissions.

Women in business are increasingly viewed as a significant community asset. There was an announcement of a supporting grant from a large local corporation to a business resource center for Hispanic women. There was also an announcement of a joint meeting of the U. S. Small Business Administration with the National Association of Women Business Owners and the Colorado Women's Chamber of Commerce for women business owners considering entering or expanding into the global market.

Notices of events included meetings of the State Association of Professional Saleswomen, the American Society of Women Accountants, the State Women's Chamber of Commerce, the metro chapter of Business and Professional Women, and various support groups for women. Notices also included the telephone numbers and locations of five regional Community

College Women's Centers providing support groups and career and educational services specifically for women.

In recent decades, in the evangelical world we have appropriately focused much of our attention and energy into efforts to counteract the antimarriage, antifamily rhetoric of the 1960s and 1970s. Hopefully, by doing so we have made some gains in reestablishing the importance of family. However, it is important to understand that we have not and cannot roll back the massive forces of change that have irrevocably shaped women's lives into new patterns. Evangelical women, too, have become a part of the complex working women's world.

In the subtle revolution, the year 1980 was an important date, as Bernard has noted. This was the year of the "tipping point," as Bernard has phrased it, the point at which more than half of all married women were employed outside the home. In 1980, being employed had become, in the real world of everyday living, ". . . a normative life style for married women as well as for married men." For the first time in recent history, married women who were *not* in the labor force had become a minority. Bernard has compared this tipping point to a great geological shift: "a whole sociological structure had tipped and its center of gravity shifted." In Bernard's opinion, this shift is likely to prove irreversible.[38]

It is important, however, to think cautiously about what such figures may mean. Taken alone, these statistics give only a cloudy view of women's choices and the motivations that shape them. The common wisdom that holds that decreasing numbers of women at home full-time means increasing numbers of women who do not care about children and family is certainly incorrect. Inflammatory rhetoric from both the left and the right has done nothing to help us understand the pressures women face in this time of transition and has done much to obscure the nature of the choices women are now forced to make.

THE WORKING MOTHER'S DILEMMA

Sylvia Hewlett is an economist who is concerned about the impact that married women's shift into the labor force has had on both the mothers and their children.[39] In a recent column Hewlett summarizes some hard economic facts that give clarity to the average working mother's dilemma.[40] According to Hewlett, in 1988 the average family income was only 6 percent higher than in 1973, though almost twice as many wives were at work. She describes economic policies and tax laws that, in her opinion, have worked to the disadvantage of families and notes that over the last twenty-five years the cost of housing has jumped 56 percent and college tuitions have rocketed 87.9 percent in real dollars. She cites one Gallup poll that shows that only 13 percent of working mothers want to work full-time, although 52 percent of them do so. Hewlett notes, "Often what keeps these mothers at work 40 hours a week is heavy mortgage payments." She concludes bluntly:

> With male wages sagging and the divorce rate at 50%, it's hard to spin out a scenario in which large numbers of women have the option of staying home full time. The trick is to spread the burden around. Employers and government both have to pull their weight. This critical task of building strong families can no longer be defined as a private endeavor, least of all a private *female* endeavor. No society can afford to forget that on the backs of its children ride the future prosperity and integrity of the nation.[41]

One may, of course, disagree with Hewlett's solution to the dilemma working mothers face. However, the facts Hewlett has assembled in *When the Bough Breaks* make it clear that telling the majority of working mothers to stay home is remarkably like Marie Antoinette recommending that the hungry eat cake if they had no bread.[42]

In response to the tension and stress they experience in the world of work, women themselves are rethinking the dilemmas they face. Despite students' initial protests, the warm response to Barbara Bush's commencement speech at Wellesley (Spring 1990) indicates that many young women are beginning to question the new mythology and what it teaches women about work.[43]

In a recent survey two out of three of the young women interviewed indicated that if they had the opportunity they would consider taking time at home out of the labor force in order to rear children.[44] What will give them the opportunity? While it is not certain what factors will shape the choices of coming generations of women, it is interesting to note that these women are beginning the process of structuring their adult lives with a commitment to family. A happy marriage and well-adjusted children were a higher priority for these young women than were career or contribution to society. At the same time it is discouraging to note that for the young men who are their potential mates, the interview indicated that their priorities ran: career, marriage, contribution to society, then children in a definite last place.

It is interesting to note the "essential requirements" which these young women listed for a spouse: faithfulness, ambition and willingness to work hard, intelligence, and a well-paying job. Such characteristics, if present in a mate, would certainly enhance the opportunity for these women to stay home and rear children. But what choices will these women make if the spouse does not have a well-paying job, or if he becomes unemployed? Or what choices will these women have if their marriages dissolve in divorce? Most of these young women (85 percent) believe that they are more likely than their parents' generation to be divorced. And what choices will they make if parenting turns out to have considerably more work and less immediate gratification than these inexperienced young women now envision it will provide? What if they are married to young men who indeed have good jobs but whose commitment to children is low or entirely absent?

Granting the limitations of such a survey, it is interesting to note that, even at this early idealistic stage of their lives, these young women indicate some awareness of a hard fact. What they want, and what they may be able to have, may not necessarily be the same, as Hewlett's data makes graphically clear. Opportunity for women rarely pivots simply around personal choice. Having watched the struggles of their mothers and older sisters, this generation is perhaps more realistic about the factors over which women have little control but which nonetheless shape their lives. While either/or choices between work and family are less likely to be necessary in the years ahead, having it all is not, and probably never has been, a viable option for women or men. However, women are confronted in unique ways with necessary compromises which are real, often painful, and always complex. Not enough counselors are presently prepared to help women deal constructively with the difficult choices such compromises inevitably entail.

Six out of ten of these young women believe it will be more difficult to be a woman than a man in the decades ahead. Nothing we now know would cause us to argue the point otherwise.

The problems that face women who work outside the home include chronic fatigue, scarcity and cost of reliable childcare. The problems also include the tension, and sometimes guilt, generated by conflicting obligations of work and family and the strain of renegotiating gender-role expectations and responsibilities. For mothers of small children in low-paying jobs (with or without a man in the household) there is also the depression associated with the exhaustion of chronic overload.

SEXUAL HARASSMENT AND DISCRIMINATION

For large numbers of women, there is also the tension of working in an environment where discrimination and sexual harassment is an emotional reality. Inappropriate touch, sexually loaded innuendos and jokes, and stereotypical remarks and attitudes continue to characterize the majority of workplaces.[45]

The fullest and most reliable assessment of sexual harassment comes from two studies undertaken by the U. S. Merit Systems Protection Board (MSPB). In both the first and follow-up MSPB studies, it was found that 42 percent of the female federal civilian employees had experienced some form of sexual harassment in the workplace during the previous two years.[46]

In many work settings there is the unspoken but constant pressure to look good, that is, to look young, sexually attractive, and fashionably dressed, not simply well-groomed. While discrimination against older workers happens to men as well as women, older women, particularly those who appear older, are more likely to become targets of discriminatory behavior, often subtle and difficult to prove.

A client, a displaced homemaker seeking reentry into the labor market, recently told me:

You have to be young, thin, sexy, and computer liter-
ate in order to have a chance. They can't ask me how
old I am—that's against the law. But they asked me
when I graduated from high school and how much
computer experience I had. The young woman who
interviewed me was dressed in an expensive new-style
suit with a very short skirt; she looked at me and asked
me if I thought I would fit into their work environment,
and then told me she'd call me if anything fitting my
qualifications came up. She made it clear I didn't need
to stay home tomorrow and wait for her call.

Discrimination is a subtle thing and difficult to understand
in its least evident forms. The personal experience of a friend
provides a helpful illustration of the problem and the difficulty
of dealing with it in a straightforward way.

For a time in her professional life Elaine held a university
appointment in a department in which she was the only
woman holding faculty rank. She soon discovered that the man
who was head of the department had established an interesting routine. Each day at 4:20 he would gather up the faculty
who were present and available at that time and then head for
Sam's Place, a neighborhood bar adjoining the university.
There, in informal and well-lubricated meetings, important information was exchanged, resources were informally allocated,
and staff conflicts and responsibilities negotiated. Agendas for
faculty meetings were informally set, the results of ongoing research debated, and the jokes that signalled insider status were
told. It was common wisdom in the department that if an individual needed to talk to the chief, the approved route was to
make the 4:20 meeting at Sam's. It was considered bad form to
spring something at a faculty meeting that had not been previously cleared at Sam's.

The point, I think, is clear: initially it was difficult, if not impossible, for Elaine to gain access to her department chairman
through the powerful, informal camaraderie routinely extended to her male peers. Women can be shut out of the
elaborate, male-dominated social systems in which much of
professional life is functionally worked out, and women can

be shut out in ways that are difficult to protest. Sex discrimination suits in federal court are obviously no solution to problems such as my friend's exclusion from the informal, daily staff meetings held at Sam's.

In such instances, women have to devise different ways to deal with such exclusion. However, the pressure and tension of struggling daily with such issues can be exhausting. If women measure success in relational terms, then the negative impact on the woman's sense of worth and competence when she is forced to deal with such discriminatory social structures over a long period of time is both destructive and incalculable.

Elaine told me of another woman who also suffered from system-based discrimination in a way that was difficult to protest. Approximately a year after Elaine joined the faculty, a new department secretary was hired. Jean was a single parent whose son, Jason, had cerebral palsy and required extensive speech and physical therapy. It was difficult for Jean to manage to pick Jason up at his special school and get him to his therapy appointments on time. One cold, snowy evening, Jean had car trouble and left early. One of the male professors complained to Elaine, "You just never can depend on women with kids; they're always wanting some special favor. I'm going to talk to Dick [the department chairman] about this."

There was no indication of any understanding on his part of the irony of his complaint. As part of the perks of his position, he could choose to leave whenever he wished to do so, whether his work was done or not. (This particular professor was notorious among students for his failure to prepare lectures properly or to return papers in reasonable time.) Jean, a woman on an hourly wage, was judged by a different standard.

The structure of the system itself made the unfairness difficult to protest. Jean's job description permitted no autonomy or self-monitoring; her coming and going was determined by the clock, not her competency in completing her work, her sense of responsibility, her integrity, or her personal judgment. Since in that particular college of the university, nearly all professorial positions were held by men and support positions were held by women on salary or hourly wage, the results of the job distribution discriminated in effect, although probably not in intent, against women. Women—most of whom had children and needed the flexibility—had the lowest paying jobs and therefore the least options and choice, while men—who had least responsibility for children—had greatest flexibility and autonomy. The system, however, made this legal.

The system structure provided no accountability for a tenured professor whom students and peers deemed politically astute and professionally irresponsible. In contrast, potentially at least, the system penalized a woman who was both a capable worker and a responsible parent. With good reason, women often experience the world of work as discriminatory in ways they themselves sometimes find difficult to describe or to understand, and impossible to protest.

Counselors of women need to develop a special sensiti·.ity to issues of discrimination and sexual harassment. Women clients often need help in exploring what it is about their work environment that triggers their stress. An awareness of injustice and discrimination and a sense of being trapped are often difficult for women to identify and express. Evangelical women often feel that if something is unfair at work, it is their responsibility to endure the injustice without complaint. If sexual harassment occurs, it is often their guilty sense that the problem is in some way the result of their bad behavior, not the responsibility of the perpetrator. Many evangelical women hold a distorted sense of what a submissive spirit is, and in an effort to be obedient to a faulty concept of biblical womanhood, passively tolerate overload, unjust differential in pay scales, and job descriptions that result in unfair deprivation of benefits and opportunities. For the most part, these women have no experience in thinking about justice, in relationship to others or to themselves, and no experience in actively seeking to make their environment different and better. For these women, it is a totally foreign concept to enter into a struggle in order to achieve conflict resolution marked by both peace and justice.

COUNSELING WOMEN WITH WORK-RELATED PROBLEMS

The problems that women face in the work environment are, of course, part of the problems they bring to the counseling process. Counselors are rarely trained, however, to identify work-related problems or to help women identify and deal with such problems.

With rare exception, women (single and married) who are struggling with work-related stress and depression, will initially report their concern to the counselor in terms of frustrated, dissatisfying relationships. If both the woman and her counselor believe the old myth that only relationships count for women, the question of work-related problems will never come up.

Counselors need to learn to ask questions about work.
• How does the woman feel about work?
• Does she (single or married) view her work as evidence she is sexually and relationally undesirable to men?
• Does she believe that good women are protected and taken care of by men and that working is evidence of lack of love or her lack of worth as a woman?
• Why is she working at the particular job at which she is employed?
• Is she an intellectually able woman trapped in a boring, dead-end job?
• Is her struggle with depression a surface issue?
• What is her theology of work?

In subtle and sometimes less than subtle ways, occupational segregation continues to shunt women into less-skilled, lower-paying jobs. Women continue to have difficulty securing admission into apprentice training programs for the skilled trades (e.g., electricians, carpenters, painters). They often experience harassment on the job when they enter these formerly male-only preserves. The glass ceiling is real, and often a significant contribution to professional women's sense of depression when they are faced with demands and choices different from those of their male colleagues.

It is amazing what begins to happen to a woman client who is stressed and depressed when she begins to realize that no one could work under the conditions with which she is struggling without experiencing serious difficulty. It is even more amazing to watch what happens to the depression, and to the need for medication, when a woman begins to believe that it is a good and godly thing to attempt to change the injurious and unjust working conditions with which she may be faced. Unfortunately, there are often limits to the environmental changes that an individual woman can achieve. However, it is astonishing how much positive internal change happens to the woman when she understands that she is struggling with issues of justice, not some spiritually disgraceful lack of faith or psychological illness. Emotional healing often begins when a woman client realizes that justice for her personally as an individual woman is of enormous importance to God.

WOMEN AT HOME

It is important to remember, however, that not all women work outside their homes. Women who are economically able to stay at home and choose to do so have their own set of problems. These women also struggle with the tensions of change and the issues of transition, even through the structure of their lives appears stable and traditional.

These women often feel unrecognized. The statistics confirming the dramatic shift of women into the labor force has tended to obscure the numbers, and the importance, of women who are choosing to devote themselves to traditional mother-homemaker roles. In a feature story focusing on contemporary women's divergent life patterns, Nina Darnton[47] organized 1988 data from the Bureau of Labor Statistics to illustrate this point as shown in Table 3.

Table 3
Mothers Who Are Employed

	In the Labor Force	At Home
Mothers with children one year old or less.	50.8%	49.2%
Mothers with children under age six	56.1%	43.9%
Mothers with children ages six to seventeen	73.3%	26.7%

SOURCE: Bureau of Labor Statistics, 1988 data, from *Newsweek*, 4 June 1990. Used by permission.

Such organization of data reminds us graphically that while more than half of mothers with children one year old or under are in the labor force, approximately 49 percent of such mothers are at home caring for their children. If less than ten out of one hundred households now consist of a breadwinner father, a homemaker mother, and children under eighteen, those women are there nonetheless.

These women feel not only unrecognized; they often feel undervalued. While mothers at home feel devalued, their childcare responsibilities help to reassure them to some degree that they are providing a valuable service to family and community. Being a stay-at-home woman is even more difficult for women who are empty-nesters or widows who choose not to enter or reenter the work force. As the balance has tipped and participation in the labor force has become normative for women, issues of identity and worth have become particularly difficult for this group, and the pattern by which they need to structure their lives has become less clear and well-defined.

The problems that face women who work within the home include their new minority status and their sometimes understandably defensive response to the transition they are experiencing. Many feel shortchanged and angry that, from their perspective, the role and services of the traditional homemaker have been and continue to be devalued, often by career women who, nonetheless, depend on the stay-at-home mothers to keep the Brownie troop, the schools, the churches, and other community organizations going with their volunteer time. These stay-at-home women often see themselves as isolated, surrounded by moms who leave home for work every day but who leave the stay-at-home mom's phone number at the school in case of their child's emergency. The stay-at-home mom's house is the one at which the UPS driver drops everyone else's packages and the one to which the latchkey kids come when they are lonely, scared, or in trouble.

Traditional homemakers know that choosing homemaking as a full-time, lifetime career is increasingly risky, even within the evangelical community. Growing numbers of displaced homemakers, including those within her church, make the stay-at-home mom feel afraid. She fears that it may be true that she is one heart attack, or one affair, away from poverty and/or forced reentry into the workplace. In the current labor market, particularly under conditions of economic recession, her experience in making Mickey Mouse birthday cakes, Ninja Turtle costumes, and serving as room mother and parent representative on the curriculum committee will qualify her for nothing more than minimum wage.

No-fault divorce laws have contributed to a world in which if her marriage fails the at-home mother can expect that the standard of living for herself and her minor children will decline 73 percent in the first year after the divorce, while that of her former husband will increase 42 percent.[48] If she is awarded child support assistance, she more likely than not will collect only a small percent, if any, of the funds legally due her and her children.[49]

"THE MOMMY WARS"

Perhaps most infuriating to at-home women is their sense that most people, including many women in the labor force, believe that the world of the stay-at-home mom is the world of June Cleaver, which despite the chaos of change has managed to survive, trouble-free, behind some magic picket fence. Perhaps most infuriating to the go-to-work mothers is their sense that most people, including the stay-at-home moms, believe that they care less for their children than for the glamour, excitement, and discretionary income they believe that the go-to-work women's employment brings.

Of course, neither the June Cleaver clone nor the glamorous working-woman stereotype represent women's lives as they are. Nevertheless, women's own misunderstanding of their divergent life patterns, and of the problems each entails, has produced tension and conflict between women themselves that has been dubbed by the media as "The Mommy Wars."[50] While such labels may sell magazines and newspapers, it has trivialized the issues with which women are struggling and obscures the common ground that women with children have with each other. Many at-home moms would work if they could find decent, part-time jobs, flexible schedules, and affordable, high-quality childcare. And many working moms would be home at least part-time if they could afford it and were provided flexible schedules and job evaluation standards that did not penalize them professionally for personal commitment to family.

In these times of transition, women agree that they need more options. It is easy to forget that choices women make in times of transition are in a very real sense forced choices. Women can choose only from the options available to them, and in the majority of instances, women feel that the options presently available to them (single and married) are far from fully satisfactory. It is not yet a user-friendly world for women—or for the most part, for the majority of men.

A MIXED MESSAGE FROM THE CHURCH

Women in the labor force who are conservative Christians often find themselves facing mixed messages. A woman may hear sermons that extol the virtues of the Proverbs 31 woman who considered a field and bought it, but feel and sometimes hear clear disapproval of her work as a real estate agent. Another woman may hear praise for the Proverbs 31 woman who stretched out her hand to the poor and needy, and criticism of her employment as a social worker. Still another may hear the Proverbs 31 woman praised for her spinning and weaving that provided clothing for her family, and hear herself scolded for her work as a retail clerk whose salary buys her children's clothing and books for school.

"From the way they talk, it isn't my work my church objects to," one woman client said wryly. "They just object to my being paid for it."

Women in the labor force who are conservative Christians often face a powerful message about their work in the structure of the church programs. These women are frequently confronted with Bible study groups that meet only mornings or afternoons, women's fellowship luncheons that are scheduled only during the week, and special programs for stay-at-home moms that are regularly listed in the church bulletin.

Such programs may well represent sound church planning. However, what are working women to think when there are no church programs focused on their interests, no scheduling that reflects the realities of their lives? What are they to conclude when the church gives no tangible recognition of either their needs or their contributions to their families? What does it mean when the breadwinning contributions of working men are publicly recognized, and the work of women is not? How can working women develop a sound theology of work and a healthy sense of biblically based self-worth in such a context?

In conservative church settings, women who work outside their homes are in many subtle and powerful ways faced with social barriers that set them apart from the women-at-home groups on which the church focuses attention and to whom, by implication, they extend their approval.

A client, a nurse who is an empty-nester who has returned to work in a local children's hospital, had a painful experience that illustrates the complexity of the issue. A young couple in the church where she attends had experienced a series of misfortunes: premature birth of twins, resulting in major medical difficulties for the mother; the young father's loss of his job; and the approaching foreclosure on their home. My client inquired one Sunday morning about the church's plans to be of assistance to this young couple. The woman she asked replied, "Oh, we've got everything worked out, and the schedule for meals and childcare is all arranged."

"What am I supposed to do?" asked my client.

"Oh, nothing," the woman replied. "We know you working women never have time to help with the work of the church."

The issue is not simple. Laying aside the possibly intentional snub inherent in the remark, it contained some difficult truth. My client, given her schedule, could *not* provide the traditional assistance of cooking and childcare. To presume, however, that in consequence she had no interest in the work of the church or that she could do nothing to help reflects aspects of the so-called Mommy Wars within the church in a particularly unfortunate form.

Most conservative churches continue to be naive at best and indifferent at worst about the complexities of programming for working women. Simply scheduling an evening edition of the same daytime programs designed for at-home moms is no solution to the needs of working women. In the first place, evening hours and energy is the one thing the at-work mother does not have. Further, mothering problems are not the only issues in which working mothers are interested. Even more importantly, not all working women are mothers.

Across the spectrum, from unskilled laborers working for minimum wage to professional women, single women at work receive little or no encouragement within the church community in dealing with their work. What are these women to think when the structure of the church program focuses exclusively upon their marital status? True, they are the "singles," but they are also women who work. How are they to understand their calling, their value as workers? They are also women often working in situations in which they are the objects of unfair labor practices, sexual harassment, and job discrimination. Is this of no interest or concern to the church?

One client, who works in a laundry/dry cleaning establishment, recently asked me, "Do you think God thinks my work is important?" I was encouraged that she felt comfortable bringing her concern to the counseling hour. However, I was and am convinced that her concerns were, for the most part, the reflection *not* of her marital status, nor of poor emotional adjustment. Rather, they reflected the failure of her church community to focus theological attention and emotional support upon the reality of her life and her needs as a working woman.

CHANGES IN THE FAMILY

During the 1960s and 1970s there was a strong outcry against marriage and family as social institutions that were limiting and destructive to women. Women were encouraged by the more radical element of the feminist left to adopt what has been called here the new mythology. Women were urged to place careers at the center of their lives (as men presumably did), to experience sex in uncommitted relationships (paralleling the supposed masculine pattern of adult sexuality), and to assign to marriage and children only incidental importance (again presumably paralleling men's life patterns). One of the more memorable slogans of that time was, "A woman needs a man like a fish needs a bicycle."

Recent history has confirmed how seriously such an approach misunderstood the goals and priorities of women. Betty Friedan has herself acknowledged the rejection of the so-called second-wave feminism of the 1960s by the large majority of women. Friedan has attributed this in part to the failure of the feminist leadership to affirm and support women's investment in families.[51]

Counselors know that whatever change the winds of transition have brought, that for the most part the women who come to the counselor's office continue to be interested in marriage and family.[52] Demographers now predict that a somewhat smaller percentage of women born recently will marry. Being single is a more socially and economically acceptable alternative for women. However, marriage is, and is likely to remain, a nearly universal experience for American women. One study suggests that approximately 90 percent of young white women and 80 percent of young black women will marry.[53] The counselor also knows, however, that the difficulty women (and men) face in forming and sustaining stable, healthy marriages is formidable. The problems which they bring to the counselor provide evidence of a changing world that in many ways appears destructive to stable family life.[54]

EXPECTATIONS FOR MARRIAGE

The winds of change have brought uncertainty about marriage itself, what it is all about, and what a woman can reasonably expect in marriage. Does marriage mean that a woman will be taken care of economically? Not necessarily. Economic stress and heightened levels of expectations, coupled with rising costs of housing and education, may well mean that she herself will be required to contribute economically to the upkeep of the household and her own needs. If the marriage fails and she becomes a female head-of-household, she may find herself the sole support of herself and her minor children and forced into America's growing ranks of the poor.

Does marriage mean that a woman's emotional needs will be met? Not necessarily. In a culture in which self-fulfillment, emotional intimacy, and personal happiness are assigned highest priority, she may find herself unexpectedly disappointed by the level of emotional closeness and sexual satisfaction the marriage partnership provides. Sexual infidelity is increasingly common in the culture at large and appears to be occurring with disappointing frequency within the evangelical community as well.

Will marriage provide social stability and a predictable life pattern? Not necessarily. Contemporary families continue to be highly mobile, moving frequently, sometimes over great distances. A woman can no longer expect to live out her married life supported by a network of longtime friends and extended family in a neighborhood she knows. Neither can she expect, even if she is a committed Christian, that marriage itself will necessarily last "until death do us part." Approximately half of all marriages end before their seventh year.[55] The rate of marriage failure within the church has risen in rough proportion to the rate of failure in the culture at large.

What has changed for women? Expectations—emotional and economic, both for themselves as individuals and for marriage as an institution. The characteristics of the world in which marriage and family must be worked out have changed as well. Frozen foods, microwave ovens, and dishwashers may expedite dinner preparation, but television is an incompetent babysitter and a poor substitute for family games; the content of television certainly does not facilitate the development of children's thinking and moral reasoning.

What does marriage and family mean for most women?

- It means struggling with the cost of housing and coping with the frightening upward spiral of cost for insurance and medical care.
- It means confronting the rising levels of concern—on the part of both parents and teachers—about adequate public school education of children, and making difficult, often costly choices about children's schooling.
- In many neighborhoods it means dealing with the threat of a subculture of drugs, alcohol, sexual promiscuity, and violence that threatens to engulf children and community.

- For at least half of all married women, it means managing both a home and the pressure of work outside the home.
- For at least half of young mothers, it means the struggle of finding and paying for adequate childcare while trying to compensate for the limited available time for the couple and for the family.
- For many women it means struggling to maintain connections with extended family separated by distance and often shattered from the separation and alienation divorce may bring.
- It means the struggle and conflict of blended families and the stress of elder care.

Such conditions do not foster easy establishment of satisfying marriages and stable families. When such difficult conditions are coupled with high levels of culturally fostered expectations for personal happiness and the good life of economic affluence and leisure, marriage and family can seem an endless round of effort that is insufficiently rewarding and undervalued by both spouse and society.

"If I'm doing it right, how come it's so hard?" a young wife and mother asked me recently. "And if I'm doing a good thing, why doesn't it feel better?"

There are additional factors that complicate marriage and family for contemporary women. The increase in options available to women in the management of their fertility provides something of the best and the worst in a particularly complex combination. New forms of contraception, new medical options for infertile couples, and the legality of abortion provide women with new parameters of moral, medical, and psychological choice.

DEALING WITH DIVORCE AND SECOND MARRIAGES

While we may all wish that this were not so, divorce, second marriages, and the challenge of establishing blended families are increasingly part of the evangelical world. These factors do not occur only out there in the culture at large.

Divorce and the massive readjustments that it necessitates produce long-term consequences for all involved.[56] Psychological, social, and economic fallout from divorce is inevitable.

The idea of a simple, consequence-free divorce is a culture-wide fantasy. While the nature and intensity of the consequences vary widely from individual to individual and case to case, regardless of the circumstances, divorce is traumatic. The trauma of children often intensifies the mother's own personal trauma, even in those instances when the dissolution of the marriage may have occurred with the full knowledge and authorization of the woman's church.

Second marriages have particular risks and challenges, and often present particularly difficult issues of adjustment. Whatever the initial romantic hope may have been, those who have survived the establishment of a blended family know that it happens only as the result of time, hard work, the grace of God, and unending willingness to try again despite hurt feelings.

Some of the old mythology can make these already painful issues even worse. If a woman believes that by her love and faith, it lies within her power to keep a marriage together regardless of circumstances or the choices of her spouse; if she believes that it is her responsibility to make life happy, productive, and stress-free for her children, then both the woman and her counselor face unique challenges in working out a productive adjustment to the trauma the woman experiences when the anticipated happy ending to her story fails to occur.

REAL WOMEN IN A CHANGING WORLD

The lives of many of my clients illustrate the world of change. One client, Jeanne, is a devout young Christian, and is just now planning her wedding. This will be the first marriage for her and for her young husband-to-be. Despite their shared faith, both she and her fiance are anxious. Jeanne's parents are divorced; both Jeanne and her fiance have siblings who are divorced; both fear that they may not be able to keep the vows they are planning to make of lifelong fidelity.

"So many people are getting divorced," Jeanne said sadly when telling me of her sister's separation and impending divorce. "I wonder if we'll be able to keep it together, even with God's help."

Ellen, too, is planning a wedding. It is a second marriage for her. She has two children from her previous marriage, and the man she is marrying also has two children from his previous marriage. "I don't know how we'll manage," Ellen said.

> I know it won't be easy, but it's sure not easy alone. I'll have to keep working—he's really faithful to pay his child support, so he doesn't have too much extra, and someday we'd like to have a child of our own. It will have to be soon, though. My biological clock is running out.
>
> I worry most, though, about his mother. She really liked Jim's first wife, and she thinks Jim would go back to her if I was out of the picture. She's already told Jim she'll never think of my kids as her grandchildren.
>
> It's going to be rough in lots of ways. We're looking for a church that will marry us even though we've both been divorced. We'd like to get our lives together and make this work. Harry [her former husband] is taking me back to court. He thinks his child support ought to be less now that I'm getting married.

Delores has chosen to stay home with her two children. Her husband, Mark, is a highly successful young attorney. Mark and Delores are high-profile members in a large, affluent suburban church. Mark cannot understand why Delores is depressed. She has a large home in an exclusive suburb, a new car, healthy children, beautiful clothes, and part-time help when they entertain. Mark's work schedule of sixty-plus hours a week means that he has little, if any, time with the children. He is too tired and too tense for good communication, companionship, or a satisfying sexual relationship. When Delores protests, Mark points out that the children were something Delores wanted, but that children were never on his life agenda. He is angry that Delores is not more excited that he is five years ahead of schedule in meeting his life goals—he has just been made junior partner in his firm. Mark has told Delores angrily that she has everything any reasonable woman could want, and what *he* needs from her is help with social obligations, appreciation of all he's giving her, and lots of peace and quiet when he comes home.

Rita is trying to get pregnant. She was referred by her physician for psychological support in dealing with the emotionally exhausting medical procedures through which she is going in her effort to conceive. She is also struggling with questions of faith: What is God's will? Are these procedures a bad substitute for faith or an expression of it?

June is a tall, dignified, beautiful woman, a grandmother, and a leader in her church's program for women. She also was referred by her physician. June had gone through a relatively symptom-free menopause, then, to her physician's bewilderment, had become seriously depressed for no medically apparent reason. Careful, patient counseling began to unravel the painful puzzle. June's husband was taking early retirement. Her fear of their new pattern of life together was rooted in the long secret years of sexual abuse she had silently endured as a Christian wife. "I cannot bear to think what may happen if he is there all day, every day," she whispered, "and there's nothing I can do."

KATHERINE'S STORY

Katherine also appeared seriously depressed. She came for counseling because her pastor, after talking with her, thought she could perhaps profit from talking with a woman. Katherine has three children, all preschoolers, and works at a print shop some distance from her home. She and her husband, Larry, grapple with the cost of day care. Katherine has worked out an informal arrangement with her sister, a neighbor, and, in the event a child is ill, her mother-in-law, who has reluctantly agreed to help out in an emergency. Larry is a construction worker, and in off-season delivers pizza and works for a janitorial firm.

Katherine's depression is, in part, due to utter exhaustion. She must be up, have the children up and dressed, and leave the house by seven every morning—earlier if snow is heavy and traffic likely to be slow. She leaves the baby with her sister, circles back to the neighbor and drops off the two other children, then checks in at work at eight o'clock. Her employer

permits her to work without a break until lunch, take a short
lunch hour, and skip her afternoon break. This enables her to
leave early to start the hour's circuit to pick up her children,
talk briefly with their caretakers, and get home to start dinner.

From Katherine's perspective, once home her time is filled
with an endless series of relational demands she is too tired to
meet and tasks that, once done, promptly need to be done
again—food preparation, laundry, housecleaning, shopping,
and childcare. She wants to give Larry and the children more
of her time and attention. She wants to be more active in her
church. All of this must be managed somehow around an
eight-hour workday in which she spends the majority of her
time doing repetitive tasks that demand relatively error-free
performance.

Katherine feels trapped and hopeless. Her hard work seems
to do little to move her family toward their goal of purchasing
a HUD house that Larry can repair and remodel; both want
desperately to move out of the cramped apartment in which
they are now living. Katherine is most concerned, however,
about the rising tension between herself and Larry. More and
more frequently they flare into quarrels that neither of them
fully understand.

They quarrel about sex. Katherine is tired, disinterested, and
afraid of another pregnancy. Larry resists emotionally any discussion of a vasectomy; women in Katherine's family have a
history of tumors, and her physician is reluctant to prescribe
the pill for her. Larry insists that his sexual needs are not being
met and that it is Katherine's biblically directed responsibility
to meet them. He believes that "the Bible says" Katherine has
no right to say no if he needs (wants) sex. Katherine feels angry, guilty, confused, and totally turned off.

They quarrel about money—there is never enough. Larry's
pride and joy, the "loaded with extras" truck he purchased
early in their marriage, now needs extensive, expensive re-
pairs. Larry and Katherine both feel trapped and angry that
they have not had a real vacation since Andrea, their second
child, was born. They dread Christmas, since it inevitably pro-
vokes an explosive confrontation between them and a
hangover budget crisis that extends into March. They feel

guilty about their erratic giving to their church and the small amount they have pledged to the building fund.

They quarrel about the division of the domestic labor, the things that always need to be done. Larry insists that he helps. Katherine insists that he does only about half as much as he says he does, and does that reluctantly, only after she nags. Further, from Katherine's viewpoint, when he does help, Larry does things in a half-way fashion that drives her frantic. Larry insists that Katherine is like her mother and makes the housework harder than it has to be. Larry also reports that Katherine occasionally refuses his help when he does offer and then gets upset because she is tired and everything is not done as she wants it. This feels to Larry like a bum rap.

Both Larry and Katherine hate the task of paying bills, so each depends upon the other to do this, and both are angry when, as is frequently the case, overdue bills result in penalties they cannot afford or unpleasant notes from creditors.

When Katherine came for counseling, her job had become the scapegoat upon which both she and Larry blamed their difficulties. Larry was quick to explain that he did not believe in women working outside the home—conveniently ignoring the fact that it was necessary to have Katherine's salary to pay the rent and buy groceries during his frequent layoffs. Their problems, however, were more complex than either initially was willing to face.

Katherine had grown up believing that being loved meant being taken care of. Consequently, she had failed to take seriously any possibility that she might need to work following marriage and so had taken vocational training lightly. She now found herself forced into a nonskilled, low-paying job with few benefits, a job which both exhausted and bored her. She had married a man with little inclination to share the responsibilities of family care, a belief system that equated maleness with exemption from so-called women's work, an appetite for the affluent, good life, and a limited understanding of himself.

Prior to marriage, Larry's estimate of his ability to provide for his family was based on an overly optimistic belief that the demand and pay for construction workers would always remain high. His belief was coupled with a naive underestimate of the costs of supporting a family. When babies arrived in close succession and a severe depression in the housing industry reduced his hours and pay, his self-confidence tumbled and his disposition soured.

Neither Katherine nor Larry were prepared for the demands of parenthood. Neither anticipated the degree to which children pulled them apart and reduced the energy, time, attention, and money that they had previously spent upon each other.

Larry was unable to acknowledge the sense of competition that he felt with his children and with Katherine. Consequently, at the end of the day he was unable to reconcile his desire for an immediate meal, undisturbed peace and quiet, and his wife's undivided attention, with the children's high levels of activity and noise, their need for his companionship, and their demands for food.

Katherine, exhausted, and caught between the demands of husband and children, added further demands on herself. She expected that as a good Christian wife and mother, she would be continuously patient, even-tempered, consistent, and kind. She expected further that her house would look like her mother's did—her mother was a fastidious stay-at-home mom—and that she would make home a haven of peace and quiet to which everyone would be happy to return at the end of the day. Secretly she feared that if she insisted that Larry help her more with childcare and the house, her demands would escalate the conflict between them to the point where he might leave her and the children.

Katherine's job was certainly a part of the problems this family faced, but the job was far from the *only* problem with which this couple needed to grapple. This case is a reminder to us as counselors that while we can err by *underestimating* the degree to which job-related stress contributes to women's emotional problems, the reverse may also be true. We can focus on the job-related stress and overlook the family-related problems that often intensify the woman's tension with her job.

Research provides some interesting insights into Katherine and Larry's problems.

In the statistically average couple in which both are employed full-time, the wife's share of domestic labor is three times greater than that of her husband.[57] While the majority of husbands of wives who are employed full-time *say* that housework should be more evenly distributed, their behavior does not reflect their belief. The types of domestic work men do tend to be intermittent (e.g., mowing the lawn, washing the car, painting the house) or associated with leisure activities (taking the kids to the mall or barbecuing).[58] The daily routine chores (vacuuming, cooking, cleaning, laundry, baby care) remain almost exclusively women's work. As a result, women add from four to six hours a day of demanding domestic labor to their time on the job, the infamous and exhausting "second shift."[59]

Studies report conflicting results in the effort to determine if men's participation in domestic labor and childcare is increasing.[60] The issue of men's participation is not so simple as it might appear, however.[61]

Larry insisted that, at least on occasion, Katherine rejected his help. Thinking of Katherine's exhaustion, such an action seems extremely improbable. However, some studies have indicated, to the surprise of the researchers, that although there has been an increase of women desiring help with housework,[62] under some circumstances some women do in fact resist their husband's help.[63]

It is clear that some types of domestic labor entail emotionally significant activities through which women (and men) establish and support gender identity.[64] For some women, some forms of housework affirm gender identity and validate their womanhood. Some forms of housework represent their creativity and their expertise. For some women, it is the domain through which they can exert influence and control over their families. As a demonstration of love, housework can express commitment and produce a sense of achievement and satisfaction.

However in many instances, unfortunately, a woman's reluctance to seek help represents her belief that seeking help will create conflict and possibly more work for herself if she does so. Some women feel that their performance of housework is a necessary exchange for the husband's continuance in the marriage and that if the woman stops doing the housework, the marriage will probably end.[65]

For both Larry and Katherine, much of the argument focused upon more equitable sharing of domestic work camouflaged a serious underlying issue: their discomfort about their sense of gender identity when their life circumstances required a change in role behaviors.[66] Each of them felt at times the confusion that change brings.[67] Was Katherine less feminine when or because she contributed substantially to the economic survival of the family? Was Larry less masculine when or because he vacuumed? Neither felt clear about such issues, and they did not know how to explore new forms of family structure that would retain and integrate their deeply held values—the importance of family and the masculine/feminine differences they both cherished.

Common sense as well as research suggested that the conflict and tension of Katherine and Larry's lives could be sharply reduced if they shared household tasks more equitably, reduced Katherine's standards of housekeeping to more reasonable levels, scheduled and organized the household tasks and routines more effectively, brought their finances under better control, and shared more fairly the parenting tasks that Katherine had, up to the time of crisis, largely taken upon herself. With some professional help, Larry and Katherine were able to do this, but only after they had taken time to develop together a clearer idea of what it was to be masculine and feminine and to understand better the significance of the changes in their roles.

They wanted and worked out a marriage and family that was based upon biblical values. However, in the process they discovered that in a world in transition it was necessary to express these values in patterns of behavior quite different than those of the highly traditional homes in which they had grown up. Larry learned to think differently than his father who continued to brag that he had never diapered a baby or dried a dish. Katherine learned to think differently than her mother who had never balanced her checkbook or filled her car with gas (and was not about to learn).

In thinking about the changes that have occurred during this time of transition, we have focused primarily on the difficulties and the struggles women face, and for an obvious reason.

These are the aspects of change with which the counselor is most likely to be confronted. There are, however, other things to consider if as counselors we are to keep a balanced view.

WOMEN WHO OVERCAME

While the counseling process brings the counselor into personal contact with the dilemmas and struggles of women in contemporary society, it also permits the counselor to know firsthand the marvelous strength and resiliency of these women. Against all human odds, many women become triumphant overcomers in the complex world of change through which they make their way.

A former client sent me a Christmas card. She was the joyful mother of a new baby. Prayer, perseverance, and new medical procedures had given her a miracle. Another wrote a note of thanksgiving. She had just passed the fifth-year anniversary of her breast surgery with no evidence of any reoccurrence of cancer. Women now have some medical options that make it a better world for them.

Another former client sent me a letter without a return address. She had divorced an abusive husband who had threatened her life. With court approval, she had then fled with her children to her extended family in another state. "Life isn't perfect," she wrote, "but we're okay. We all sleep good now, and Dana's stopped having bad dreams. Emily has a good teacher and is doing good at school and doesn't worry about me like she used to. The church helps out with food, and my Sunday school class is a real support. My job isn't much, but we get by, and I thank God every night for all the good things He's done for us."

This is a far from perfect solution, but unlike Hannah (in Elizabeth's family Hall of Fame), death was not the only option this woman could choose. Public awareness of the problem and better legal options have opened a narrow door of escape for women caught in domestic violence, although their resources remain tragically small.

And there are more:

- A former client sent news of a fellowship grant to pursue an advanced degree in mathematics.

- Another has finished her residency and opened her practice as a pediatrician.
- Another, who has followed a traditional path as an at-home wife and mother, has been recognized by her denomination for volunteer work with drug-addicted newborns.
- Another has retired from a long and distinguished career in the public schools and has been honored for the contribution she has made.
- Another has negotiated an agreement with her firm to do a major portion of her work at home via computer so that she can spend a greater amount of time with her young children.
- Another, with the practical and cheerful encouragement of her husband, has returned to work as a nurse on the burn unit of a local children's hospital.
- Another has been accepted by her seminary of choice and is following her calling to work within the church.
- Still another is well on her way to an advanced degree that will qualify her as a researcher and therapist.
- Still another, who was a high school dropout and heavy drug user, has stopped taking drugs, earned her GED, and is taking a parenting class at the community college. She hates books and loves cars; she has been accepted into the auto mechanics course at the vocational school. When she has graduated, she plans to get a new job, one that will pay more than her present minimum wage, then move herself and her two children out of the public housing project where they now live.

A friend came one spring day to take me to lunch to celebrate her thirtieth wedding anniversary. "I've come to remind you," she said, "that lots of good marriages are doing quite well in a crazy world."

Women have resources and opportunities now that only a short time ago were not open to them. The available options and choices are not always what women or their counselors would wish. But when we think of transition and change, we would do well to remember the words of the old writer in Ecclesiastes, "There is a time for everything," he reminds us, ". . . a time to plant and a time to uproot, . . . a time to tear down and a time to build, . . . a time to keep and a time to

throw away. . . . " And in the great cycle of gain and loss in
life, God "has made everything beautiful in its time."[68]

NOTES

1. Jessie Bernard, "Women's Mental Health in Times of Transition," in
Women and Mental Health Policy, ed. L. E. Walker, Sage Yearbooks in
Women's Policy Studies, vol. 9 (Beverly Hills, Calif.: Sage, 1984), 184.
   2. Ibid.
   3. Francine D. Blau and Anne E. Winkler, "Women in the Labor Force:
An Overview," in *Women: A Feminist Perspective*, 4th ed., ed. Jo Freeman
(Mountain View, Calif.: Mayfield, 1989), 265–86.
   4. Ibid., 269–70.
   5. Ibid., 269.
   6. Ibid., 271.
   7. Ibid.
   8. Ibid.
   9. U.S. Bureau of Labor Statistics, 1988 data as cited in Nina Darnton,
"Mommy vs. Mommy," *Newsweek*, 4 June 1990, 66.
   10. Blau and Winkler, 272.
   11. The 9 to 5 National Association of Working Women, 1990 Annual Profile of Working Women, as cited in Sara Frances, "A Tribute to Working
Women," *Colorado Women News* 5, no. 9 (September 1990): 12-14.
   12. Ibid.
   13. Ibid.
   14. Ibid.
   15. "Trading Places," *Newsweek*, 16 July 1990, 48–54.
   16. Ibid., 49.
   17. Ralph E. Smith, *The Subtle Revolution* (Washington, D.C.: The Urban Institute, 1979).
   18. Blau and Winkler, 277, 280–83.
   19. Jean Baker Miller, *Toward a New Psychology of Women*, 2nd ed. (Boston:
Beacon Press, 1986), xii–xiii.
   20. U.S. Bureau of Labor Statistics, March 1988, as cited in E. N. Glenn and
R. L. Feldberg, "Clerical Work: The Female Occupation," in Freeman, 287–
311 (statistics cited from 288). Glenn and Feldberg's study of women as
clerical workers is comprehensive, carefully documented, and helpful reading for counselors seeking to understand women's work related stress.
   21. Ibid., 301.
   22. 9 to 5 National Association of Working Women, *National Survey on
Women and Stress* (1984), as cited by Glenn and Feldberg, 303.
   23. B. A. Reskin and H. I. Hartmann, eds., *Women's Work, Men's Work: Sex
Segregation on the Job* (Washington, D.C.: National Academy Press, 1986).
   24. C. M. Renzetti and D. J. Curran, *Women, Men, and Society: The Sociology
of Gender* (Boston: Allyn and Bacon, 1989), 183.

25. Susan A. Basow, *Gender Stereotypes: Traditions and Alternatives*, 2nd ed. (Pacific Grove, Calif.: Brooks/Cole, 1986), 252.

26. Renzetti and Curran, 179.

27. A Saltzman, "Trouble at the Top," *U.S. News and World Report*, 17 June 1991, 40–41.

28. The following general references provide helpful overviews of the complex issues of women's work: B. Reskin and H. Hartmann, eds., *Women's Work, Men's Work*; B. Vetter and E. Babco, *Professional Women and Minorities*, 7th ed. (Washington, D.C.: Commission on Professions in Science and Technology, 1987). See also, R. Sidel, *Women and Children Last* (New York: Penguin, Books, 1986).

29. Debra Renee Kaufman, "Professional Women: How Real Are the Recent Gains?" in Freeman, 329–46.

30. Ibid., 332.

31. Ibid., 330.

32. Ibid., 334.

33. Anne Fausto-Sterling, *Myths of Gender: Biological Theories about Women and Men* (New York: Basic Books, 1985), 32–33.

34. Kaufman, 329, 341, 343.

35. Saltzman, 40–48.

36. K. A. Samon, "Great Expectations: An Update on the Wharton Women of '80," *Working Woman* 16, no. 7 (July 1991): 66–69, 92.

37. Sara Frances, "A Tribute to Working Women," *Colorado Women News* 5, no. 9 (September 1990): 12–14.

38. Bernard, 191.

39. Sylvia Ann Hewlett, *A Lesser Life* (New York: Morrow, 1986). See also Sylvia Ann Hewlett, *When the Bough Breaks: The Cost of Neglecting Our Children* (New York: Basic Books, 1991).

40. Sylvia Ann Hewlett, "Running Hard Just to Keep Up," *Time Special Issue: Women, the Road Ahead* 136, no. 19 (Fall 1990): 54.

41. Ibid.

42. Hewlett, *When the Bough Breaks*.

43. Margaret Carlson, "What's Love Got To Do With it?" *Time*, 7 May 1990, 35. See also "A Job Wellesley Done," *Newsweek*, 11 June 1990, 26.

44. "What Youth Thinks," a survey by Yankelovich Clancy Shulman as reported in Nancy Gibbs, "The Dreams of Youth," *Time Special Issue: Women, the Road Ahead* 136, no. 19 (Fall 1990): 10–14 (chart 14).

45. Susan Ehrlich Martin, "Sexual Harassment: The Link Joining Gender Stratification, Sexuality, and Women's Economic Status," in Freeman, 57–75.

46. U.S. Merit Systems Protection Board, *Sexual Harassment in the Federal Workplace: Is It a Problem?* (Washington D.C.: U.S. Government Printing Office, 1981). U.S. Merit Systems Protection Board, *Sexual Harassment in the Federal Government: An Update* (Washington D.C.: U.S. Government Printing Office, 1988).

47. Nina Darnton, "Mommy vs. Mommy," *Newsweek*, 4 June 1990, 66.

48. L. Weitzman, *The Divorce Revolution* (New York: Free Press, 1985).

49. Hewlett, *When the Bough Breaks*, 88–90.

50. Darnton.

51. Betty Friedan, *The Second Stage* (New York: Summit Books, 1981), 94–99, 354–66.

52. Naomi Gerstel and Harriet Engel Gross, "Women and the American Family: Continuity and Change," in Freeman, 89–120.

53. Arthur J. Norton and Jean E. Moorman, "Current Trends in Marriage and Divorce Among American Women," *Journal of Marriage and the Family* 49 (February 1987): 3–14.

54. Hewlett, *When the Bough Breaks*.

55. Renzetti and Curran, 131.

56. Judith S. Wallerstein and Sandra Blakeslee, *Second Chances: Men, Women and Children a Decade After Divorce* (New York: Ticknor and Fields, 1989). See also Weitzman, *Divorce Revolution*, and Hewlett, *When the Bough Breaks*, 88–94.

57. Joseph H. Pleck, *Working Wives/Working Husbands* (Beverly Hills, Calif.: Sage, 1985). See also Catherine E. Ross, "The Division of Labor at Home," *Social Forces* 65 (March 1987): 816–33.

58. Shelley Coverman, "Women's Work Is Never Done: The Division of Domestic Labor," in Freeman, 356–68.

59. Arlie Hochschild and Anne Machung, *The Second Shift: Working Parents and the Revolution at Home* (New York: Viking, 1989).

60. Coverman, 36.

61. M. Shaevitz, "If She's Out Hunting Tigers, Why Won't He Clean Up the Hut?", chapter 6 in *Sexual Static: How Men Are Confusing the Women They Love* (Boston: Little, Brown and Co., 1987), 85–103.

62. Pleck, 82–90.

63. Myra Marx Ferree, "The Struggles of Superwoman," in *Hidden Aspects of Women's Work*, ed. Christine Bose, Roslyn Feldberg, and Natalie Sokoloff (New York: Praeger, 1987), 161–80. See also Joanne Vanek, "Household Work, Wage Work, and Sexual Equality," in *Families in Transition*, ed. A. S. Skolnick and J. Skolnick (Boston: Little, Brown and Company, 1983), 176–89.

64. Sara F. Berk, *The Gender Factory: The Apportionment of Work in American Households* (New York: Plenum, 1985).

65. Gerstel and Gross, 101.

66. Donna Hodgkins Berardo, Constance L. Shehan, and Gerald R. Leslie, "A Residue of Tradition: Jobs, Careers, and Spouses' Time in Housework," *Journal of Marriage and Family* 49 (May 1987): 381–90. See also Dana Hiller and W. W. Philliber, "The Division of Labor in Contemporary Marriage: Expectations, Perceptions, and Performance," *Social Problems* 33 (February 1986): 191–201.

67. Jessie Bernard, "The Good Provider Role: Its Rise and Fall," *American Psychologist* 36 (January 1981): 1–12.

68. Ecclesiastes 3:1–3,6,11 (NIV).

Chapter Nine

Unique Individuals in the Common Bond of Womanhood

THERE IS A FAST-FOOD RESTAURANT not far from my office. An apartment complex nearby the restaurant provides a secluded, tree-lined parking lot, which customers and neighborhood residents use as an informal park. One day while eating my lunch in this park, I watched the women gathered there.

A skillful young woman was kicking a soccer ball in one corner of the lot. Another young woman was sitting in a car with a young man, listening to a radio, her head leaning against his shoulder. An exasperated mother was feeding french fries to her toddler daughter who cheerfully persisted in wiping catsup on her shirt. Two comfortably middle-aged women were sitting in the shade where the trees were thickest. They were laughing together, sharing sack lunches. There was a sign on their comfortably middle-aged car that said, "Ask me about my grandchildren." A woman in a car parked diagonally from mine was intently studying *The Wall Street Journal*—the local office of a large brokerage firm is in a building nearby. A woman with beautiful white hair was sitting in the dappled sunlight by the fence, drinking coffee and sorting coupons— there is a large grocery not far away.

Another woman finished jogging her last lap around the lot and started back to work. I recognized her as the receptionist in the doctor's office on the corner. One woman sat in the most distant corner of the lot, isolated from all activity and possible contact with people. I could not see her clearly, but from time to time I saw her wipe her eyes in a way that made me think that she was crying. Two women drove into the lot and parked near the driver's license bureau. They entered the building to- gether, laughing. Their physical resemblance made me wonder if they were a mother and daughter, perhaps sharing a rite-of- passage in which the daughter had come to exchange her learner's permit for her first driver's license. And I was there, sitting with my coffee and over-stuffed briefcase, watching and thinking.

We were a highly diverse group of individuals, of differ- ing ages, ethnic backgrounds, and interests, engaged in differing tasks. It was intriguing to consider the astonishing variability represented in this small group of women. How different we were, gathered by chance and geography for a brief sunny interval in this informal public square.

Mentally reviewing the manuscript on which I had been working, I wondered: had I emphasized sufficiently the neces- sity for the counselor to be alert and responsive to the wide range of significant individual differences that characterize women clients? The effective counselor of women counsels women as individuals, not as generic representatives of a gendered group.

And yet, watching the group, I was struck by the degree to which, in an equally intriguing way, our diversity was also bound together in a common bond of womanhood. Different as we were, we were all working out our lives as women. While willing to celebrate our common humanity with men, most of us, I suspected, would also have expressed a strong, distinctive group identity as women. In mentally reviewing my manuscript, that strongly gendered group identity also made me wonder. Had I represented faithfully the importance of this common bond, the distinctive significance and meaning of being a woman?[1]

For the counselor this tension is a continuing challenge. With every woman client, the counselor faces difficult questions: How do I help this woman as a woman, and do so in a way that reflects both her unique individuality and her identity as a woman? And how do I affirm her distinctive identity as a woman without distorting the common humanity she holds with all men as well? And how do I as a counselor help both the client and myself respond to her distinctive identity as a woman without unwittingly perpetrating the stereotypic concepts of womanhood to which we have all been exposed?

For all of us, the distortions of both the old and the new mythologies confuse and mislead us, client and counselor alike, unless we continue to examine carefully the belief systems about women that we hold. As the previous discussion has made clear, it is my basic assumption that neither the client nor the counselor can deal effectively with gender identity or individual differences unless the stereotypic, destructive mythology that has clustered around our concepts of women is cleared away.

As we have seen, this process is not easy for client, counselor, or scientist. The social context of the culture in which we live shapes our sense of what women are or ought to be and teaches us to see in stereotypic ways. These distorted concepts then continue to influence our thinking in powerful, and often unconscious, ways unless we are deeply committed to an ongoing examination of our beliefs and the sources from which they spring.

THE MYTHOLOGY PROBLEM

Consequently, the misbeliefs that women hold about themselves—and, unfortunately, that the counselor also may hold—form a core portion of the problems with which counselor and client must struggle. It is difficult to emphasize sufficiently how powerful and subtle these myths are, and how challenging the task of identifying them can be. The following example illustrates something of the problem that client and counselor can face.

The myth that women are of less value than men appears on the surface so obviously incorrect that no one, client or counselor, would believe it to be true. If the counselor simply asks a woman client, "Do you think women are of less value than men?" the answer, with rare exception, will be a somewhat bewildered, "No," and then a pause while both client and counselor think what to do next. Myths can rarely be flushed out and made emotionally present in the counseling hour by such a head-on attack.

Within the counseling process, however, this particular myth often surfaces naturally in those sessions in which family history is discussed. For example, asking a woman about the circumstances of her birth and her parents' response to her gender will sometimes open the floodgates of feeling and memory of family circumstances in which the myth was formed.

In the lives of many clients, the roots of the myth reach back before the woman's conscious memory. At the time of the woman's birth, the announcement that the newborn child was a girl may have evoked a sense of disappointment in her parents, at least initially, particularly if she was a firstborn. (One study indicated that 90 percent of men and 92 percent of women desired that the first baby be male.)[2]

I have asked many women clients how their parents felt about their gender. A common response runs something like, "Oh, I know my parents love me, but I think they would have rather had a boy," or "Oh, I think it's all right that I was a girl, at least later after my brother came along." Women who have older siblings will sometimes say, "Well, they already had one girl, so I think they wished I had been a boy." or "Oh, yes, it was all right because I already had a brother."

Such responses are not true in all instances, of course, but it is nevertheless an eye-opening experience for most counselors to listen over a period of time to various women's experiences of parent attitude toward their sex/gender. It is astonishing to discover how frequently the birth of a girl evoked such negative or ambivalent responses on the part of the parents that knowledge of the parent's attitude was openly communicated to the woman as a part of her life history.

In the process of gently exploring the pain linked with such responses, the woman's belief in her devalued worth will often surface. One client recently said, "Well, I never have felt like I was worth very much. I think I got part of my attitude from my father. I suppose he loved me, but the girls didn't matter to him like the boys did, and I guess when I was a youngster, I decided girls weren't worth much."

I am certain that this woman, if asked directly if women were as valuable as men, would have answered, "Yes." *Yes* was, indeed, what she *wished* with all her heart that she could think about herself; it was not, however, what she actually believed. Yet it was only as we explored together her parents' value system, the attitudes they had expressed, and the pain these attitudes caused, that she was able to recognize in herself her long nonverbalized belief that to have been born female was to have been born into a permanent second-class.

If the counselor wishes to be effective with a woman client and appropriately responsive both to gender and individual differences, knowledge of the destructive mythology (old and new) is necessary. The counselor must additionally develop the self-knowledge necessary to identify such misbeliefs in her/himself and the clinical skills required to enable the client to uncover and explore these misbeliefs which are often deeply buried and covered with pain.

Such work cannot occur except within the context of a healing relationship. Establishment of a therapeutic relationship between the counselor (female or male) and woman client is itself a complex and delicate task.

THE COUNSELING RELATIONSHIP

If the counselor wishes to be effective with women clients, attention must be paid to the special requirements of a productive therapeutic relationship for women. For women clients, the counseling relationship is most effective when built upon high levels of counselor respect for the woman's ability to set her own goals for growth and achievement and to govern her life. Such counselor attitudes, of course, are also helpful to men clients. For the most part, however, such attitudes automatically characterize the counselor's work with men. We assume a man's ability to govern his life unless there is clear evidence to the contrary. Such an assumption is often not made with women clients.

The counseling process appears to be most effective for women when the counselor *with the client* develops a nonhierarchical relationship characterized by equality, mutuality, and appropriate counselor self-disclosure.[3] Healing is enhanced when the counselor views the goal of the relationship *not* in terms of expressing the counselor's status, power, or skills, but rather in terms of empowering the client, increasing *her* resources, *her* capabilities, and *her* effectiveness and ability to act.

The empathic quality of the relationship between the counselor and the woman client is crucial. In developing therapeutic processes consistent with the Stone Center approach to women's development, Kaplan noted, "An empathic bond between client and therapist is essential [in order] for the therapist to hear and validate the client's own experience as *she, not the therapist,* constructs it."[4]

The traditional model of therapy (the one to which most counselors are exposed in the course of professional training) stresses objective, unemotional, impersonal attitudes on the part of the counselor. This model reflects a relational style uncongenial to women, who appear to thrive in a more egalitarian, mutual, emotionally genuine therapeutic interaction.[5]

For the Christian counselor confronted with the hurt and wounded sufferer, the relationship must also incorporate, in client-appropriate ways, the presence of the healing, compassionate Christ. While the spiritual journey of the client and the counselor may (and often does) lie along different paths, it is my assumption that Christian spirituality makes psychological sense and distinctively shapes the therapeutic relationship undertaken by the Christian counselor.

Psychotherapy and spiritual guidance are not synonymous. Responsible professionals in both fields observe distinctive differences in practice. Nevertheless, as Benner has pointed out in his discussion of these differences, psychotherapy, with rare exception, deals with a sufficiently wide slice of life that spiritual considerations are inevitably involved.[6]

By definition, the Christian counselor enters into a healing partnership with the client in which, to borrow Propst's apt phrase, the presence of the Christ "forms the backbone of the counseling relationship,"[7] including those instances in which he, through his Holy Spirit, is at work "'anonymously' in the healing and growth of all individuals who are anywhere struggling."[8]

In general terms, to be most effective with women clients the therapeutic relationship must be characterized by equality, mutuality, and respect, and it must be responsive to women's gender-specific characteristics and needs. Additionally, however, the Christian counselor is called to rely upon more than human discernment and clinical skill, even while seeking to develop these, and, in the practice of caregiving and the art of intervention, to hold her/himself accountable to the ultimate Higher Authority, as well as to the highest standards of the profession through which we seek to serve.

THE PROBLEM OF THE SOCIAL CONTEXT

As counselors, dealing with stereotypic concepts and responding to individual differences provides a sufficient challenge for most of us. As Christian counselors, however, we are faced with an additional problem which poses a particular difficulty all its own.

Throughout the earlier discussion of sex and gender differences, I have emphasized the growing understanding of scientists and clinical practitioners that the social environment influences and, in some instances, controls the expression or inhibition of gendered behavior. The old assumption that the social environment need not be considered a significant variable in the understanding of sex and gender is now viewed by most, if not all, scientists as seriously incorrect. Gendered behaviors do not lie *in* the individual in a fashion parallel to the way in which chromosomes or hormones are *in* the individual. Gender is something that results from what is *in* the individual—chromosomes, hormones, and learning—*in interaction with* the social environment in which that individual lives and functions.

In the personal example given earlier, my ability and willingness to change a fuel pump—instrumental masculine behavior—was certainly more likely to emerge when I was in need, alone on a country road, than when I was with my football hero date.

A recent study of women's competitive behaviors provides an additional case in point. Traditionally, it has been assumed that women are less competitive than men, and, as noted in the discussion of aggression research, current studies appear to confirm this belief. However, a different finding appeared in the work of two researchers who recently studied the competitive behaviors of women in the academic world.[9]

The women studied were insiders, that is, they were women who had attained positions that placed them within reach of rewards such as grants, prestigious jobs, and peer recognition. In the academic world, such resources and rewards are usually regarded as scarce. The researchers discovered that *in that environment* the competitive behaviors of these particular women for these scarce resources did not differ significantly from those of their male peers.

In my opinion, such fiercely competitive behavior is not a desirable thing for either men or women. However, the point I wish to emphasize here is that it was not until women were studied *in that kind of environment* that new information about women's competitive behavior emerged. This study is only one example of the large body of evidence that led Maccoby (among others) to point out that gendered behavior emerges primarily in social situations and varies in relation to the composition of the group or dyad.[10]

We must face responsibly the clear evidence of the significance of the social environment on gendered behavior. This evidence leads us, as counselors who see religiously committed clients, to an important and complex question. What is the impact of the religious community—specifically the evangelical community, for those of us who practice there—upon the gendered behaviors of the religiously committed women who form the majority of the clients whom we serve?

In most instances, our professional training encourages us to regard the impact of social environment on gendered behavior as having little importance. We may be willing to concede that the way in which women behave may be significantly impacted by some special social context "out there"—the academic world, for example—but we are slow to consider the inescapable fact of our own reality. The women we see are women, granted, but they are *religiously committed women whose lives are shaped in interaction with the religious community of which they and we are a part.*

What does this mean?

We do not know. As discussed earlier, the impact of the religious community and the significance of the spiritual dimension of women's lives have been almost totally ignored in sociological study of women's life patterns, and psychological study of their mental health.[11] However, common knowledge of the conventional therapeutic practice calling for "hands off" regarding spiritual/religious issues often leads the religiously committed woman to seek out a Christian counselor.

To my knowledge, there has been no formal study of the impact on the client-therapist relationship in those instances when the basis of the client's choice of therapist has incorporated the client's perception of the therapist as affiliated with a congruent religious value system. In fact, as counselors, we do not know what it means to the therapeutic process to have been chosen by the client as a *Christian* counselor, nor have the implications of such a position been sufficiently spelled out. However, it would appear reasonable to expect that the counselor who has been chosen on such a basis may well (at least in the client's mind) carry extended responsibility in the counseling process. For the religiously committed client, the Christian counselor may in fact occupy a special position of trust and obligation.

Having been chosen, at least in part, because of the client's desire for a religiously congruent therapist, one might well

question the ethical propriety of a Christian counselor know-
ingly accepting a religiously committed woman client, then
failing in the counseling process to deal straightforwardly with
the reality and impact of the religious community with which
the client interacts. A rough parallel might be a therapist chosen by the client for skill in family therapy but who then avoids
in the therapeutic process all talk about family. It is not just
the internal spiritual processes of the client, and counselor, that
become relevant to the counseling process. The social impact
of the religious community, of which both client and counselor
are a part, also influences the counseling process and the issues which surface there.

A client, depressed and discouraged, was working as a
church secretary forty-plus hours a week at less than minimum
wage. Following some thoughtful discussion in several counseling sessions, she sought to renegotiate her contract with the
church. In the negotiation process, she was told (1) if she had
"really turned her life over to God" she would regard her work
as a ministry (read: do it for no pay at all), and (2) since she
had a husband, her present pay was more than adequate unless she was developing a materialistic attitude toward life.
There was some implication that this latter was believed to be
the case since she had, presumably, already demonstrated lack
of spiritual maturity by going to see a counselor.

In cases such as this, and others entailing even more complex issues, as counselors we must face the hard questions:
How can the religiously committed woman client's trauma
be dealt with honestly without consideration of the fact that
she is a religiously committed woman and that it is her *religious community*—in this case the church itself—that has
impacted her life in an injurious way? What is the psychological impact upon a religiously committed client when it is
her religious community or church that is the source of her
injury?

And what does it mean in the therapeutic process that the
woman has brought her pain to her Christian counselor? In
many instances, this action reflects the woman's belief that she
can trust her Christian counselor to help her work out a solution that will not injure herself or her church because she sees

her counselor as a member of the larger religious community to which she belongs.

In such instances it is clear that the social environment (i.e., the religious community) does indeed impact the woman's behavior in her initial choice of therapist, her concept of justice for women, her expectation that the therapist will help her work out a solution consistent with the value system of which she is a part, and other complex issues (e.g., the significance of women's wages within the marriage contract).

However, we are faced as counselors with the fact that we, too, are a part of that environment and influenced by it in our behaviors, both as individuals and as counselors. When we act as though being a Christian counselor is only a matter of theology, we deny the clear findings of science. By being a Christian counselor we become a part of a specialized group, a designated community, and influenced by the social environment of which we are a functioning member. Only by confronting the impact of the religious community on *both* the counselor's and the client's behavior can the counselor keep faith with the client's trust in the counselor's integrity.

The failure to study the impact of the religious community on the life and functioning of the religiously committed woman has left us with serious and complex questions. What happens psychologically to a religiously committed woman who works out an identity and gender-role prescription rejected by the majority of her religiously committed peers and the authority structure of her church? What is the psychological impact upon a religiously committed woman who worships regularly in a church that emphasizes exclusively the male attributes of God and is controlled and led by an all-male clergy? What happens in the therapeutic relationship if the woman client begins to move toward a position to which the *counselor* is *religiously* opposed?

How can we use the strengths and assets of the religious community to aid and strengthen the client? In what ways can the spiritual strengths of the client be utilized in the healing process? How can our membership in the religious community be used to strengthen ourselves as individuals and as counselors to become more spiritually mature and more effective participants in the healing process? We have many assumptions regarding such matters but little established information to guide us.

Gendered behaviors emerge in a social environment in the context of relationships is that both inhibit and foster their expression. In general, we do not know specifically what that means if the social environment is that of a religious community and the counseling relationship is one based on a common religious value system. More specifically, we do not know to what degree and in what ways the evangelical community shapes, encourages, or inhibits the gendered behaviors of women. And we are not clear about the ways in which the evangelical community influences the responses of its counselors to the women whom they see. There are no definitive studies to help us as counselors find our way in this complex and potentially emotionally conflicted situation. Denying the impact of the social environment on either the client or the counselor is, however, no solution to the dilemma.

This book has focused on information *about* women—women as consumers of mental health services, women as women (the sex and gender studies), and women as individuals, rich in diversity of gifts and pain. Accompanying this emphasis on information has been a serious concern about *mis*information about women—the misbeliefs or mythology that confuses and misleads us in our relationships, women with women, women with men, and counselors with clients. My primary purpose in dealing with both information and misinformation has been to establish a sound foundation for the counseling process.

It is my hope, however, that this information will also prove useful in a broader perspective than that of counseling. We live in a time of social change and challenge. Within the church we live in a time when the nature and roles of men and women are frequently debated, often with insufficient attention to the degree to which the thinking of the participants in the debate (on both sides) are shaped by the stereotypes of the culture.

Personal piety and good intentions do not protect any of us from absorbing the errors of our culture. Only truth can do that. It is my hope that this book will help us to identify the truth we know and the questions we cannot yet answer. It is also my hope that in so doing we will, women and men alike, take a significant step toward eliminating those misbeliefs about women which exist within the church and which by their presence prevent women from being valued and respected as equals within the family of God.

NOTES

1. The specific impact of sex and gender in the counseling process is considered at length in a forthcoming second volume by M. Gay Hubbard.
2. C. C. Peterson and J. L. Peterson, "Preference for Sex of Offspring as a Measure of Change in Sex Attitudes," *Psychology* 10 (1973): 3–5.
3. Alexandra G. Kaplan, "Dichotomous Thought and Relational Processes in Therapy," *Work in Progress*, no. 35 (Wellesley, Mass.: Stone Center, 1988).
4. Alexandra G. Kaplan, "The Self-in-Relation: Implications for Depression in Women," *Work in Progress*, no. 14 (Wellesley, Mass.: Stone Center, 1984), 13, italics mine.
5. Irene P. Stiver, "The Meaning of Care: Reframing Treatment Models," *Work in Progress*, no. 20 (Wellesley, Mass.: Stone Center, 1985).
6. David G. Benner, *Psychotherapy and the Spiritual Quest* (Grand Rapids, Mich.: Baker, 1988), 154.
7. L. Rebecca Propst, *Psychotherapy in a Religious Framework: Spirituality in the Emotional Healing Process* (New York: Human Sciences Press, 1988), 14.
8. Bernard Tyrrell, as quoted by Benner, 160.
9. E. F. Keller and H. Moglen, "Competition and Feminism: Conflicts for Academic Women," *Signs* 12 (1987): 492–511.
10. E. E. Maccoby, "Gender and Relationships," *American Psychologist* 45, no. 4 (April 1990): 513–20.
11. See chapter 3, pages 57–61.

Bibliography

"A Job Wellesley Done." Newsweek, 11 June 1990, 26.

Alsdurf, Jim, and Phyllis Alsdurf. *Battered Into Submission.* Downers Grove, Ill.: InterVarsity, 1989.

Baltes, P. B. "Life-span Developmental Psychology: Some Converging Observations on History and Theory." *Life-Span Development and Behavior,* edited by P. B. Baltes and O. G. Brim. Vol. 2. New York: Academic Press, 1979.

Bannon, J. A., and M.L. Southern. "Father-Absent Women: Self-Concept and Modes of Relating to Men." *Sex Roles* 6 (1980): 75–84.

Basow, Susan. *Gender Stereotypes: Traditions and Alternatives.* 2d ed. Pacific Grove, Calif.: Brooks/Cole, 1986.

Bates, Carolyn M., and Annette M. Brodsky. *Sex in the Therapy Hour.* New York: Guilford, 1989.

Baumrind, Diana. "Sex Differences in Moral Reasoning: Response to Walkers (1984) Conclusions That There Are None." *Child Development* 57 (1986): 511–21.

Belle, Deborah. "Inequality and Mental Health: Low Income and Minority Women." *Women and Mental Health Policy*, edited by Lenore E. Walker. Sage Yearbooks in Women's Policy Studies, vol. 9. Beverly Hills, Calif.: Sage, 1984.

Bem, Sandra. "Androgyny and Gender Schema Theory: A Conceptual and Empirical Integration." *Nebraska Symposium on Motivation*, 1984: Psychology and Gender, edited by T. B. Sonderegger. Lincoln, Neb.: University of Nebraska Press, 1985.

————. "Gender Schema Theory: A Cognitive Account of Sex-typing." *Psychological Review* 88 (1981): 354–64.

————. "Gender Schema Theory and Its Implications for Child Development: Raising Gender-Aschematic Children in a Gender-Schematic Society." *Signs* 8, no.4 (1983): 598–616.

————. "The Measurement of Psychological Androgyny." *Journal of Consulting and Clinical Psychology* 42 (1974): 155–62.

Benbow, C. P., and J. C. Stanley. "Consequences in High School and College of Sex Differences in Mathematical Reasoning Ability: A Longitudinal Perspective." *American Educational Research Journal* 19 (1982): 598–622.

————. "Sex Differences in Mathematical Reasoning Ability: More Facts." *Science* 222 (1983): 1029–31.

————. "Sex Differences in Mathematics Ability: Fact or Artifact?" *Science* 210 (1980): 1262–64.

Benderly, Beryl Lieff. "Don't Believe Everything You Read." *Psychology Today* 23, no.11 (November 1989): 67–69.

————. *The Myth of Two Minds: What Gender Means and Doesn't Mean*. New York: Doubleday, 1987.

Benner, David G. *Psychotherapy and the Spiritual Quest*. Grand Rapids, Mich.: Baker, 1988.

Berardo, Donna Hodgkins, Constance L. Shehan, and Gerald R. Leslie. "A Residue of Tradition: Jobs, Careers, and Spouses' Time in Housework." *Journal of Marriage and Family* 49 (May 1987): 381–90.

Bergman, Stephen. "Men's Psychological Development: A Relational Perspective." *Work in Progress*, no. 48. Wellesley, Mass.: Stone Center, 1991.

Berk, Sara F. *The Gender Factory: The Apportionment of Work in American Households*. New York: Plenum, 1985.

Bernard, Jessie. "The Good Provider Role: Its Rise and Fall." *American Psychologist* 36 (January 1981): 1–12.

———. "Women's Mental Health in Times of Transition." *Women and Mental Health Policy*, edited by Lenore E. Walker. Sage Yearbooks in Women's Policy Studies, vol. 9. Beverly Hills, Calif.: Sage, 1984.

Bernardez, Teresa. "Women and Anger—Cultural Prohibitions and the Feminine Ideal." *Work in Progress*, no. 31. Wellesley, Mass.: Stone Center, 1988.

Biller, H. B. "The Father and Sex Role Development." *The Role of the Father in Child Development*. 2d ed. Edited by M. Lamb. New York: Wiley, 1986.

Blau, Francine D., and Anne E. Winkler. "Women in the Labor Force: An Overview." *Women: A Feminist Perspective*. 4th ed. Edited by Jo Freeman. Mountain View, Calif.: Mayfield, 1989.

Bleier, Ruth. "Gender Idealogy and the Brain." *The Wisconsin Alumnus* (July/August 1987): 11–13.

———. *Science and Gender: A Critique of Biology and Its Theories on Women*. New York: Pergamon, 1984.

Block, J. H. "Debatable Conclusions about Sex Differences." *Contemporary Psychology* 21 (1976): 517–22.

Bobgan, Martin, and Deidre Bobgan. *Psychoheresy: The Psychological Seduction of Christianity*. Santa Barbara, Calif.: Eastgate, 1987.

Boston Women's Health Collective. *The New Our Bodies, Our Selves*. New York: Simon and Schuster, 1984.

Bouhoutsos, Jacqueline C. "Sexual Intimacy Between Psychotherapists and Clients: Policy Implications for the Future." *Women and Mental Health Policy*, edited by Lenore E. Walker. Sage Yearbooks in Women's Policy Studies, vol. 9. Beverly Hills, Calif.: Sage, 1984.

Bower, Bruce. "Females Show Strong Capacity for Aggression." *Science News* 140, no. 22 (November 30, 1991): 359.

———. "Teenage Turning Points." *Science News* 139, no. 12 (March 23, 1991): 184–86.

Boyce, Mary E. " Female Psychosocial Development: A Model and Implications for Counselors and Educators." *Counseling and Human Development*, no. 6 (February 1985): 1–12.

Brodsky, Annette. "A Decade of Feminist Influence on Psychotherapy." *Psychology of Women Quarterly* 4 (1980): 331–344.

Brodsky, Annette, and Rachel T. Hare-Mustin. "Psychotherapy and Women: Priorities for Research." *Women and Psychotherapy*. New York: Guilford, 1980.

———, eds. *Women and Psychotherapy: An Assessment of Research and Practice*. New York: Guilford, 1980.

Broverman, I. K., D. M. Broverman, F. E. Clarkson, P. S. Rosenkrantz, and S. R. Vogel. "Sex-role Stereotypes and Clinical Judgments of Mental Health." *Journal of Consulting and Clinical Psychology* 28 (1972): 1–7.

Buczek, T. C. "Sex Biases in Counseling: Counselor Retention of the Concerns of a Female and Male Client." *Journal of Counseling Psychology* 28 (1981): 13–21.

Budd, B. E., P. R. Clance, and D. E. Simerly. "Spatial Configurations: Erikson Reexamined." *Sex Roles* 12 (1985): 571–77.

Bustanoby, Andre. "Counseling the Seductive Female." *Leadership* 9, no. 1 (Winter 1988): 51.

Caplan, Paula J., Gael M. Macpherson, and Patricia Tobin. "Do Sex-Related Differences in Spatial Abilities Exist?" *American Psychologist* 40, no. 7 (July 1985): 786–99.

Carlson, Margaret. " What's Love Got To Do With It?" *Time*, 7 May 1990, 35.

Chesler, Phyllis. *Women and Madness.* New York: Doubleday, 1972.

Chodorow, Nancy. *The Reproduction of Mothering: Psychoanalysis and the Sociology of Gender.* Berkeley: University of California Press, 1978.

Clark, Mary Franzen. *Hiding, Hurting, Healing: Restoration for Today's Woman.* Grand Rapids, Mich.: Zondervan, 1985.

Colby, A., and W. Damon. "Listening to a Different Voice: A Review of Gilligan's: *In A Different Voice.*" *Merrill-Palmer Quarterly* 29 (1983): 473–81.

Collier, Helen. *Counseling Women: A Guide for Therapists.* New York: Free Press, 1982.

Collins, Gary. *Can You Trust Psychology? Exposing the Facts and the Fictions.* Downers Grove, Ill.: InterVarsity, 1988.

———. *Christian Counseling: A Comprehensive Guide.* Rev. ed. Dallas, Tex.: Word, 1986.

———. "How Common is Pastoral Indiscretion?" *Leadership* 9, no. 1 (Winter 1988): 12–13.

———. "A Letter to Christian Counselors." *Journal of Psychology and Christianity* 9, no. 1 (Spring 1990): 37–39.

Conarton, S., and L. K. Silverman. "Feminine Development through the Life Cycle." *Feminist Psychotherapies: Integration of Therapeutic and Feminist Systems*, edited by M. A. Douglas and L. E. Walker. Norwood, N. J.: Ablex, 1989.

Costrick, N., J. Feinstein, L. Kidder, J. Marecek, and L. Pascale. "When Stereotypes Hurt: Three Studies of Penalties for Sex-role Reversals." *Journal of Experimental Social Psychology* 11 (1975): 520–30.

Couper, Sarah J. "Prelude to Equality: Recognizing Oppression." *Gender Matters: Women's Studies for the Christian Community,* edited by June Steffensen Hagen. Grand Rapids, Mich.: Zondervan, 1990.

Coverman, Shelley. "Women's Work Is Never Done: The Division of Domestic Labor." *Women: A Feminist Perspective.* 4th ed. Edited by Jo Freeman. Mountain View, Calif.: Mayfield, 1989.

Darnton, Nina. "Mommy vs Mommy" *Newsweek,* 4 June 1990, 66.

Darpoe, K. P., and R. L. Olney. "The Effect of Boys' or Girls' Toys on Sex-Typed Play in Preadolescents." *Sex Roles* 9 (1983): 507–18.

Deaux, K. "From Individual Differences to Social Categories: Analysis of a Decade's Research on Gender." *American Psychologist* 39, no. 2 (February 1984): 105–16.

Deaux, K., and B. Major. "Putting Gender into Context: An Interactive Model of Gender-Related Behavior." *Psychological Review* 94 (1987): 473–81.

Dobson, James C. "Biology Determines Gender Roles." *Male/Female Roles: Opposing Viewpoints,* edited by Neal Bernard and Terry O'Neill. Opposing Viewpoints Series. San Diego, Calif.: Greenhaven Press, 1989.

Dohrenwend, B. P., and B. S. Dohrenwend. "Sex Differences and Psychiatric Disorders." *American Journal of Sociology* 81 (1976): 1447–54.

Doyle, James. *The Male Experience.* Dubuque, Iowa: Brown, 1983.

———. *Sex and Gender: The Human Experience.* Dubuque, Iowa: Brown, 1985.

Eagly, A. H. *Sex Differences in Social Behavior: A Social-Role Interpretation.* Hillsdale, N. J.: Erlbaum, 1987.

Eagly, A. H., and V. J. Steffen. "Gender and Aggressive Behavior: A Meta-Analytic Review of the Social Psychological Literature." *Psychological Bulletin* 100 (1986): 309–30.

Eccles (Parsons), J. "Expectancies, Values, and Academic Behaviors." *Achievement and Achievement Motivation,* edited by J. T. Spence. San Francisco: Freeman, 1983.

Eccles (Parsons), J., T. F. Adler, and C. M. Kaczala. "Socialization of Achievement Attitudes and Beliefs: Parental Influences." *Child Development* 53 (1982): 310–21.

Eccles (Parsons), J., and J. E. Jacobs. "Gender Differences in Math Ability: The Impact of Media Reports on Parents." *Educational Researcher* 14 (1985): 20–25.

———. "Social Forces Shape Math Attitudes and Performance." *Signs* 11 (1986): 367–89.

Edelwich, Jerry, and Archie Brodsky. *Sexual Dilemmas for the Helping Professional.* 2d ed. New York: Brunner/Mazel, 1991.

Edwards, Carolyn P. "Societal Complexity and Moral Development: A Kenyan Study." *Ethos* 3 (1975): 505–27

Erikson, Erik. *Childhood and Society.* 2d ed. New York: Norton, 1963.

———. "Inner and Outer Space: Reflections on Womanhood." *Daedalus* 93 (1964): 582–606.

———. "Once More the Inner Space." *Life History and the Historical Moment.* New York: Norton, 1975.

Eysenck, H. J. "The Effects of Psychotherapy: An Evaluation." *Journal of Consulting Psychology* 16 (1952): 319–324.

Fackelmann, Kathy. "The Safer Sex? Probing a Cardiac Gender Gap." *Science News* 139, no. 3 (January 19, 1991): 40–41.

Fausto-Sterling, Anne. *Myths of Gender: Biological Theories about Women and Men.* New York: Basic Books, 1985.

Feingold, A. "Cognitive Gender Differences Are Disappearing." *American Psychologist* 43 (1988): 95–103.

Ferree, Myra Marx. "The Struggles of Superwoman." *Hidden Aspects of Women's Work,* edited by Christine Bose, Roslyn Feldberg, and Natalie Sokoloff. New York: Praeger, 1987.

Fidell, L. S. "Put Her Down on Drugs: Prescribed Drug Usage in Women." Paper presented at the Western Psychological Association Meeting, Anaheim, Calif., April 1973.

———. "Sex Differences in Psychotropic Drug Use." *Professional Psychology* 12 (1981): 156–62.

Forbes, Cheryl. *The Religion of Power*. Grand Rapids, Mich.: Zondervan, 1983.

Fortune, Marie M. *Is Nothing Sacred? When Sex Invades the Pastoral Relationship*. New York: Harper and Row, 1989.

Foster, Richard. *The Challenge of the Disciplined Life: Money, Sex and Power*. New York: Harper and Row, 1988.

Frances, Sara. "A Tribute to Working Women." *Colorado Women News* 5, no. 9 (September 1990): 12–14.

Freud, Sigmund. As quoted in Juanita Williams, *Psychology of Women*. 3d ed. New York: Norton, 1987.

——— "New Introductory Lectures on Psychoanalysis" (1933). As quoted in M. Matlin, *The Psychology of Women*. Fort Worth, Tex.: Holt, Rinehart and Winston, 1987.

Frieden, Betty. *The Second Stage*. Rev. ed. New York: Summit Books, 1986.

Frieze, I. H., J. Parsons, P. Johnson, D. Ruhle, and G. Zellman. *Women and Sex Roles*. New York: Norton, 1978.

Frodi, A., J. Macaulay, and P. P. Thome. "Are Women Always Less Aggressive than Men? A Review of the Experimental Literature." *Psychological Bulletin* 84 (1977): 634–660.

Garnet, L., and J. Pleck. "Sex Role Identity, Androgyny, and Sex Role Transcendence: A Sex Role Strain Analysis." *Psychology of Women Quarterly* 3 (1979): 270–83.

Gerstel, Naomi, and Harriet Engel Gross. "Women and the American Family: Continuity and Change." *Women: A Feminist Perspective*. 4th ed. Edited by Jo Freeman. Mountain View, Calif.: Mayfield, 1989.

Gilbert, L. A. "Toward Mental Health: The Benefits of Psychological Androgyny." *Professional Psychology* 12 (1981): 29–38.

Gilligan, Carol. *In a Different Voice: Psychological Theory and Women's Development*. Cambridge, Mass.: Harvard University Press, 1982.

————. "In a Different Voice: Women's Conceptions of Self and Morality." *Harvard Educational Review* 47 (1977): 481–517.

————. *Making Connections: The Relational Worlds of Adolescent Girls at Emma Willard School.* Cambridge, Mass.: Harvard University Press, 1990.

————. "Moral Orientation and Moral Development." *Women and Moral Theory,* edited by E. F. Kittay and D. T. Meyers. Savage, Md.: Rowman and Littlefield, 1987.

————. "Remapping the Moral Domain: New Images of the Self in Relationship." *Mapping the Moral Domain,* edited by C. Gilligan, J.V. Ward, and J.M. Taylor. Cambridge, Mass.: Harvard University Press, 1988.

————. "Reply." *Signs* 11, no. 2 (Winter 1986): 325–33.

Gould, R. L. *Transformation: Growth and Change in Adult Life.* New York: Simon and Schuster, 1978.

Gove, W. R. "Mental Illness and Psychiatric Treatment Among Women." *Psychology of Women Quarterly* 4 (1980): 345–62.

————. "Mental Illness and Psychiatric Treatment Among Women." *Psychology of Women: Ongoing Debates,* edited by Mary Roth Walsh. New Haven, Conn.: Yale University Press, 1987.

————. "Sex, Marital Status, Psychiatric Treatment: A Research Note." *Social Forces* (1979): 89–93.

Gove, W. R., and J. F. Todor. "Adult Sex Roles and Mental Illness." *American Journal of Sociology* 78 (1973): 812–35.

Greeno, C. G., and E. Maccoby. "How Different is the 'Different Voice?'" *Signs* 11, no. 2 (Winter 1986): 310–16.

Greenspan, Miriam. *A New Approach to Women and Therapy.* New York: McGraw-Hill, 1983.

Halpern, D. F. "The Disappearance of Cognitive Gender Differences: What You See Depends on Where You Look." *American Psychologist* 44 (August 1989): 1156–58.

————. *Sex Differences in Cognitive Abilities.* Hillsdale, N. J.: Erlbaum, 1986.

Halstein, Constance. "Development of Moral Judgement: A Longitudinal Study of Males and Females." *Child Development* 47 (1976): 51–56.

Hancock, Emily. *The Girl Within*. New York: Ballantine Books, Random House, 1989.

Hare-Mustin, Rachael T. "An Appraisal of the Relationship Between Women and Psychotherapy: 80 Years After the Case of Dora." *American Psychologist* 38 (May 1983): 593–601.

Harris, L. J. "Sex Differences in Spatial Ability: Possible Environmental, Genetic, and Neurological Factors." *Asymmetrical Function of the Brain*, edited by M. Kinsbourne. New York: Cambridge University Press, 1987.

Hart, Archibald. "Private Sins of Public Ministry." *Leadership* 9, no. 1 (Winter 1988): 23.

Hendricks, Maureen. "Women, Spirituality, and Mental Health." *Women and Mental Health Policy*, edited by Lenore E. Walker. Sage Yearbooks in Women's Policy Studies, vol. 9. Beverly Hills, Calif.: Sage, 1984.

Henley, N. M. "Psychology and Gender." *Signs* 11 (1985): 101–19.

Hewlett, Sylvia Ann. *A Lesser Life*. New York: Morrow, 1986.

———. "Running Hard Just to Keep Up." *Time Special Issue: Women, the Road Ahead* 136, no. 19 (Fall 1990): 54.

———. *When the Bough Breaks: The Cost of Neglecting Our Children*. New York: Basic Books, 1991.

Hiller, Dana, and W. W. Philliber. "The Division of Labor in Contemporary Marriage: Expectations, Perceptions, and Performance." *Social Problems* 33 (February 1986): 191–201.

Hochschild, Arlie, and Anne Machung. *The Second Shift: Working Parents and the Revolution at Home*. New York: Viking, 1989.

Holroyd, J. C., and A. M. Brodskey. "Psychologists' Attitudes and Practices Regarding Erotic and Nonerotic Physical Contact with Patients." *American Psychologist* 32 (1977): 843–49.

"How Common Is Pastoral Indiscretion?" Results of a Leadership Survey. *Leadership* 9, no. 1 (Winter 1988): 12–13.

Hunt, Dave, and T. A. McMahon. *The Seduction of Christianity.* Eugene, Oreg.: Harvest House, 1985.

Huston, A. C. "The Development of Sex-Typing: Themes from Recent Research." *Developmental Review* 5 (1985): 1–17.

Hutchinson, M. C. *Transforming Body Image: Learning to Love the Body You Have.* Freedom, Calif.: The Crossing Press, 1985.

Hyde, J. S. "How Large Are Cognitive Gender Differences? A Meta-Analysis." *American Psychologist* 36 (1981): 892–901.

———. "How Large Are Gender Differences in Aggression? A Developmental Meta-Analysis." *Developmental Psychology* 20 (1984): 722–36.

Hyde, J. S., and M. Linn. "Gender Differences in Verbal Ability: A Meta-Analysis." *Psychological Bulletin* 104, no. 1 (1988), 53–69.

Jacklin, C. N. "Epilogue." *Sex Related Differences in Cognitive Functions,* edited by M. A. Wittig and A. C. Petersen. New York: Academic Press, 1979.

———. "Female and Male: Issues of Gender." *American Psychologist* 44, no. 2 (February 1989): 127–33.

Johnson, Marilyn. "Mental Illness and Psychiatric Treatment Among Women; A Response." Psychology of Women: Ongoing Debates, ed. Mary Roth Walsh. New Haven, Conn.: Yale University Press, 1987.

Jordan, Judith. "Empathy and Self Boundaries." *Work in Progress,* no. 16. Wellesley, Mass.: Stone Center, 1984.

———. "The Meaning of Mutuality." *Work in Progress,* no. 23. Wellesley, Mass.: Stone Center, 1986.

———. "Relational Development: Therapeutic Implications of Empathy and Shame." *Work in Progress,* no. 39. Wellesley, Mass.: Stone Center, 1989.

Jordan, Judith, Alexandra Kaplan, and Janet Surrey. "Empathy Revisited." *Work in Progress,* no. 40. Wellesley, Mass.: Stone Center, 1990.

Josselson, Ruthellen. *Finding Herself: Pathways to Identity Development in Women*. San Francisco: Jossey-Bass, 1987.

Kagan, Jerome. As quoted in Laura Shapiro, "Guns and Dolls." *Newsweek*, 22 May 1990, 81.

Kahn, A. "The Power War: Male Response to Power Loss Under Equality." *Psychology of Women Quarterly* 8 (1984): 234–47.

Kamin, Leon. Cited by Mary Stewart VanLeeuwen in *Gender and Grace: Love, Work and Parenting in a Changing World*. Downers Grove, Ill.: InterVarsity, 1990, 18–19.

Kaplan, Alexandra G. "Dichotomous Thought and Relational Processes in Therapy." *Work in Progress*, no. 35. Wellesley, Mass.: Stone Center, 1988.

———. "Female or Male Psychotherapists for Women: New Formulations." *Work in Progress*, no. 2. Wellesley, Mass.: Stone Center, 1984.

———. "Female or Male Therapists for Women: New Formulations." *Work in Progress*, no. 5. Wellesley, Mass.: Stone Center, 1984.

———. "The Self-in-Relation: Implications for Depression in Women." *Work in Progress*, no. 14. Wellesley, Mass.: Stone Center, 1984.

Kaplan, M. "A Woman's View of DSM-III." *American Psychologist* 38 (1983): 786–92.

Kaufman, Debra Renee. "Professional Women: How Real Are the Recent Gains?" *Women: A Feminist Perspective*, 4th ed. Edited by Jo Freeman. Mountain View, Calif.: Mayfield, 1989.

Keller, E. F., and H. Moglen. "Competition and Feminism: Conflicts for Academic Women." *Signs* 12 (1987): 492–511.

Kerber, L. D. "Some Cautionary Words for Historians." *Signs* 11, no. 2 (Winter 1986): 304–10.

Kerber, L. D., C. G. Greeno, E. Maccoby, Z. Luria, C. Stack, and C. Gilligan. "On In A Different Voice: An Interdisciplinary Forum." *Signs* 11, no. 2 (1986): 304–33.

Kimura, Doreen. "Are Men's and Women's Brains Really Different?" *Canadian Psychology* 28 (1987): 133–47.

———. "How Sex Hormones Boost–or Cut–Intellectual Ability." *Psychology Today* 23, no. 11 (November 1989): 62–66.

Kohlberg, L. "A Cognitive-Developmental Analysis of Children's Sex-Role Concepts and Attitudes." *The Development of Sex Differences*, edited by E. E. Maccoby. Stanford, Calif.: Stanford University Press, 1966.

———. "The Development of Children's Orientation Toward a Moral Order: I. Sequences in the Development of Human Thought." *Vita Humana* 6 (1963): 11–33.

———. *The Philosophy of Moral Development: Moral Stages and the Idea of Justice: Essays on Moral Development*. Vol. 1. San Francisco: Harper and Row, 1981.

———. *The Psychology of Moral Development: Moral Stages and the Idea of Justice: Essays on Moral Development*. Vol. 2. San Francisco: Harper and Row, 1984.

Konner, Melvin. *The Tangled Wing; Biological Constraints on the Human Spirit*. New York: Holt, Rinehart and Winston, 1982.

Lenney, E. "Androgyny: Some Audacious Assertions Toward Its Coming of Age." *Sex Roles* 5 (1979): 703–19.

Lerman, Hannah. "From Freud to Feminist Personality Theory: Getting Here from There." *Psychology of Women Quarterly* 10 (1986): 1–18.

———. *A Mote in Freud's Eye: From Psychoanalysis to the Psychology of Women*. New York: Springer, 1986.

Lerner, Harriet Golhor. *Women in Therapy*. New York: Harper and Row, 1988.

Levinson, D. J. *The Seasons of a Man's Life*. New York: Knopf, 1978.

Lifton, Peter D. "Individual Differences in Moral Development: The Relation of Sex, Gender, and Personality to Morality." *Journal of Personality* 53, no. 2 (June 1985): 306–34.

Linn, M. C., and A. C. Petersen. "Emergence and Characterization of Sex Differences in Spatial Ability: A Meta-Analysis." *Child Development* 56 (1985): 1479–98.

———. "A Meta-Analysis of Gender Differences in Spatial Ability: Implication for Mathematics and Science Achievement." *The Psychology of Gender: Advances through Meta-Analysis*, edited by J. S. Hyde and M. C. Linn. Baltimore: John Hopkins University Press, 1986.

Long, Patricia. "A Woman's Heart." *In Health* 5, no. 2 (March/April 1991): 52–58.

Luria, Zella. "A Methodological Critique." *Signs* 11, no. 2 (Winter 1986): 316–21.

MacArthur, John, Jr. *Whatever Happened to the Holy Spirit?* Panorama City, Calif.: Grace to You, 1989.

McBroom, W. H. "Parental Relationships, Socioeconomic Status, and Sex Role Expectations." *Sex Roles* 7 (1981): 1027–33.

McBurney, Louis. *Counseling Christian Workers.* Dallas, Tex.: Word, 1986.

Maccoby, Eleanor. "Gender and Relationships: A Developmental Account." *American Psychologist* 45, no. 4 (April 1990): 513–20.

———. "The Role of Gender Identity and Gender Constancy in Sex-Differentiated Development." *New Directions for Child Development* 47 (1990): 5–20.

Maccoby, Eleanor, and C. N. Jacklin. *The Psychology of Sex Differences.* Stanford, Calif.: Stanford University Press, 1974.

———. "Sex Differences in Aggression: A Rejoinder and Reprise." *Child Development* 51 (1980): 964–80.

MacHaffie, Barbara J. *Her Story: Women in Christian Tradition.* Philadelphia: Fortress Press, 1986.

McKenna, W., and S. J. Kessler. "Experimental Design as a Source of Sex Bias in Social Psychology." *Sex Roles* 3 (1977): 117–28.

Maloney, H. Newton. "Codes of Ethics: A Comparison." *Journal of Psychology and Theology* 5, no. 3 (Fall 1986): 94–101.

Marshall, Diane. "Current Issues of Women and Therapy." *Journal of Psychology and Christianity* 4, no. 1 (Spring 1985): 62–72.

Matlin, Margaret W. *The Psychology of Women.* Fort Worth, Tex.: Holt, Rinehart and Winston, 1987.

Miller, Jean Baker. "Connections, Disconnections and Violations." *Work in Progress,* no. 33. Wellesley, Mass.: Stone Center, 1988.

———. "The Construction of Anger in Women and Men." *Work in Progress,* no. 4. Wellesley, Mass.: Stone Center, 1983.

———. "The Development of Women's Sense of Self." *Work in Progress,* no. 12. Wellesley, Mass.: Stone Center, 1984.

———. *Toward a New Psychology of Women.* Boston: Beacon Press, 1976.

———. *Toward a New Psychology of Women.* 2d ed. Boston: Beacon Press, 1986.

———. "What Do We Mean by Relationships?" *Work in Progress,* no. 22. Wellesley, Mass.: Stone Center, 1986.

———. "Women and Power: Some Psychological Dimensions." *Work in Progress,* no. 1. Wellesley, Mass.: Stone Center, 1982.

Miller, Jean Baker, Judith V. Jordan, Alexandra G. Kaplan, Irene P. Stiver, and Janet L. Surrey. "Some Mis-Conceptions and Re-Conceptions of a Relational Approach." *Work in Progress,* no. 49. Wellesley, Mass.: Stone Center, 1991.

Mitchell, J. *Psychoanalysis and Feminism.* New York: Grossman, 1974.

Money, J. *Love and Love Sickness: The Science of Sex, Gender Difference and Pair Bonding.* Baltimore: John Hopkins Press, 1980.

Money, J., and A. Ehrhardt. *Man and Woman, Boy and Girl.* Baltimore: John Hopkins Press, 1972.

Money, J., and P. Tucker. *Sexual Signatures: On Being a Man or a Woman.* Boston: Little, Brown and Co., 1975.

Money, J., and C. Wiedeking. "Gender Identity/Role: Normal Differentiation and Its Transpositions." *Handbook of Human Sexuality*, edited by B. Wolman and J. Money. Englewood Cliffs, N. J.: Prentice Hall, 1980.

Morecek, Jeanne, and Marilyn Johnson. "Gender and the Process of Therapy." *Women and Psychotherapy*, edited by Annette Brodsky and Rachel Hare-Mustin. New York: Guilford, 1980.

Moyer, K. E. "Sex Differences in Aggression." *Sex Differences in Behavior*, edited by Richard C. Friedman, Ralph M. Richart, and Raymond L. Vande Wiele. New York: Wiley, 1974.

Murphy, Cullen. "Men and Women: How Different Are They?" *The Saturday Evening Post* (October 1983): 211–15.

Naditch, S. F. "Sex Differences in Field Dependence: The Role of Social Influence." Paper presented at the meeting of the American Psychological Association, Washington, D. C., September 1976.

National Association of Working Women, 9 to 5. 1990 Annual Profile of Working Women. Cited in Sara Frances, "A Tribute to Working Women." *Colorado Women News* 5, no. 9 (September 1990): 12–14.

Neely, James C. *Gender, The Myth of Equality*. New York: Simon and Schuster, 1989.

Neugarten, Bernice L., ed. *Middle Age and Aging*. Chicago: University of Chicago Press, 1968.

———. "A New Look at Menopause." *The Female Experience*, edited by C. Tavris. Del Mar, Calif.: Communications/Research/Machines, 1973.

———. "Summary and Implication." *Personality in Middle and Late Life*, edited by Bernice L. Neugarten and Leon Stein. New York: Atherton, 1964.

Norton, Arthur J., and Jean E. Moorman. "Current Trends in Marriage and Divorce Among American Women." *Journal of Marriage and the Family* 49 (February 1987): 3–14.

"Our Bodies, Their Selves: Bias Against Women in Health Research." *Newsweek*, 17 December 1990, 60.

Peterson, C. C., and J. L. Peterson. "Preference for Sex of Offspring as a Measure of Change in Sex Attitudes." *Psychology* 10 (1973): 3–5.

Phillips, R. D., and F. D. Gilroy. "Sex Bias in Counseling and Clinical Judgments of Mental Health: The Broverman Findings Reexamined." *Sex Roles* 12 (1985): 179–93.

Pleck, J. H. *Working Wives, Working Husbands*. Beverly Hills, Calif.: Sage, 1985.

Plomin, R., and T. Foch. "Sex Differences and Individual Differences." *Child Development* 52 (1981): 383–85.

Polan, Mary Lake. "Gender Bias in Medical Research Is Putting Women's Health at Risk." *The Denver Post*, 2 March 1991.

Pope, K. S., P. Keith-Spiegel, and B. G. Tabachnick. "Ethics of Practice: The Beliefs and Behaviors of Psychologists as Therapists." *American Psychologist* 42 (1987): 993–1006.

———. "Sexual Attraction to Clients." *American Psychologist* 41, no. 2 (1986): 147–58.

Prescott, S. "Why Researchers Don't Study Women: The Responses of Sixty-two Researchers." *Sex Roles* 4 (1978): 899–905.

Propst, L. Rebecca. *Psychotherapy in a Religious Framework: Spirituality in the Emotional Healing Process*. New York: Human Sciences Press, Inc., 1988.

Radloff, L. S. "Sex Differences in Depression: The Effects of Occupation and Marital Status." *Journal of Sex Roles* 1 (1975): 249–65.

Rebecca, M., R. Hefner, and B. Oleshansky. "A Model of Sex-Role Transcendence." *Beyond Sex-role Stereotypes: Readings Toward a Psychology of Androgyny*, edited by A. G. Kaplan and J. P. Bean. Boston: Little, Brown and Co., 1976.

Renzetti, C. M., and D. J. Curran. *Women, Men, and Society: The Sociology of Gender*. Boston: Allyn and Bacon, 1989.

Reskin, B. A., and H. I. Hartmann, eds. *Women's Work, Men's Work: Sex Segregation on the Job.* Washington, D.C.: National Academy Press, 1986.

Riessman, Catherine K., and Naomi Gerstel. *Social Science and Medicine.* Quoted in "The Costly Retreat from Marriage." Bryce J. Cristensen. *The Saturday Evening Post* (January/February 1990): 32.

Rosewater, Lynne Bravo. "Feminist Therapy: Implications for Practitioners." *Women and Mental Health Policy,* edited by Lenore E. Walker. Sage Yearbooks in Women's Policy Studies, vol. 9. Beverly Hills, Calif.: Sage, 1984.

Ross, Catherine E. "The Division of Labor at Home." *Social Forces* 65 (March 1987): 816–33.

Russo, N. F., ed. *A National Agenda to Address Women's Mental Health Needs.* Washington D.C.: American Psychological Association, 1985.

Rutter, Peter. *Sex in the Forbidden Zone: When Men in Power—Therapists, Doctors, Clergy, Teachers, and Others—Betray Women's Trust.* Los Angeles: Jeremy P. Tarcher, 1989.

Saltzman, A. "Trouble at the Top." *U.S. News and World Report* 110, no. 23 (June 17, 1991): 40–41.

Samon, K. A. "Great Expectations: An Update on the Wharton Women of '80." *Working Woman* 16, no. 7 (July 1991): 66–69, 92.

Shaevitz, M. "If She's Out Hunting Tigers, Why Won't He Clean Up the Hut?" Chapter 6. In *Sexual Static: How Men Are Confusing the Women They Love.* Boston: Little, Brown and Co., 1987.

Shapiro, D. A., and D. Shapiro. "Meta-analysis of Comparative Therapy Outcomes Studies: A Replication and Refinement." *Psychological Bulletin* 92 (1982): 581–604.

Sheehy, G. *Passages: Predictable Crises of Adult Life.* New York: Dutton, 1974.

Sherif, C. "Needed Concepts in the Study of Gender Identity." *Psychology of Women Quarterly* 6 (1982): 375–98.

Sherman, Julia A. "Therapist Attitudes and Sex-Role Stereotyping." *Women and Psychotherapy*, edited by Annette M. Brodsky and Rachel Hare-Mustin. New York: Guilford, 1980.

Sherman, Julia A., C. Koufacos, and J. A. Kenworthy. "Therapists: Their Attitudes and Information About Women." *Psychology of Women Quarterly* 2 (1987): 299–313.

Shulman, Yankelovich Clancy. "What Youth Thinks." In Nancy Gibbs, "The Dreams of Youth." *Time Special Issue: Women, the Road Ahead* 136, no. 19 (Fall 1990): 10–14.

Sidel, R. *Women and Children Last*. New York: Penguin Books, 1986.

Simpson, Elizabeth L. "Moral Development Research: A Case Study of Scientific Cultural Bias." *Human Development* 17 (1974): 81–106.

Smith, M. L. "Sex Bias in Counseling and Psychotherapy." *Psychological Bulletin* 87 (1980): 392–407.

Smith, M. L., G. V. Glass, and T. I. Miller. *The Benefits of Psychotherapy*. Baltimore: Johns Hopkins University Press, 1980.

Smith, Ralph E. *The Subtle Revolution*. Washington, D. C.: The Urban Institute, 1979.

Stack, Carol B. "The Culture of Gender: Women and Men of Color." *Signs* 11, no. 2 (Winter 1986): 321–24.

Steinke, Peter. "Clergy Affairs." *Journal of Psychology and Christianity* 8, no. 4 (Winter 1989): 56–62.

Stericker, A., and S. LeVesconte. "Effect of Brief Training on Sex-Related Differences in Visual-Spatial Skill." *Journal of Personality and Social Psychology* 43 (1982): 1018–29.

Stewart, Abigail J., and M. Brinton Lykes, eds. *Gender and Personality: Current Perspectives on Theory and Research*. Durham, N.C.: Duke University Press, 1985.

Stiver, Irene. "The Meaning of Care: Reframing Treatment Models." *Work in Progress*, no. 20. Wellesley, Mass.: Stone Center, 1985.

———. "Work Inhibitions in Women: Clinical Considerations." *Work in Progress*, no. 3. Wellesley, Mass.: Stone Center, 1983.

"Student Researchers Win Top STS Awards." *Science News* 139, no. 10 (March 9, 1991): 150.

Sturdivant, Susan. *Therapy with Women.* New York: Springer, 1980.

Surrey, Janet L. "Relationship and Empowerment." *Work in Progress*, no. 30. Wellesley, Mass.: Stone Center, 1987.

———. "Self-in-Relation: A Theory of Women's Development." *Work in Progress*, no. 13. Wellesley, Mass.: Stone Center, 1985.

Swift, Carolyn. "Women and Violence: Breaking the Connection." *Work in Progress*, no. 27. Wellesley, Mass.: Stone Center, 1987.

Tannen, D. *That's Not What I Meant: How Conversational Style Makes or Breaks Your Relations with Others.* New York: Murrow, 1986.

———. *You Don't Understand: Women and Men in Conversation.* New York: Ballantine Books, 1990.

Tavris, Carol. "Co-dependency: A Guilt Trip for Women." *The Denver Post*, 18 March 1990.

Thorne, Barrie, Cheris Kramarae, and Nancy Henley. "Language, Gender and Society: Opening a Second Decade of Research." *Language, Gender and Society*, edited by B. Thorne, C. Kramarae and N. Henley. Rowley, Mass.: Newbury House, 1983.

Tieger, T. "On the Biological Basis of Sex Differences in Aggression." *Child Development* 51 (1980): 943–63.

Tobin, P. "The Effects of Practice and Training on Sex Differences in Performance on a Spatial Task." Master's Thesis, University of Toronto: Toronto, Canada, 1982.

Towson, S. M. J., and M. P. Zanna. "Toward a Situational Analysis of Gender Differences in Aggression." *Sex Roles* 8 (1982): 903–14.

"Trading Places." *Newsweek*, 16 July 1990, 48–54.

Tyrrell, Bernard. Quoted by David Benner, *Psychotherapy and the Spiritual Quest*. Grand Rapids, Mich.: Baker, 1988.

U. S. Bureau of the Census. *Poverty in the United States.* Current Population Reports, Consumer Income, series P-60, no. 175. Washington, D. C.: U. S. Department of Commerce, 1991.

U. S. Bureau of Labor Statistics. Cited in E.N. Glenn and R.L. Feldberg, "Clerical Work: The Female Occupation." *Women: A Feminist Perspective.* 4th ed. Edited by Jo Freeman. Mountain View, Calif.: Mayfield, 1988.

U. S. Bureau of Labor Statistics. 1988 data as cited in Nina Darnton. "Mommy vs Mommy." *Newsweek,* 4 June 1990, 66.

U. S. Merit Systems Protection Board. *Sexual Harassment in the Federal Government: An Update.* Washington, D. C.: U. S. Government Printing Office, 1988.

U. S. Merit Systems Protection Board. *Sexual Harassment in the Federal Workplace: Is It a Problem?* Washington, D. C.: U.S. Government Printing Office, 1981.

Utian, Wulf. *Managing Your Menopause.* Englewood Cliffs, N. J.: Prentice Hall, 1990.

Vaillant, G. *Adaptation to Life.* Boston: Little, Brown and Co., 1977.

Vanek, Joanne. "Household Work, Wage Work, and Sexual Equality." *Families in Transition,* edited by A. S. Skolnick and J. Skolnick. Boston: Little, Brown and Co., 1983.

Van Leeuwen, Mary Stewart. "The Christian Mind and the Challenge of Gender Relations." *Reformed Journal* (September 1987).

———. "The Female Reconstructs Psychology." *Journal of Psychology and Christianity* 3, no. 2 (Summer 1984): 20–32.

———. *Gender and Grace: Love, Work and Parenting in a Changing World.* Downers Grove, Ill.: InterVarsity, 1990.

———. "Making Baskets or Building Houses." *Daughters of Sarah* 15 (September/October 1989): 3–7.

———. "Selective Sociobiology, and Other Follies." *Reformed Journal* 38, no. 2 (February 1988): 24–28.

———. *Sex, Gender and Christian Freedom.* Downers Grove, Ill.: InterVarsity, 1990.

Vetter, B., and E. Babco. *Professional Women and Minorities.* 7th ed. Washington, D. C.: Commission on Professions in Science and Technology, 1987.

Vinson, J. S. "Use of Complaint Procedures in Cases of Therapist-Patient Sexual Contact." *Professional Psychology: Research and Practice* 18, no. 2 (1987): 159–64.

Walker, Lenore E. "Sex Differences in the Development of Moral Reasoning: A Critical Review." *Child Development* 55 (1984): 677–91.

———. *Terrifying Love.* New York: Harper and Row, 1989.

Wallerstein, Judith S., and Sandra Blakeslee. *Second Chances: Men, Women and Children a Decade After Divorce.* New York: Ticknor and Fields, 1989.

Walsh, Mary Roth, ed. *The Psychology of Women: Ongoing Debates.* New Haven, Conn.: York University Press, 1987.

Weitzman, L. *The Divorce Revolution.* New York: Free Press, 1985.

Welter, Barbara. "The Cult of True Womanhood." *Dimity Convictions: The American Woman in the Nineteenth Century,* edited by Barbara Welter. Athens, Ohio: Ohio University Press, 1976.

White, Burton L. "Should You Stay Home With Your Baby?" *The Psychology of Women: Ongoing Debates,* edited by Mary Roth Walsh. New Haven, Conn.: Yale University Press, 1987.

Women's Realities, Women's Choices. Hunter College Women's Studies Collective. New York: Oxford University Press, 1983.

Williams, Juanitay. *Psychology of Women: Behavior in a Biosocial Context.* 3d ed. New York: Norton, 1987.

Winfrey, Joan. "Gender Studies: A Review of the Literature and Some Implications for the Church." *Journal of Biblical Equality* 1 (1989): 50–60.

Wolfman, Brunetta. "Women and Their Many Roles." *Work in Progress,* no. 7. Wellesley, Mass.: Stone Center, 1984.

Wright, H. Norman. *Always Daddy's Girl.* Ventura, Calif.: Regal Books, 1989.

Author Index

Edwards, Carolyn P., 149
Erikson, Erik, 157–59, 160, 173
Eysenck, H. J., 71

Fackelmann, Kathy, 152
Fausto-Sterling, Anne, 104, 110–11, 121, 134, 135, 195
Feingold, A., 135
Ferree, Myra Marx, 222
Fidell, L. S., 2
Forbes, Cheryl, 50
Fortune, Marie M., 80
Foster, Richard, 50
Frances, Sara, 197
Freud, Sigmund, 6–7, 18–19, 28, 100, 149, 156–57, 158, 160
Freudian, 6, 7, 8, 16, 67, 77, 148, 157, 185
Friedan, Betty, 47, 56, 213
Frieze, I. H., 128
Frodi, A., 130

Garnet, L., 52
Gerstel, Naomi, 213, 222
Gibbs, Nancy, 200–1
Gilbert, L. A., 52
Gilligan, Carol, 55, 74, 149, 166, 170–72
Glenn, E. N., 192
Gould, R. L., 146
Gove, W. R., 1, 3–4, 7–8
Greenspan, Miriam, 9, 49, 66

Halpern, D. F., 132, 136
Halstein, Constance, 149
Hancock, Emily, 173
Hare-Mustin, Rachel T., 96, 177
Harris, L. J., 132
Hart, Archibald, 82
Hefner, R. R., 52
Hendricks, Maureen, 61

Henley, N. M., 52
Hewlett, Sylvia A., 199–200, 209, 213
Hiller, Dana, 223
Hochschild, Arlie, 222
Holroyd, J. C., 2, 79
Hubbard, M. Gay, 231
Hunt, Dave, 112
Huston, A. C., 126
Hutchinson, M. C., 151
Hyde, J. S., 126, 127, 128, 132, 134, 135, 138

Jacklin, C. N., 94, 119, 120–22, 126, 132, 134, 135, 136, 138
Jacobs, J. E., 137
Johnson, Marilyn, 8
Jordan, Judith, 168, 169
Josselson, Ruthellen, 173

Kagan, Jerome, 160, 163
Kahn, A., 49
Kamin, Leon, 119, 154
Kaplan, Alexandra G., 52, 77, 168, 169, 234
Kaplan, M., 5
Kaufman, Debra Renee, 194–95, 196
Keller, E. F., 236
Kimura, Doreen, 105–7, 108, 109
Kohlberg, L., 149, 161–62, 170–71
Konner, Melvin, 111–12, 120
Kroeger, Catherine, 32

Lenney, E., 52
Lerman, Hannah, 7, 157
Lerner, Harriet Golhor, 16, 67–68
Levinson, D. J., 146
Linn, M. C., 132, 134
Long, Patricia, 152

Subject Index